European and American
Snuff Boxes
1730-1830

I Frontispiece (*overleaf*)

a Gold, with diamond thumbpiece, on the cover, an enamel miniature of a lion hunt. *Maker* A.P.C. Probably Swiss, 1765–70.

b Gold, silver and paste diamonds. *Maker* Jean Moynat (m. 1745, d. 1761.) Paris, 1754–5.

c Gold with enamelled scenes by the unidentified artist Le Sueur, signed *L. E. Sueur*. Paris, 1750–1.

d Gold. Paris, 1756–62.

e Onyx and enamelled gold. *Maker* D.P. Paris, 1738–9.

f Gold and enamel, the cover set with portrait miniature. *Maker* Louis Ouizille (m. 1768, living 1790). Paris 1775–6.

All boxes Courtesy of The Trustees of The Wallace Collection, London

a	
b	*c*
d	
e	*f*

European and American
Snuff Boxes
1730-1830

Clare Le Corbeiller

A Studio Book
THE VIKING PRESS · New York

Published in 1966 by The Viking Press, Inc.
625 Madison Avenue, New York, N.Y. 10022

Library of Congress catalog card number: 66-16384

Reproduced and printed in Great Britain by
Redwood Press Limited, Trowbridge & London

Contents

Preface

It is my hope that readers of this book will discover snuff boxes both pleasantly familiar and pleasantly strange. While I have tried to present a complete record of the production of snuff boxes during their liveliest century, I am sensible to the innumerable variations that can be rung on a single theme, and acknowledge with regret that some may have escaped me.

A word may be in order concerning the arrangement of this book. In the free exchange of idioms that allows motifs to be passed on from one medium to another in the decorative arts there still, in a given period, is generally a dominant style. Such, among snuff boxes, is the Parisian gold *tabatière* whose pervasive influence is visible in boxes of all materials. The presentation has therefore been arranged according to the materials of which the boxes were made; these have then been grouped in ways which, it is hoped, will shed light on their technical similarities as well as on their stylistic relationship to the gold *tabatière*.

A great number of persons, by their generously shared time and knowledge, have made this book possible. My first debt is to Mr Perry O'Neil and his assistant, Mr Paul Goren, for permitting me to explore at leisure the invaluable storehouse of materials gathered in the Arents Collection of the New York Public Library. I should also like to thank Mr Paul Schaffer of A La Vieille Russie, Mr Hanns Weinberg of The Antique Porcelain Company and Mrs Hedy Backlin, The Cooper Union Museum, for allowing me to study boxes in their collections.

To Mr Henry Hawley of the Cleveland Museum of Art; Miss Margaret Greenshields, Cecil Higgins Museum, Bedford; Dr Robert Wark of the Henry E. Huntington Library and Art Gallery; Mr Marvin D. Schwartz, Brooklyn Museum; Miss Margaret Stearns, the Museum of the City of New York; Mr Kenneth Snowman, Wartski, London; Mr Cyril Aldred and Miss Patricia M. Ford of the Royal Scottish Museum, Edinburgh; and Mr G. Balaud-Spooner of the Sheffield City Museum I am indebted for information and for photographs, many of which they kindly arranged to have taken for me.

Much of the information in these pages was obtained from correspondents; for their kindness in answering my inquiries I wish to thank Mrs Yves Henry Buhler, Museum of Fine Arts, Boston; Mr John Emerson Langdon; Mr John Devereux Kernan; Marquesa Zenaide Giunta di Roccagiovine; Mr Ross Watson of the Birmingham City Museum and Art Gallery; Mr R. J. Charleston, Victoria and Albert Museum; Professor Giovanni Mariacher; Mme Charles-Henri Lerch; and Mr Edward H. Pinto.

Mr David DuBon of the Philadelphia Museum of Art, Mr Paul Grigaut of the Virginia Museum of Fine Arts and Mr Norman S. Rice of the Albany Institute of History and Art made it possible for me to illustrate boxes in private collections.

I wish also to thank Mrs Stephen P. Kelner for her patient and exemplary typing.

Finally, to Mr F. J. B. Watson, The Wallace Collection, London; to Mr John Goldsmith Phillips, The Metropolitan Museum of Art; and to my husband I owe my especial gratitude for their continued encouragement and advice.

New York
1966

C.L.C.

Acknowledgment

The Author and Publishers wish to thank the following for permission to reproduce the illustrations appearing in this book:
The Metropolitan Museum of Art, New York, for *Portrait of Maria Luisa of Parma* (Bequest of Annie C. Kane, 1926); figs. 10, 13, 14, 20, 21, 34, 53–5, 58, 67–9, 94, 95, 98, 99, 106, 120, 126, 135, 141, 162, 170, 192, 193, 202, 308, 314, 319 and 422 (Bequest of Catherine D. Wentworth, 1948); 15, 245, 673 and 674 (Bequest of Kate Read Blaque, 1938, in memory of her husband, Valentine Alexander Blaque); 29, 38–40, 44, 48, 49, 59, 60, 79, 87, 88, 101, 110, 112, 127, 129, 133, 134, 144–6, 159, 163, 174, 179, 185, 194, 198, 213, 214, 217, 219–21, 227, 237, 238, 247, 249, 250, 252, 255, 260, 288, 294, 312, 342, 448, 455, 528, 602, 604, 610–14 and 645 (Gift of J. Pierpont Morgan, 1917); 80 (Gift of James Donahue, 1954); 136 (Gift of Frederic E. Gilbert, 1959); 180 (Gift of Giulia Morosini, 1932); 195 (Bequest of Edward C. Post, 1915); 207 (Bequest of Mary Martin, 1938); 242, 257 (The Moses Lazarus Collection, Gift of Misses Sarah and Josephine Lazarus, 1888); 263 (Bequest of Isaac D. Fletcher, 1917); 304 (Gift of Mrs Henry Scholtz, 1946); 305 (Gift of Miss Helen O. Brice, 1942); 360, 361 (Bequest of Mary Strong Shattuck, 1935); 366, 371, 372, 416, 417, 426, 427, 431, 432, 623 and 625 (Bequest of John L. Cadwalader, 1914); 370 (Bequest of A. T. Clearwater, 1933); 439 (Gift of C. Gustave Mouraille, 1957, in memory of his sister, Miss M. Mathilde Mouraille); 498, 511, 527, 530, 533 and 544 (Gift of R. Thornton Wilson, 1955, in memory of Florence Ellsworth Wilson); 529 (Gift of Mrs Morris Hawkes, 1924); 595 and 622 (Gift of Mrs Lucy W. Drexel, 1889); 609 (Bequest of Mary Clark Thompson, 1924); 618 (Bequest of W. Gedney Beatty, 1941).
The Walters Art Gallery, Baltimore, for figs. 1, 76–8, 114, 123, 293, 303, 345, 346, 428–30, 480 and 676.
Wartski Ltd., London, for figs. 2, 3, 161, 169, 190, 233, 246, 265, 284, 292, 302, 328, 336, 337, 445, 454, 476, 477, 484 and 627.
Archives Photographiques, Paris, and the Musée du Louvre, Paris, for figs. 4, 5 (photographs by Maurice Chuzeville), 17, 18, 24, 25, 30, 35, 36, 43, 62, 85, 89–91, 100, 108, 115, 117–19, 125, 128, 131, 132, 137, 150, 155, 166, 175, 188, 196, 200, 201, 203, 208–10, 222, 223, 231, 236, 239, 254, 264, 318, 341, 343, 350, 414, 450, 460, 461, 463, 474, 482, 483, 485, 505, 663–5, 668, 669, 671 and 675.
The Trustees of the British Museum, London, for figs. 6, 19, 22, 171, 226, 243, 244, 251, 273, 274, 278, 279, 281, 282, 352, 570, 642–4, 646, 690–2, 694 and 695.
The Director of the Staatliche Kunstsammlungen, Dresden, for figs. 7, 447 and 637.
Musée Cognacq-Jay, Paris, for figs. 8, 26, 27, 45, 51, 121, 140, 143, 147, 172, 173, 186, 187, 206, 216 and 473.
Mr and Mrs Charles B. Wrightsman, for figs. 9, 31, 32, 41, 52, 56, 83, 152, 160 and 253.
Sotheby and Co., London, for figs. 11, 16, 23, 33, 37, 50, 102, 113, 116, 139, 148, 183, 205, 211, 266, 272, 275, 280, 296, 300, 307, 317, 333, 344, 452, 453, 495, 496, 499, 501–3, 513, 514, 537, 560, 561, 568, 572, 573, 633, 634, 636, 638, 640 and 654.
A La Vieille Russie Inc., New York, for figs. 12, 28, 97, 109, 157, 204, 218, 232, 235, 259, 283, 285–7, 289, 323–5, 331, 332, 415, 418, 421, 459, 466–70, 569, 619–21 and 653.
The Trustees of the Wallace Collection, London, for figs. 42, 65, 86, 151, 256 and 457; and for the illustrations on the jacket and frontispiece.
The Trustees of The Henry E. Huntington Library and Art Gallery, San Marino, California, for figs. 46, 81, 82, 92, 96, 107, 158, 165, 167, 177, 184 and 327.
The Trustees of the Victoria and Albert Museum, London, for figs. 47, 130, 178, 224, 225, 228, 230, 258, 271, 315, 349, 462, 475, 481, 487, 490, 493, 494, 526, 576, 591, 592, 594, 596, 597, 599, 600, 603, 605, 608, 656, 688, 702 and 703.
The California Palace of the Legion of Honor, San Francisco, for figs. 57, 105 and 149.
Antique Porcelain Company, New York, for figs. 61, 142, 164, 176, 269, 276, 299, 313, 330, 446, 449, 451, 458, 478, 491, 492, 513, 514, 524, 525, 577, 578, 629 and 672.
The Director-General of the Rijksmuseum, Amsterdam, for figs. 63, 93, 111, 154, 261, 262, 267, 268, 316, 358, 359 and 362.
The Bowes Museum, Barnard Castle, for fig. 64.
The Museum of Fine Arts, Boston, for figs. 66, 277 and 353.
Mrs Harvey A. Firestone, Jr., for figs. 71–3, 103, 104, 531, 532, 534, 535 and 635.
A La Vieille Cité, Paris, for fig. 70.
Madame H. Collin du Bocage, Paris, for figs. 74 and 75.
The Taft Museum, Cincinnati, for fig. 84.
The Cleveland Museum of Art, for figs. 122, 189, 234 (Gift of Mrs Edward B. Greene); 347 (Anonymous Gift); 579 and 580 (Gift of Mr and Mrs J. H. Wade).
The Keeper of the Nationalmuseum, Stockholm, for fig. 124.
The Art Institute of Chicago, for figs. 138, 156, 168, 212, 240, 241, 301, 322, 326 and 456.
The Director of the Royal Scottish Museum, Edinburgh, for figs. 181, 182, 191, 197, 229, 297, 348, 472 and 486.
The Brooklyn Museum, for figs. 199, 364, 382, 419, 574, 641, 662 and 666.
Christie, Manson and Woods, Ltd., London, for figs. 215, 270, 306, 309, 320 and 321; and for colour plates II and III.
The Director of Verwaltung der Staatlichen Schlösser und Gärten, Berlin, for figs. 248, 464, 465 and 471.
Charles Angell, Bath, for fig. 290.

Acknowledgment

The Trustees of The Cooper Union Museum, New York, for figs. 291, 571, 601, 655, 660 and 667.

The Trustees of The Lady Lever Art Gallery, Port Sunlight, for fig. 295.

The Provost of The Queen's College, Oxford, for fig. 298.

The Director of the Museum of Decorative Art, Copenhagen, for figs. 310 and 311.

Mr E. Markus and Harvey and Gore Ltd., for fig. 329.

The Director of the State Hermitage Museum, Leningrad, for figs. 334, 335, 338–40, 488, 489, 542 and 554–9.

The Director of the Museo Stibbert, Florence, for fig. 351.

Mr Philip Hammerslough, for figs. 355, 385, 387, 397–9, 401, 402, 406 and 408.

The New-York Historical Society, New York City, for figs. 356, 357 and 405.

The Master and Fellows of St John's College, Cambridge, for fig. 363.

The Wardens of The Worshipful Company of Goldsmiths, London, for figs. 365 and 639.

The Director of the City of Norwich Museums, Castle Museum, Norwich, for figs. 367–9, 615, 626, 628 and 631.

The President of Magdalen College, Oxford, for fig. 373.

The Director of Sheffield City Museum, for figs. 374–7.

The Henry Ford Museum, Dearborn, Michigan, for figs. 378–81, 400, 407, 412 and 413.

Yale University Art Gallery, for fig. 383; and for fig. 624 (The Mabel Brady Garvan Collection).

Henry Francis du Pont Winterthur Museum, for figs. 384 and 390–2.

Mr John Devereux Kernan, for figs. 386, 388, and for figs. 389 and 393 (photographs by Charles Gunn).

Philadelphia Museum of Art, for figs. 394 and 395 (photographs by A. J. Wyatt, Staff Photographer).

Mr Elliott Richardson, Jr., for fig. 396.

The Norfolk Museum, for figs. 403 and 404.

Mr Paul Gouin, for fig. 409.

Musée de la Province de Quebec, for figs. 410 and 411.

The Director of the Museo Nazionale, Naples, for figs. 423, 500, 510, 512, 538, 539, 543, 545–9, 567, 575, 630, 632, 657 and 686.

The Director of the Röhsska Konstslöjdmuseet, Göteborg, for figs. 424 and 425.

The Director of the Schweiz. Landesmuseum, Zurich, for figs. 433, 562–4 and 649.

The Director of the Museo del Palazzo di Venezia, Rome, for fig. 434.

Museum of the City of New York, for figs. 435, 617, 659 and 670.

Colonial Williamsburg, Virginia, for figs. 436 and 440–4.

The Curator of the Musée Le Secq des Tournelles, Rouen, for figs. 437 and 438.

The Curator of the Musée Nissim de Camondo, Paris, for fig. 479.

The Cecil Higgins Art Gallery, Bedford, for figs. 497, 504, 509, 593, 598 and 616.

The Director of the Württembergisches Landesmuseum, Stuttgart, for figs. 506–8.

The Director of the Landesgewerbeamt Baden-Württemberg, Stuttgart, for figs. 515 and 677–9.

Leitung der Grossherzoglichen Privatsammlungen, Darmstadt, for figs. 516–20.

The Curator of the Musée des Arts Décoratifs, Paris, for figs. 521–3.

The Director of the Cahiers de la Céramique du Verre et des Arts du Feu, Sèvres, for fig. 536.

The Director of the Museo Arquelógico Nacional, Madrid, for figs. 550–3.

The Syndics of the Fitzwilliam Museum, Cambridge, for figs. 565 and 566 (Glaisher Bequest).

The Director, Rosenborg Castle, Copenhagen, for figs. 581–6.

Manchester City Art Gallery, for figs. 587–90 and 606 (Raby Bequest).

Beauchamp Galleries, London, for fig. 607.

The Trustees of The London Museum, for figs. 647 and 648.

Mrs H. B. Findlay, for figs. 650–2 and 701.

The Director of the Österreichische Tabakregie, Vienna, for figs. 658 and 661.

The National Museum of Wales, Cardiff, for figs. 680–2.

The Curator of the State Museum, Brunswick, for figs. 683–5.

City Museum and Art Gallery, Birmingham, for fig. 687.

The Pinto Collection of Wooden Bygones, for figs. 689, 693 and 696–700.

The Publishers are especially grateful to Christie, Manson and Woods, Ltd., for the loan of the colour blocks which appear as Plates II and III.

I Introduction

Few of the dreams and expectations that called explorers westward to America were of more lasting consequence than the unforeseen discovery of tobacco. Whether as medicine or sport, whether snuffed or chewed, whether smoked in a pipe or in a cigarette, tobacco has been, and continues to be, a determining force in the economies and tastes of the West.

The history of tobacco in Europe falls into three distinct consecutive periods. The first comprises the 60-odd years between its discovery in 1492 by two of Columbus's crewmen, and its first general use beginning *c.* 1570. The way was prepared for the acceptance of tobacco by such a large number of first- and second-hand accounts by travellers and herbalists that it seems surprising that it should have taken so long to be recognised. In this period of intensive exploration smoking was observed by Pedro Alvarez Cabral and Nicolas Durand de Villegagnon in Brazil (1500, 1555); by Bernal Diaz del Castillo (*c.* 1492–1581) in Mexico; by Alvar Nuñez Cabeça de Vaca in what is now Texas (1528–34); by Jacques Cartier in Canada (1534), Fernando de Alarcón in California (1540), and René de Laudonnière and Sir John Hawkins in Florida (1564). The first account of tobacco to be published in Europe was that included in Martin Waldseemüller's *Cosmographia introductio* of 1507. It was followed, over the next 50 years, by a number of accounts of which several—notably Oviedo y Valdes' *Historia general de las Indias*—were reprinted, translated and freely borrowed. Despite these early accounts it was only in the decade 1560–70 that tobacco was discovered, all over Europe, as a consumer product. It was by then being grown in Portugal: the first tobacco plants or seeds to be seen in Europe are thought to have been brought to that country from Brazil, probably before 1548, by Luis de Goes. It was his kinsman, the archivist Damião de Goes, who showed some plants to the French ambassador Jean Nicot in 1560, an occasion that resulted in the introduction of tobacco at the court of Catherine de' Medici. (There is, however, no evidence—as S. A. Dickson has shown in *Panacea or Precious Bane*—to support the traditional story that snuff was widely adopted in France, or even used generally at court, as an immediate result of this event.) From Portugal, also, tobacco was introduced into Spain, probably between *c.* 1565 and 1571.

Leaving aside the conflicting claims of precedence which a number of writers have advanced, it may be said that 1570 was the turning point in the acceptance of tobacco in Europe. The published account of Nicot's discovery of it first appeared in the 1570 edition of *L'Agriculture et la maison rustique*, a continuation by Jean Liébault of a work by his late father-in-law, the physician and polymath Charles Estienne. Early in the following year, Pierre Pena and Matthias de l'Obel published, in London, *Stirpium adversaria nova*, the first herbal to consider tobacco as a separate plant (rather than as a variety of henbane). In the same year, in Seville, Nicolas Monardes published his *De la cosas que se traen de nuestras Indias Occidentales*. This proved to be the pivotal account of tobacco, being translated into Latin and Italian and being issued on the Continent in no fewer than ten editions before 1600; the first French translation appeared in 1602. In 1577, an English translation by John Frampton was published as *Ioyfull newes out of the newe founde worlde*.

With the publication of these volumes the account of tobacco enters its second phase, during which period—which lasted until *c.* 1630–5—it was prized as a medicament. It had been as an Indian medicinal drug and as a narcotic in ceremonies that smoking had come to the attention of Europeans; its curative powers were accepted as a matter of course. Monardes and Nicot both stressed the usefulness of tobacco as a cure-all; Henry Buttes, writing in 1599 (*Dyets Dry Dinner*), declared that it

> cureth any griefs, dolour, opilation, impostume, or obstruction, proceeding of cold or winde: especially in the head or breast: the leaues are good against the Migram, cold stomackes, sick kidnies, tooth-ache, fits of the moother, naughty breath, scaldings or burnings . . . The fume taken in a Pipe is good against Rumes, Catarrhs, hoarsenes, ache in the head, stomacke, lungs, breast: also in want of meat, drinke, sleepe or reast.

But this phase was relatively short-lived. Even Buttes admitted that tobacco

> Mortifieth and benummeth: Causeth drowsinesse: troubleth and dulleth the sences: makes (as it were) drunke: dangerous in meale time.

Perhaps the most violent objections were those of James I, whose *Counterblaste to tobacco* (1604) incorporated the resentment of the Church of England against the narcotic properties of tobacco associated with heathen rituals and magic and a thinly disguised attack on Sir Walter Ralegh who had been the first to popularise smoking in England:

> A custome loathsome to the eye, hatefull to the nose, harmefull to the braine, dangerous to the lungs, and in the black stinking fume thereof, neerest resembling the horrible Stigian smoake of the pit that is bottomlesse.

By *c.* 1625 tobacco as a preventive or curative medicine was largely discredited, although the Plague in England in 1665 revived interest in its supposed virtues. But even though tobacco was no longer respectable as a medicament, it had become necessary. Far from being abandoned, it was consumed in ever-increasing quantities, and while there were sporadic attempts in the course of the next century to justify it on medical grounds, tobacco had become a frankly social, pleasurable obsession.

It is with this third phase of the history of tobacco that the present volume is concerned, specifically the universal custom of snuff taking.

Snuffing had been observed as early as 1493 by Friar Ramón Pane, who had accompanied Columbus and remained behind as a missionary. It is from his report that the first published account of snuff taking, among the Taino Indians of Haiti, was provided, in 1511, in *De orbe novo decades* by Pietro Martire d'Anghieri (the translation is by Richard Eden in 1555):

> ... as often as the kynges aske counsaile of their *Zemes* [fetishes] as concerning their warres, increase of fruites or scarsnes, or health and sickenes, they enter into the house dedicate to theyr *Zemes*, where, snuffinge vp into theyr nose-thryls the pouder of the herbe cauled *Cohobba* [the Arawak name for tobacco] ... they say that immediately they see the houses turne topsy turuye, and men to walk with theyr heeles vpwarde: of suche force is this pouder vtterly to take away all sense.

It was not generally adopted, however, until much later in the century. Buttes, in 1599, described tobacco 'compiled very close ... most perspicuous and cleare: which the Nose soonest taketh in snuffe'. His remark, however, should not be taken to imply the existence of a popular social custom in England at so early a date, but rather the acceptance of the medicinal virtues of snuff. That there immediately developed a ritual analogous to (and the undoubted precursor of) snuff taking is evident from the appearance, 1597–8, of the first part of *Henry IV* in which Hotspur described (I.iii) 'a certain lord, neat, and trimly dress'd',

> *And 'twixt his Finger and his Thumbe, he held*
> *A Pouncet-box: which euer and anon*
> *He gaue his Nose, and took't away againe:*
> *Who therewith angry, when it next came there,*
> *Tooke it in Snuffe. And still he smil'd and talk'd ...*

It is tempting to assert that Shakespeare was referring to tobacco, but the allusion is almost certainly to some other aromatic powder.

It was not until 1612, when John Rolfe planted the first seeds of West Indian tobacco in Virginia with a view to making the colony a profitable venture, that tobacco became an important element in the English economy and social life. Up to that time, tobacco (largely for smoking) was being imported into England from Spain: in 1615, 50,000 lb. of Spanish tobacco as against only 2,300 lb. of Virginian were brought in. But by 1618 the American colony yielded over 20,000 lb. and from the following year England began to import more tobacco from her own colony than from Spain. Elsewhere in Europe, Spain enjoyed a virtual monopoly of the tobacco trade, and the progressive rise of snuff taking on the Continent can be traced to its Portuguese and Spanish origins: prior to 1650, in Western Europe, it is only in the Roman Catholic countries—Spain, Italy and Ireland—that snuffing was well estab-lished. (That it was also popular in Russia this early is apparent from an observation made in 1647 by Adam Oelschlager (Olearius) that 'Tobacco was heretofore so common there, that it was generally taken, both in smoak and powder' and that the poorer people were spending so much on it that in 1634 the sale and use of snuff was forbidden.) In a remark that provides an unexpected transcription of Hibernian sternutation as heard by Gallic ears, the French traveller La Boullaye Le Gouz noted in 1644 that among the Irish one had 'but to draw a box of sinisine (i.e., *snisín*, snuff) and offer it to them' to receive the greatest attention from the inhabitants. And two years later John Raymond, in his *Itinerary* of a visit to Italy made in 1646 and 1647, wrote:

> We din'd at Poggio Bonci, a place noted for the perfumed tobacco composed there; which the Italians through custome take in powder as profusely as we in England doe in the pipe.

(Poggibonsi, some 40 miles from Florence, remained the centre of snuff manufacture in Italy through the eighteenth century.) Moreover, it is from the Church itself that we first learn of the uses and abuses of snuff. Her attempts to suppress the habit, associated with heathen witchcraft, were totally ineffective, even amongst the clergy and within the precincts of the churches. Snuff taking during Mass had evidently reached such proportions that in 1624 Pope Urban VIII felt compelled to issue a bull excommunicating those who took snuff in church; and in 1635 Tomas Ramón (*Nueva prematica de Reformacion*) declared that

> It is an abomination in the sight of God that the clergy take snuff at ecclesiastical councils.

Papal wrath culminated in a bull of 1690 which, prohibiting snuff within the walls of Saint Peter's, was (according to Misson)

> founded upon the Holy Father's being inform'd that a certain voluptuous Priest, while he was saying Mass in this very Church, had his snuff-box open upon the Altar, and took Snuff many Times. As the least Inattention is sufficient to spoil the Design and the Success of Transubstantiation, has not the prudent Pope done very wisely?

But habit was too strong: in 1709 (2 March) the *Tatler* spoke out against the freedom with which women took snuff in church; while Joseph Baretti, in 1768, remarked of the Italian friars:

> As they all take snuff, those who have no great means of buying it, apply carefully to the cultivation of tobacco, and make it themselves.

Evidently the greatest co-operation the Church could expect to receive was during Lent. C. F. P. Masson, in his description of Russia published in 1800, observed that

> The common people observe with the most scrupulous exactness the four grand Lents which are enjoined them. Their superstition carries them so far, that they abstain even from their wives or their snuff-boxes.

Although tobacco had been known in France for about a hundred years, it is not until 1655 that snuff was first described, in *Traicté du tabac* by Louis Ferrant, who treated it entirely as a sternutatory. Within ten years it had become a matter for social comment. Jean-Baptiste Lully's *Ballet de l'Impatience* (1661) included a three-voice choral canzonetta of the 'snuff takers'; in 1665 Molière opened his play *Dom Juan* with a panegyric on snuff, '*la passion des honnestes gens'*. Little was said of snuff during the reign of Louis XIV, to whom it was notoriously distasteful. It nonetheless enjoyed an unofficial vogue, to judge by the popularity of Simon Barbe's *Le parfumeur françois*, a recipe book for scenting snuffs, which went into four editions between 1693 and 1698.

From France snuff spread to northern Europe and England, making its appearance in Holland about 1665, and in Germany about ten years later. It is said to have been introduced into the latter country by Huguenot refugees who were, at least in Cologne, the first snuff takers and manufacturers. It is interesting to note, however, that an edict of the Elector of Bavaria dated 2 December 1675 granted a monopoly of all tobacco and plain snuff to an Italian named Bignami. Bignami was evidently only the first of a succession of Italian tobacco merchants in Germany: nearly a century later, Baron Caspar Riesbeck, travelling through Germany in 1780, commented on an ostentatious villa near Höchst, the property of one Bolongaro who 'made his fortune entirely by the snuff which bears his name, which is still extremely liked throughout all Germany'.

In other regions of the Continent, snuff taking as a social custom appears also to have become known during the last quarter of the seventeenth century. Pierre Martin de La Martinière, who published his account of a journey from Norway to Siberia in 1671, emphasised throughout his narrative the prevalence of smoking and the eagerness with which roll tobacco was sought after from the travellers. But already by 1698 snuff was included among the goods imported into Denmark. Switzerland was the last country to take up snuff: strict sumptuary laws prevented its adoption before *c.* 1775.

As on the Continent, the first use of snuff in England was for its curative powers and it is mentioned in this respect, as has been seen, as early as 1599. The medicinal approach was still in evidence in 1633 when Stephen Bradwell, in *Helps for Suddain Accidents*, recommended 'powder of strong Tobacco' as a poison antidote. As a social pastime, snuff taking appeared in England still later. A proposal issued in 1797 (later remembered by the diarist William Hone) to publish a two-volume history of tobacco and snuff (a proposal evidently never fulfilled) included in the table of contents 'Snufftakers in the Parliamentary army. . . . Oval Snuff-boxes first used by the Rounde-heads. . . .' A different origin was offered in 1708 by a writer in the *British Apollo* who asserted that

> Snuff, tho' the Use of it has been long known to such, as were by Marchandizing or other means, familiar with the Spanish Customes, has been till lately, a perfect stranger to the Practice of the British Nation, and like our other Fashions, came to us from *France*.

In support of the latter theory it may be noted that the earliest discovered use of the word 'snuff box' occurs only in 1681, and that literary references to snuff taking begin to appear regularly only in the final quarter of the century. (Samuel Butler's scathing reference, in *Hudibras*, to 'snuff-mundungus'—a term reserved for the very worst quality of tobacco— may be counterbalanced by the enthusiasm of his contemporary, John Dryden, who appears to have been the first in a long line of compulsive snuff takers in England.) The Dutch derivation of the word 'snuff' (*O.E.D.*) suggests that the habit may also have been adopted on a popular level through trade associations between Holland and England: it was through clandestine trade mediated by the Dutch East India Company during the Civil War that American tobacco reached England.

While snuff had enjoyed a not inconsiderable market for over half a century, its commercial availability and popularity in Europe increased suddenly in the first decade of the eighteenth century as a result of two events. The first, which affected England alone, was the capture in 1702 of about 50 tons of snuff from Spanish ships at Port St Mary and Vigo Bay. According to Charles Lillie, the contemporary London perfumer and tobacconist who tells the story,

> This sort of bale snuff had never been seen or known in England before, except through some Spanish Jews, who, in the present case, bought up almost the whole quantity at a considerable advantage. . . . From [this] quantity of different snuffs, thus distributed throughout the kingdom, novelty being quickly embraced by us in England, arose the custom and fashion of snuff taking.

The second event was the Union of England and Scotland in 1707, as a result of which Glasgow became the link between the supply of American tobacco and the Continental market. Hitherto, the chief source had been the Brazilian tobacco imported by Spain and Portugal. (Small amounts of tobacco were grown in almost every country on the Continent, although it was strictly forbidden in England in deference to the colonial trade.) But the Union enabled Scotland to trade directly with America for the first time, and to take advantage of her ready access to Continental ports. Within 16 years the Glasgow tobacco lords—who, distinguished by their scarlet cloaks and gold-headed canes, were to make the city famous for the prosperity they brought it—had 23 ships. Their industry succeeded in severely diminishing the trade of the English ports of Bristol and Whitehaven; by 1771–2 no less than 35,659,347 lb. of American tobacco were exported from Glasgow to such diverse parts of Europe as Leghorn, Bordeaux, Dieppe, Mahon, Amsterdam, Göteborg, Copenhagen, Bergen and Dublin. In addition, 5,769 lb. were re-imported into America and 23,873 lb. to the West Indies. Not all of this tobacco, of course, was converted into snuff. The lingering competition of the pipe is evident in the popularity of miniatures of domestic peasant scenes adapted from Teniers (*80*), which are commonly found on Continental gold boxes *c.* 1760. (It is curious that pipe smoking should have been so conspicuous a subject in the decoration of snuff boxes, while snuff taking is scarcely ever represented.) It was only in 1773 that Dr Johnson remarked, with regret, that 'Smoking has gone out': in Holland it remained more popular than snuff throughout the century, while in America chewing tobacco was preferred. But until *c.* 1830 snuff constituted the most important part of the tobacco trade. The records of the London tobacconists Fribourg and Treyer reveal that from 1720 to 1820 snuff accounted for 90 per cent. of their retail trade, and that it was only after 1850 that it comprised less than half of that trade.

In America, snuff taking appeared earliest, and survived the most vigorously, in cities where the influence of Dutch or English customs was most persistent, as in Albany and Boston. The habit must have attained some currency for an advertisement of 1734 to identify the waistcoat of a runaway servant as 'Snuff coloured'. Even as early as 1726, in Burlington, New Jersey, the ladies of the Society of Friends were warned against the

> Use [of] ye Irreverent practice of taking Snuff, or handing Snuff boxes one to another in Meetings.

Snuff was never generally accepted in the eighteenth century, however, smoking and chewing tobacco being preferred. Moreau de Saint-Méry, visiting the country in 1793–8, reported that

> an American of either sex who uses snuff is a sort of phenomenon, and the women never deform or dirty their noses by using this powder so cherished by Europeans.

A little snuff was manufactured in the colonies; the most renowned, and possibly the earliest, snuff mill was that established by Gilbert Stuart's father, shortly before 1755, near Kingston, Rhode Island. The elder Stuart had been persuaded to emigrate from Glasgow in the hope of duplicating the thriving snuff-making industry for which his native city was well known. Although a few other mills were founded later in the century, chiefly in New York City, Albany and Philadelphia (where, in 1790, there were 20 snuff manufacturers), native commercial production was hardly warranted. The smallness of the demand is clearly indicated by the fact that of the American tobacco exported by the Glasgow merchants in 1771–2, 194 lb. of snuff were sent back to New York, 432 lb. to Philadelphia, and 817 lb. to Virginia. Snuff taking became more general during the second quarter of the nineteenth century, a period in which a number of mills were founded, chiefly in the north-east. In 1814 (16 July), John Adams wrote to Thomas Jefferson that one of the things he had learned from Plato (*Symposium*, 185–9) was

> that sneezing is a cure for the Hickups. Accordingly I have cured myself and all my Friends of that provoking disorder, for thirty Years with a Pinch of Snuff.

By the following year, it is said, snuff accounted for a larger share of the industry than tobacco for smoking and chewing.

As it increased in respectability, snuff taking became perhaps the most common topic of conversation and satire in the eighteenth century, one to which allusions could be shared by everyone. Lady Mary Wortley Montagu wrote her sister in 1723, that 'making verses is almost as common as taking snuff'; and Horace Walpole observed to George Selwyn (3 April 1766) that 'Hearts do not snap like a tortoise-shell snuff-box'. But the enthusiasm for snuff was not limited to the virtuosi: in 1773, a peasant woman in the Scottish Highlands refused Dr Johnson's offer of a shilling, preferring snuff instead. Of particular concern to snuff takers and satirists was the snuff box, which was no mere container for the powdered herb, but the focus of an elaborate social ritual and the symbol of vanity and fashion.

Snuff was not always taken from a box. The Indian method, which was understandably not adopted in Europe, was to inhale the powder through a forked tube, the two arms of which 'they put in their nostrils and the other end in the smoke of the burning herb'. It was this pipe, according to Oviedo who gives the account of it, that was called by the Indians *tabaco*, and not the plant itself. But the confusion had already been established and the misnomer has remained. In Europe, in addition to boxes, snuff bottles and jars were in use. Charles Darwin, although he possessed a silver snuff box given him by his mother-in-law, Mrs Wedgwood of Maer, 'generally took snuff from a jar on the hall table, because having to go this distance (from his study) for a pinch was a slight check'. Snuff containers peculiar to Scotland were mulls, formed of rams' horns fitted with silver lids and tips. And H. G. Graham (*Social Life of Scotland in the Eighteenth Century*) noted, as part of the costume of the ladies of Edinburgh, that 'by their side hung the little bags which held the snuff they freely used'. Dr Johnson, Frederick the Great and Napoleon are all traditionally (and unreliably) said to have carried snuff loose in their pockets. But from the middle of the seventeenth century, the most common container for snuff was a box evoking a possessive pride most feelingly summed up by George Eliot:

> . . . the most glutinously indefinite minds enclose some hard grains of habit;
> and a man has been lax about all his own interests except the retention of his
> snuff box, concerning which he was watchful, suspicious, and greedy of clutch.

It is not surprising, given the early acceptance of snuff there, to find the first description of boxes in Italy. In 1636, the variety of materials used in their manufacture was enumerated in *La Tabaccheide*, a poem by Francesco Zucchi. In it, he described

> *Tabbachieri d'osso,*
> *Di lupini indiani, altri di creta,*
> *Di Cristallo, d'Auorio, altri di Bosso*
> *Si porta in Alabastro, e non si vieta*
> *Metterlo in vasi ancor d'Ebeno moro,*
> *In limoni [?], in Aranci di Gaeta*
> *Bella d'argento son, più belli d'Oro.*
> *In Castagne del'India, in Cocche, in Pine*
> *Si Serba e in Noci ancor d'alto lauoro*
> *Se ne vedono assai d'ossi marini,*
> *Di Matreperle, e di Conchiglie, ornate*
> *De la Natura di lauro fini.*

Zucchi concluded his catalogue with a long section in praise of horn as the material most suitable for snuff boxes.

Concerning the sizes and shapes of these and later seventeenth-century boxes little more than conjecture can be offered. Assuming the relatively small scale of the tobacco trade and the novelty of the habit, it is not likely that boxes exceeded about $2\frac{1}{2}$ inches in their greatest dimension. (A gold box cited in the *London Gazette* in 1682 weighed one ounce and was probably under two inches.) In this, early snuff boxes must have been all but indistinguishable from boxes used for pounce, sweetmeats or patches. It is only during the period *c.* 1730–*c.* 1775 that the larger size of the snuff box—from three to four inches—makes it more readily distinguishable from other boxes that could be found on a fashionable dressing table of the period. During the last quarter of the eighteenth century, snuff boxes again became smaller as the habit gradually declined.

In general, a tightly closing hinged cover has always been characteristic of snuff boxes, although in Holland tobacco boxes were often hinged. Spring hinges were a common feature of early boxes, being alluded to as early as 1665 by Karel van Mander, but they are not mentioned after *c.* 1715. Circular boxes, being generally constructed with lift-off lids, were less suitable for protecting the moisture of the snuff and relatively few were made. (The small capacity of the circular papier-mâché boxes common in the nineteenth century would have offset the somewhat loose fit of their covers.)

Only a suggestion of the variety of shapes of seventeenth-century boxes can be gathered. James Howell wrote that the Irish, whom he visited in 1639, commonly 'take out their boxes of smutchin [i.e., snuff, a corruption of the Gaelic *smuiteán*] and draw it into their nostrils with a quill', a custom that was elaborated on nearly a century later in *Whipping Tom: or, a Rod for a Proud Lady* (6th edition, 1722) in which the anonymous author observed that

> In the primitive Times of taking this exotick, or outlandish commodity, it was
> sparingly taken out of a Spring-Pipe fixed to a wooden Box in the shape of a
> Pear . . .

(Quills and snuff spoons were common accessories of the snuff box on the Continent, but rarely occur in England. In the eighteenth century the spoon was perhaps used as much for stirring the snuff—which according to some contemporary writers had to be moistened every few hours to retain its aroma—as for raising it to the nostrils. Until *c.* 1710 snuff rasps, with which a person grated his own roll tobacco, were in general use.) Octagonal boxes were mentioned as a fashionable novelty by van Mander in 1665. Louvois, said to have been the first Frenchman to possess a snuff box, owned (according to Mme de Genlis) a gold-mounted lacquer box in the shape of a heart. Oval boxes are commonly mentioned in England at the end of the century and remained the predominant shape until *c.* 1780, when they were superseded by oblong ones. Shell- or cartouche-shaped boxes came into fashion in the first quarter of the eighteenth century: '*tabatières à coquille*' are mentioned most often in the 1723 inventory of the Duchesse d'Orléans, which also included circular and oblong boxes, a gold box '*en trèfle*' and a double box '*en gondolle*'. Among other fanciful shapes are book-shaped boxes (first mentioned in 1710), and boxes in the form of sedan chairs (*414*); a snuff box '*en étoile*' advertised in the *Mercure de France* of December 1717 is perhaps of the same shape as that '*à soleil*' in the Orléans collection. Boxes modelled in the form of animals or human figures, their flat hinged bases serving as covers, have been variously called snuff boxes and *bonbonnières*. That some may be included in the former group can be assumed from an entry in the daybook of the Parisian *marchand mercier* Lazare Duvaux (p. 21) in 1757:

> *Mme la Marq. de Pompadour . . . La garniture en or à gorge & charnière d'un petit chat de lacq, formant une tabatière.*

Similar boxes carved in hardstone were undoubtedly intended to hold snuff. Less certainly *tabatières* are the many smaller boxes, of porcelain and enamel, modelled as shepherds (*526*), Oriental figures, animals, etc. Originating in the French porcelain factories, they were imitated (and sometimes copied literally) in England, first at Chelsea where they were always referred to as *bonbonnières*: whatever their original function, it was likely to have been borrowed together with the style of these boxes. In America, however, the goldsmith Edmond Milne advertised in the *Pennsylvania Gazette* in 1763 (15 December) that he had just imported from London 'enamell'd snuff boxes; in the shape of birds fruit and flowers; and some shoe fashion. . . .' The last-named design occurs about the middle of the century as a *sabot*, being altered with successive styles of costume well into the Victorian era.

In considering the varied shapes of snuff boxes and their decoration, the pressure of fashion is everywhere evident. 'You need not be in dread of true architecture', Walpole wrote Anne Pitt (19 January 1766). 'It appeared here for a moment as a mode, and consequently spread itself like wildfire into their snuff-boxes, china and dress; for whether composed of gauze or marble, no fashion is meant to last longer than a lover—it is the form is considered, not the materials.' For each box of apparently unique shape, it may be presumed that parallels exist in other materials. The Parisian silver sedan chair (*414*) has also been seen in German enamel; Louvois' heart-shaped box reappears in Parisian gold, Mennecy and Meissen porcelain and in American silver (*392*). Book-shaped boxes have been cited in silver, pottery and leather; boat-shaped ones in silver, hardstone and base metal. In like manner, a prevailing decorative style may be found on virtually all boxes of a given period, whatever their material. The lack of examples of snuff boxes from certain countries, notably Italy and Spain, should not be understood to indicate that they were not made, but simply that lack of interest has so far prevented their coming to light. A gold box in the French taste possibly made in Kaschau (Košice) in what was then northern Hungary (*352*) may serve to exemplify the perhaps unexpectedly wide diffusion of a decorative style. Some of this diffusion can be accounted for by the prevalence of engravings, especially pattern books for goldsmiths and jewellers. Among the earliest relevant here were two volumes, containing designs suitable for engraving on snuff boxes and similar objects of *bijouterie*, published in London in 1682 and 1697 by Simon Gribelin (1662–1733): *A Book of seuerall Ornaments* and *A Book of Ornaments useful to Jewellers Watchmakers and all other Artists*. In France, several artists included designs for boxes in their work, among them Jean Berain the Elder (1638–1710) and his brother, Claude (living 1726); the Parisian goldsmith Jean Bourguet (m. 1689,[1] living 1723) who issued two editions of his *Livre de Taille d'épargne* in 1702 and 1723, respectively; Jean du Viviers (1687–1761) whose designs for '*Dessus de Tabatières*' are included in a volume (Bibl. Nat. Paris) entitled *Manières et façons dont les tabatières sont faites en 1719 et 1720;* the unidentified Mondon whose signature occurs on engravings of *Tabatières à pierreries* and *Tabatières de Paysages et de Ruines;* Juste-Aurèle Meissonnier (1693–1750) and P. Moreau (w. 1771[1]). The architect Paul Decker (1677–1713) published in Germany a set of designs for snuff boxes of which one, a shell-shaped example divided into panels of strapwork on alternately light and dark grounds, was clearly designed with tortoiseshell *piqué* in mind and may have served as the prototype for many similar boxes of the period (*619, 622*). Somewhat later, Jean-Christophe Weigel (d. *c.* 1746) published his *Neu inventirte Schnup Toback Dosen von allerhand Künstler*, and Jean Leonhard Wuest (w. *c.* 1730) included snuff boxes in his *Groezt od' Geschnittent Gallanteries*. More elusive, but scarcely less important as sources of decoration, were the countless ornamental engravings suitable (as Walpole emphasised) for application to any medium or technique. The arabesques and palmettes of Berain and Daniel Marot (1650–1712) are to be found in their designs for ceilings, vases, boxes, embroidery, guns, triumphal arches and gardens. The adaptability of particular designs, and the freedom with which artists borrowed them for their own purposes has been neatly demonstrated by Geoffrey de Bellaigue (*Burlington Magazine*, May 1965), who has followed the transformation of a hunting scene painted by Jean-Baptiste Oudry in 1723 and engraved by N.-C. Silvestre. As altered by the unidentified artist Roch, it was re-engraved by one Daumont. It was this later engraving that may have served as the model for an anonymous drawing of the subject, altered still further to adapt it to the lid of a snuff box; the subject occurs once again in marquetry on a chest of drawers at Waddesdon Manor.

Book ornament and illustration were used equally freely. The garland-hung medallions of trophies engraved as head-pieces by Pierre-Philippe Choffard (1729–1809) are echoed in the Parisian gold boxes of the same period (*141, 158*); song-book illustrations are transposed on to English enamel boxes (*604*). Supreme borrowers that they were, the English turned out, in the second half of the eighteenth century, hundreds of pattern books with engravings after French, Flemish and Dutch painters as well as after such native designers as Robert Hancock, James Gwin and Charles Fenn. Intended primarily for the painters of porcelain and enamel, they are discussed more fully in Chapter VIII and are mentioned here to emphasise the ready exchange of decorative motifs between countries.

A third source of stylistic diffusion is the custom of copying actual boxes. Such a practice, which is extremely difficult to document, is premised on three circumstances: (1) the phenomenon of fashion, which insists on repetition until an enthusiasm has run its course; (2)

---

[1] m. is used to indicate the year in which a goldsmith became a master, w. the year in which he was last known to be working.

the close ties that unite any guild or union; (3) trade. Three versions of a box by Charles Le Bastier (*160*) may serve to illustrate the first point (it is also apparent that a replica of a box was sometimes executed by a different maker, e.g., *91, 92*). As an example of the second, we may cite the Parisian goldsmiths, most of whom lived and worked on the Ile Saint-Louis or near and on the Pont Neuf. Records of apprenticeship, among the many documents published by Nocq (*Le poinçon de Paris*), offer a suggestion of stylistic influence (P.-F.-M. de Beaulieu was apprenticed to Jean George; P.-F. Drais and Louis Roucel both worked for Jean Ducrollay); so also do those of intermarriage and of the attainment of mastership by the sons of goldsmiths. Certainly the recurrence of decorative motifs on snuff boxes is occasionally due to the inevitable familiarity amongst the goldsmiths of one another's work.

The influence of commerce is immediately apparent in the English figural *bonbonnières* that have been mentioned above. As an example of direct quotation, we may mention a swan-shaped enamel box in the Victoria and Albert Museum (Schreiber Collection, cat. no. 83), which duplicates a Mennecy version mounted in Paris silver dating 1744–50. On an even more piratical level, the close relation between trade and decorative styles is suggested by *A Letter to the Right Honourable Sir Robert Walpole* published in 1732. Its author, Charles Foreman, was protesting the restrictions against the exportation from England into France of 'All Sorts of fine *Hard-ware* and *Bijouteries* with Gold and Silver Ornaments, such as *Snuff Boxes, Tobacco Boxes*, &c.'; he noted that the result of the ban was simply that the Dutch bought up the English goods and then sold them in France as Dutch. From his brief description it may be hazarded that Foreman was referring to boxes of tortoiseshell *piqué*, which are never marked and which display such a remarkable uniformity of style as to make attribution of their provenance extremely difficult.

The imitation of actual boxes is most likely to have occurred in those countries where snuff taking and/or luxury manufactures were less developed than in France and England. It is apparent from the newspaper advertisements of American jewellers that most of the work for sale in their shops was imported from England. Daniel Fueter announced in *The New-York Gazette or the Weekly Post-Boy* (10 March 1763) that he had just imported 'Snuff Boxes of curious Workmanship'; a 'great choice of curious snuff boxes' from London was offered by Thomas Richardson in 1770 (*The New-York Gazette and the Weekly Mercury*, 12 November). In Philadelphia five years later, Nicolas Brooks advertised for a sale a 'curious collection of Goods, viz. . . . . paper, wood, ennamel and tortoise-shell snuff boxes' which we may safely assume were imported. The similarity of style between American base-metal boxes of the early nineteenth century and English versions in silver and pewter is surely accountable for by example.

The appearance of snuff boxes was affected by fashions not only in decoration but in usage. The refinements that accompanied the possession of a snuff box were apparently limitless, and worthy of the satirical comment they elicited. Steele genially offered the readers of the

Spectator (8 August 1711) lessons in the 'Exercise of the Snuff-Box', while the author of *Whipping Tom* (1722) contemptuously described the mannerisms that accompanied snuff taking:

> . . . some only just dip the Tip of the middle Finger into the Box . . . then this Nostrill's play'd with, then t'other. . . . Others take a Pinch betwixt the Thumb and fore Finger, which apply'd to the right Nostril with the Palm upwards, and to the left Nostril, with the Back of the Hand outward; some betwixt Finger and Thumb hold it perhaps a Quarter or half an Hour, not snuffing it, but daubing it with . . . unbecoming Airs (especially the Female Sex) under their Nostrills. . . .

The complete ritual was outlined in an anonymous French pamphlet of *c.* 1750:

1. *Prenez la Tabatière de la main gauche.*
2. *Passez la Tabatière dans la main gauche.*
3. *Frapez sur la Tabatière.*
4. *Ouvrez la Tabatière.*
5. *Presentez la Tabatière à la Compagnie.*
6. *Retirez à vous la Tabatière.*
7. *Tenez toûjours la Tabatière ouverte.*
8. *Rassemblez le Tabac dans la Tabatière, en frapant la Tabatière à côté.*
9. *Pincez le Tabac proprement de la main droite.*
10. *Tenez quelque tems le Tabac dans les doigts, avant que de le porter au nez.*
11. *Portez le Tabac au nez.*
12. *Reniflez avec justesse des deux narines, & sans grimace.*
13. *Eternuez, toussez, crachez.*
14. *Fermez la Tabatière.*

Tapping the box thrice to settle the snuff was an essential preliminary: Fanny Burney reports that Mrs Schwellenberg, Lady of the Bedchamber to Queen Charlotte (herself a notorious snuff taker for whose sake the King—who detested it—would take a pinch in order to please her), kept a pair of frogs of which she boasted 'I can make them croak when I will, when I only go so to my snuff-box, knock, knock, knock, they croak all what I please'. Another step in the ritual that is frequently mentioned in England *c.* 1715 was to admire oneself in the mirror-lined cover of the box. From the scarcity of surviving examples it must be concluded that most of these looking-glasses have been broken, or replaced—when fashion directed— by miniatures; they have been seen, however, on a Paris gold box dated as late as 1738–9.

Nothing was more generally distasteful to the pamphleteers than the adoption of snuff by women. Steele protested in the *Spectator* (4 April 1712) against 'an impertinent Custom the Women, the fine Women, have lately fallen into, of taking Snuff', especially during meal-times—when 'an upper Lip mixed with Snuff and the Sauce, is what is presented to the Observation of all'—and church services. Women were, in fact, among the earliest collectors of snuff boxes. Sixty-seven are listed in the Orléans inventory (1723); and Horace Walpole, writing to his cousin Thomas (8 April 1786) noted that

> The catalogue of the Duchess of Portland's collection is come out. . . . There are hundreds of old-fashioned snuff-boxes that were her mother's [wife of the Earl of Oxford, Queen Anne's Prime Minister], who wore three different every week.

Walpole's choice of verb is interesting, suggesting that the snuff box was an essential part of the toilette. In 1712, while describing his new gold snuff box to Stella, Swift informed her that 'the Dutchess of Hamilton has made me Pockets for like a woman's, with a Belt and Buckle, for you know I wear no wastcoat in Summer; & there are severall divisions, and one on purpose for my box, oh ho . . . '. That boxes were not always carried loose is suggested by the notice, in the *Daily Courant* of 14 July 1710, of the loss of 'a Dimmity Pocket with a Silver Snuff-Box', which seems to refer to an individual bag that protected the box against scratching. The remarkably good condition of eighteenth-century enamelled gold boxes may perhaps be attributed, at least in part, to the continued use of just such a protective 'pocket'.

As women took up snuffing and as the habit became increasingly profitable for the makers of boxes, distinctions began to be made (especially in Paris) amongst boxes for particular sexes, seasons and costumes.

The difference between snuff boxes for men or women was determined sometimes by size, sometimes by shape or decoration. In 1761 J.-J. Barrière consigned to one Cotteau, for engraving, an oval box of varicoloured gold '*à usage de femme*', with a fable subject on the bottom. This is a type of box common enough at that time (*100*), and it was probably its size that designated its use. Similarly, '*Une boeste d'homme, à cage avec placques de cailloux de sardoine*' in the collection of Madame de Pompadour, was probably merely larger than the '*boete pour femme, à baste pleine en or de coulleur, le dessus et dessous de composition*' from the same collection. In other instances, it was obviously the shape of the box or its decoration that determined its use. The goldsmith Jean George in 1764 lost two gold boxes '*en baignoire, pour homme*'; the shape (*86*) would not have been considered appropriate for women. In 1763 J.-M. Tiron advertised for the recovery of '*Une boîte d'homme, carrée . . . avec un secret dessous à ressort d'acier pour un grand portrait*', which suggests a desire to conceal a miniature of one's mistress or some more illicit subject. The use of double lids and false bottoms for such a purpose is evident from the beginning of the eighteenth century. The name of Carl Gustave Klingstedt (1657–1734) has been traditionally associated with amorous scenes concealed in snuff boxes of the *Régence*. And in England in 1719 James Arbuckle (*Snuff/a Poem*) took note of

> *Soft Couches, Beds of Doun, and easy Chairs,*
> *Where lock'd in Bliss, the wanton Pencil feigns*
> *Consenting Dam'sels, and dissolving Swains.*
> *Instructive Scenes, that give the Youth t'improve*
> *In the Mysterious Ways and Rites of Love . . .*

(The snuff box with a hidden compartment also had a political use, enabling the Jacobites in England, and the Royalists and Bonapartists in France, to carry undetected portraits of their respective heroes.)

Snuff boxes to match the season or one's costume were a matter for comment by the middle of the eighteenth century. Mercier, in his *Tableau de Paris*, observed that the winter snuff box was heavy, the summer one light, and that the man of taste owned a different box for each day of the year. This was a well-known extravagance of Count Heinrich von Brühl (d. 1763), Prime Minister of Saxony and director of the Meissen porcelain factory from 1733 to 1756. According to Dr John Moore (1779) Brühl possessed

> at least three hundred Suits of clothes. . . . A painting of each suit, with the particular cane and snuff-box belonging to it, was very accurately drawn in a large book, which was presented to his Excellency every morning by his Valet de Chambre, that he might fix upon the dress in which he wished to appear for the day.

Boswell counted 'upwards of seven hundred snuff-boxes in gold, and many of them very rich with diamonds' when he attended the sale of Count Brühl's effects in Leipzig in 1764.

Further distinctions in snuff boxes are less easily identified. The Orléans collection included a '*Tabatière de chasse d'or en gondolle à deux tabacs*'; later in the century, the term '*journée de chasse*' occurs in connection with boxes of gold or porcelain. Contrary to the natural assumption, the term clearly had nothing to do with the decoration of the box. Among the 47 boxes in Mme de Pompadour's collection were eighteen *journées de chasse* of such varied styles as gold-mounted malachite, '*vernis noir, avec papillon noir*', '*de bois de raport, à figures chinoises*' and of lacquer '*fond d'or à dragons*'. The name is probably allusive to the size of the boxes, and suggests they were designed to hold just the amount of snuff required for the day's chase.

Other boxes were (especially in Paris) designated by particular names that were the invention of the moment, intended to sustain interest in a luxury market. Thus, in 1770, Isaac-Nicolas Roger (m. 1768) advertised in *L'Avant-coureur* his 'tabatiere optique'

> où un cercle, placé sous le couvercle, fait apparaitre, parmi les ornemens fixes, successivement quatre portraits ou sujets differents, qu'on peut changer si l'on veut.

The previous year, Henry-Daniel Robineau (m. 1754) had announced his invention of a snuff box which opened in ten different ways without affecting the decoration. The *marchand mercier* Compigné, in the rue Greneta, offered *tabatières de deuil* in 1774, and in 1776 snuff boxes called *platitude* or *turgotine* were in fashion. These were essentially topical boxes made of inexpensive materials (cf. *439, 690*) and were sold by the European and American merchants on an equal footing with those of gold. Indeed, though so highly prized, gold boxes by no means enjoyed the exclusive favour of eighteenth-century collectors. Madame de Pompadour and the duc d'Aumont possessed boxes of ivory, tortoiseshell, porcelain and hardstone as well as gold; and Grancher, at whose shop in 1773 Mrs Thrale 'long'd for a snuff box of exquisite beauty' advertised '*Une grande quantité de tabatières, depuis les plus bas prix jusqu'à celles d'or émaillé*', including those of tortoiseshell, leather, steel and *vernis Martin*. Although such boxes had been made since the seventeenth century they became common only after *c.* 1775, largely as a result of cheaper materials and industrial methods of production. The assembling of snuff boxes on a piece-work basis will be seen (Chapter II) to have been a standard practice in eighteenth-century Paris: but where the Parisian *marchand mercier* combined gold and Sèvres porcelain and diamonds for the wealthy few, the Birmingham merchants dealt in steel and enamel and agate for the bourgeoisie. By 1770 Matthew Boulton (1728–1809) was employing 'seven or eight hundred' artisans in the manufacture of goods which included (according to Dr Erasmus Darwin who visited the Soho factory in 1768)

> toys and utensils of various kinds, in gold, copper, tortoiseshell, enamels, and many vitreous and metallic compositions, with gilt, plated, and inlaid wares.

Among these may be counted gilt metal and tortoiseshell snuff boxes which Boulton had begun to make the previous year. It is probable also that he was active in the mass production of enamel snuff boxes and that, about 1772, in collaboration with Josiah Wedgwood, he mounted the potter's jasper cameos in snuff boxes as well as in necklaces and bracelets. This is necessarily somewhat conjectural, as the diversity of Boulton's interests, the absence of identifying marks, and the scale of the factory system all but preclude individual attribution. (Nor, after all, was Boulton the only wholesaler who turned his attention to snuff boxes: John Taylor, John Baskerville, and Henry Clay are the best known of the many rival factories.) Despite this elusiveness of attribution the importance of Matthew Boulton and his colleagues must not be underestimated, for by their use of the latest advances in techniques (the rose-engine lathe, transfer printing) and materials (steel, enamel, papier-mâché) they helped transform the snuff box from an object of luxury to one of common possession. Further, commercial contacts spread the work of the Birmingham hardwaremen all over Europe and America. It appears that most of the cheaper snuff boxes for sale in America in the last quarter of the century were imported from Birmingham and London; and the demand for Birmingham work in Russia was such that Boulton and Wedgwood retained an agent in St Petersburg to take orders. (In this connection, it may be noted that in 1777 snuff boxes valued at no less than £241 15s.—about 1610 boxes, at a presumed average price of 3s.—were imported into that city from England.)

This democratisation was of course only possible in a social climate which considered the luxurious gold boxes of mid-century Paris as symbols of wasteful royal extravagance. The social influence of the Parisian gold box was essentially over by about 1775. It had been for about a century an object of the most coveted favour and, as such, had been the dominant stylistic force. The royal gift of a gold snuff box was certain to have a direct effect on current manners and tastes. Goldsmith, in his biography of Beau Nash, reported that in 1738, upon the gift by the Prince of Orange of 'a very fine snuff-box . . . some of the nobility thought it would be proper to give snuff-boxes too; they were quickly imitated by the middling gentry, and it soon became the fashion to give Mr. Nash snuff-boxes'. The presentation by Louis XV in 1760 to '*Mme Brona, cantatrice italienne*' of '*une tabatière d'or, pour femme, émaillée, à figures flamandes*' was sure to stimulate the demand for similar boxes: it may be observed that almost all 'Teniers' boxes date *c.* 1760 (*88*). In Paris, the presentation of a gold box had been, since 1668 when the custom is first recorded, the most acceptable gesture of esteem, suitable for ambassadors, the nobility, singers and even (1682) 'une musicienne anglaise'. The gold box was an essential part of the royal *corbeille de mariage*: that of Maria Josephine of Saxony, second wife (in 1747) of the Dauphin, included '*Une parure complète comprenant tabatière, boîte à mouches, panier . . .*' in which the '*tabatière*' was in fact 36 gold boxes. In Great Britain and America, the Freedom of a city was presented enclosed in a gold box; and gold boxes were frequently used to hold more tangible gifts: at a garden party of the Empress Amelia's in Vienna, in 1716, Lady Mary Wortley Montagu wrote her sister that the prize for a certain game was 'a fine ruby ring' in a gold snuff box. In 1735, the Prince of Wales presented the *castrato* Farinelli 'with a richly wrought gold snuff-box set with rubies and diamonds, containing a pair of diamond knee-buckles and a purse of 100 guineas'. It is true that gold boxes continued to be of ceremonial importance for some time. In 1806, Bernard–Armand Marguerit furnished Napoleon with 100 gold portrait boxes, and even during the Hundred Days four boxes were completed to order by the firm of Nitot et Fils. Also in 1815, Viscount Castlereagh was presented with 22 diamond-set gold boxes at the conclusion of the Congress of Vienna. (Their fate should be described, as it is probably typical of boxes of this type, of which so few survive. Broken up, some of the diamonds were incorporated into the Viscountess' jewellery; the gold was reserved for Castlereagh's sword and for an inkstand made by Paul Storr and Philip Rundell in 1818–20. Similarly, Queen Victoria melted down the large collection of George IV's gold boxes.) But already by the last quarter of the eighteenth century the gold *tabatière* was losing its prestige. In Paris itself, the glamour that had surrounded the most celebrated *marchands merciers*—Lazare Duvaux, Grancher, Poirier, Madame du Lac and Jabac— was lost in the bustle that filled the *cour d'honneur* of the Palais Royal, portions of which were leased in 1793 to shopkeepers and restaurateurs. It was there—among the several hundred shops of painters, glovesellers and jewellers, among the libraries, cafés and gaming rooms— that one went to buy the latest novelties in snuff boxes. For by the turn of the century they were often no more than souvenirs. Snuff taking was declining: cigarettes had been introduced in the last quarter of the eighteenth century, and in 1804 the German playwright Kotzebue wrote that in Paris 'to take snuff is getting rather out of fashion, while smoking is coming into vogue in its stead'. The symbolic importance of the snuff box persisted well into the nineteenth century: shortly after 1830, a silver box was the means of honouring Dr T. B. Wilson for his introduction of the honey bee into Tasmania; still later, in America, the first specimens of the California Gold Rush were forwarded to the east in a snuff box. Snuff is still enjoyed, but not for nearly two centuries has it been the universal passion to which the box in its varied forms bears witness.

II French Gold Boxes

Snuff boxes of gold were probably not made before about 1660. In the literature of the few countries where snuff taking was well established before that date—Italy, Spain and Ireland —gold boxes are not mentioned, while those of simpler materials such as shell, ivory and horn are often described. The earliest known description of gold boxes occurs in 1665 in a poem published in Holland; its author, Karel van Mander, speaks of

> *Daer menign doosje wort geleeght en overmant*
> *Van silver en van gout, beset met diamanten,*
> *Sapphir en Ametist, geciert aen alle canten . . .*

Boxes of this grandeur are not known to have been made in Holland this early; van Mander is undoubtedly alluding to the Parisian *boîtes à portrait*, records of which exist from 1668. A document of 23 August 1668 cited by Nocq contains the earliest known reference to Parisian box makers: on that date

> *Une boîte à portrait d'or émaillé a été saisie chez Pierre de la Fresnaye, 28 ans,*
> *demeurant chez sa mère, quai de l'Horloge; il ne la connaît pas, ayant rendu à sa mère*
> *toutes les boîtes de son père, décédé depuis 7 ans.*

Nothing further is known of Lafresnaye's father who had presumably been making gold boxes for several years prior to his death in 1661.

The *boîte à portrait* was not, officially at least, a snuff box. As late as 1694 '*tabaquière ou tabatière*' was defined by Antoine Furetière (*Dictionaire universel*) as a small box made of the '*fruits des Indes*' (hardstones and, possibly, shells), ivory or silver while a '*boeste ou boiste*' was a small covered container exemplified by '*Une boeste a portrait. Une boeste de diamants.*' Further, it is unlikely that Louis XIV, whose detestation of snuff was well known, would have chosen a snuff box as the vehicle for conferring royal favours. Nevertheless, the *boîte à portrait* was certainly the springboard for the *industrie de luxe* with which the word snuff box is traditionally associated. The presentations of *boîtes à portrait* are recorded from 1668 to 1786 in the *Comptes des Menus-Plaisirs*. They are uniformly described as being of gold, set with diamonds and a portrait miniature of the king. In this they appear to be little different from the 'Snuff Boxes of Gold; Sett with Diamonds' lost by the Marquis de Sessac in London in 1682. The number and size of the diamonds varied with the importance of the recipient. Thus on the occasion of the peace of Ryswick in 1697, Mme Lillerot, wife of the Swedish ambassador, received a *boîte à portrait* with 77 diamonds costing 36,315 livres; the Count de Cili, who carried the news of the peace, was rewarded with a box set with 14 diamonds, worth 9,090 livres. The miniaturists who painted the royal portraits for these boxes are not mentioned in the records. Jean Petitot (1607–91) was the most important of those working

18

for Louis XIV at the turn of the seventeenth century, and portraits of the royal family by him and his followers survive in gold boxes made at the end of the following century and during the Restoration. The *boîtes à portrait* were, of course, thinly disguised presents of cash; their obvious convertibility explains why none from the reign of the Sun King is known to exist, while their miniatures, of comparatively little value, have been retained.

Although no seventeenth-century gold boxes have survived, their general style may be inferred from examples made during the reign of Louis XV. A box of 1726–7 (4), bearing a portrait of the king inside the lid, is the earliest known *boîte à portrait*. It is the work of Daniel Govaers (m. 1717, d. after 1737), one of the court goldsmiths who is recorded from 1725—when he furnished a number of boxes for the *corbeille de mariage* of the queen—to 1735. Among the boxes he made for the king were *boîtes à portrait* with miniatures by Jean-Baptiste Massé (1687–1767) and the unidentified artist Ducanel; a gold box *'de couleur'* (which undoubtedly refers to varicoloured gold, a technique which did not become widespread until after 1750); a small double gold box and one with plaques of tortoiseshell piqué. Govaers' career ended abruptly in bankruptcy in 1736, and the following year he fled Paris to escape his creditors. His death is unrecorded.

Only a few snuff boxes survive from the 1720s. The variety of boxes made in that decade is suggested by the inventory of the Duchesse d'Orléans, drawn up in 1723, which mentions gold *tabatières* for four and five tobaccos, a trefoil-shaped box for three tobaccos, a circular box enamelled in green, four boxes *'à coquille'*, a double box *'en gondolle'* and one *'à soleil émaillé de vert'*. The specific mention of a circular box with a cover *'à charnière'* suggests that the precise integral hinge so characteristic of French gold boxes was just becoming standard. A circular box of 1722–6 (2) with miniatures after Watteau and Lancret is an unusually early example of miniature painting outside of royal portraiture. A box of 1723–4 in the Walters Art Gallery (1) may be taken as representative of the snuff box *'à coquille'*.

The word *tabatière*, curiously, does not occur in the *Comptes des Menus-Plaisirs* until 1726: a *'tabatière à portrait du Roi'* was furnished by Govaers in February of that year. From this date until the Revolution the two terms, *boîte à portrait* and *tabatière*, appear concurrently and, at first, apparently interchangeably. By the middle of the century the former was reserved for gold boxes set with diamonds and a royal portrait, while *tabatière* denoted boxes of gold combined with other materials such as tortoiseshell, enamel, etc. During the First Empire both types of boxes were called *tabatières*.

Gold boxes of the 1730s differ little from those of the preceding decade. Several by Govaers are notable for their use of strips of small diamonds to define scrollwork or other details (10), a style that was to continue in favour in Paris in the 1740s and which reappears as late as 1759–60 on a box by Dominique François Poitreau in the Louvre. Like all his work, these boxes of Govaers' are signed 'Gouers a Paris' on the front rim. Enamelled decoration, although mentioned in the inventory of the duchesse d'Orléans' collection in 1723, is not known on boxes dating before the mid-1730s. Boxes by Gabriel Gallois (Louvre;

formerly Beatty collection) and Noel Charles Laget (Metropolitan Museum) are similar in their borders of flowers rather stiffly enamelled in bright opaque colours. A more relaxed style of flower painting, recalling the grace and naturalism of enamelled watch cases of nearly a century earlier, is characteristic of boxes of about 1743–6 by Jean Moynat (*34*); according to the *Comptes des Menus-Plaisirs* he continued to make boxes of this type as late as 1754. Hardstone boxes (see Chapter VII) mounted in simple gold rims were fashionable from 1736 to 1744.

By 1740 the social necessity of the snuff box was accepted. The demand for snuff boxes effected an important change in their manufacture and appearance. This year may be taken as a convenient, and reasonably precise, date to mark the industrialisation of the manufactture of snuff boxes in Paris. Hitherto, most boxes were composed only of gold, or of gold and precious stones (which the goldsmiths were permitted to cut and set themselves) and were the work of a single craftsman. Chased and engraved decoration, it is true, was occasionally farmed out to specialists: at the time of Govaers' bankruptcy two of his boxes were at the shop of Gerard Debèche waiting to be engraved. Debèche (w. *c.* 1730–*c.* 1775) was a member of the guild of *tailleurs-graveurs-ciseleurs* which, established in 1631, had long provided engraved ciphers, armorials, etc., for the goldsmiths. By their statutes of 1737 they were formally authorised to

> *graver, ciseler, tant en or, argent, cuivre, laiton qu'autres métaux et matieres, les*
> *sceaux . . . vaisselles, tabatieres . . . et autres bijoux.*

(The detailed sculptural scenes on two boxes of 1757–8 and 1758–9 (*79, 76*) by Jean George, which are quite unrelated stylistically to other boxes by the same maker, are perhaps the work of a *tailleur-graveur-ciseleur*.) About 1740 the making of snuff boxes became a specialised profession exercised by goldsmiths who made only boxes. Earlier box makers had executed *vaisselle* (tableware) as well: Govaers supplied the king not only with gold boxes but, in 1727, with a silver table service. After 1740, very few goldsmiths who worked primarily with large-scale silver pieces also made gold boxes. The exceptions are André Louis Cassé (*103*), Jean-François Garand, François-Thomas Germain (*49*), Jean Antoine Bourguet, Pierre-Aymé Joubert, Jacques-Malquis Le Quin (*36*) and Robert-Joseph Auguste. A further specialisation is apparent from the boxes themselves which, after 1740, are frequently constructed of a gold frame fitted with panels of one or more of a variety of materials: hardstones, lacquer, tortoiseshell, porcelain, *vernis Martin*, and miniature paintings on vellum, ivory or enamelled copper. The invention of these *tabatières à cage* is attributed to the Parisian *marchands merciers*. The existence of their guild is first recorded by Etienne Boileau *c.* 1260 when a single merchant, according to a contemporary poem, *Dits d'un mercier*, sold such diverse goods as gloves, buckles, flutes, soaps, knives, buttons, figs, children's shoes, jewels, flags and pewter ware. A royal edict of 1570 defined their role as

> *marchans grossiers, merciers et jouailliers, de maniere que soubs cest estat de grossier*
> *on este comprins de tout temps les marchans de drap d'or, d'argent . . . tapisseries,*

*jouailleries, espiceries, merceries . . . auxquels il n'est permis de faire manufacture
quelconque, mais seulement de vendre, achepter, estaller, parer et enjolliver de toutes
especes de marchandises.*

In subsequent decrees they were forbidden to sell objects of French gold or silver but were
permitted to sell foreign plate (1579), and were granted the right to trade in and set semi-
precious stones (1613). In 1292 there were 199 merchants in France. By 1754, when it was
estimated that there were nearly 2,000, the *corporation* had become unofficially divided into
20 classes, each with its special merchandise. Snuff boxes were sold chiefly by the *marchands
petits merciers* or *marchands de bimbeloterie*. The role of the merchants in the manufacture of
gold snuff boxes can be surmised from the record books of one of the most influential
Parisian *merciers*. Lazare Duvaux (*c.* 1703–58) was active as a merchant by 1743 and in 1755
was appointed *orfèvre-joaillier du roi*. The king and Mme de Pompadour were his chief
customers; to them and to other members of the royal family and nobility he sold furniture,
porcelains, crystal lights, ornamental sculpture and snuff boxes. That Duvaux was important
as an arbiter and not a mere retailer of style is indicated by his weekly visits to Vincennes to
ensure that the productions of the porcelain factory—newly established under royal patronage—were in the best taste.

The snuff boxes recorded in Duvaux's day books—which cover the period 1748–58—
were composed primarily of the materials in which he traded: hardstones, oriental lacquer,
vernis Martin, tortoiseshell and porcelain. Some of these he acquired on his own account,
e.g., hardstones, and Japanese lacquer which the *merciers* imported through the Dutch East
India Company. For some other materials, the merchants were dependent on, and sometimes
in competition with, the *tabletiers*. The members of this guild were originally, in the thir-
teenth century, makers solely of ivory writing tablets. Their gradual expansion into other
activities was formally recognised only in 1741 when an edict directed that they

*mouleront de tous contours l'écaille, tourneront de toutes façons ou modes, monteront,
garniront et enjoliveront les croix . . . tabatieres, tablettes . . .*

The right to manufacture *vernis Martin*, hitherto the exclusive privilege of the painters, was
granted in 1749.

The incorporation of all these materials into gold boxes was accomplished in a variety of
ways. Simple boxes of ivory, composition or tortoiseshell requiring only gold rims were
mounted by goldsmiths who specialised in *garnitures*. (In what was clearly the continuation
of a traditional division of labour nearly 50 such goldsmiths are recorded in 1810 in the
Almanach des Fabricans.) These boxes would have been assembled and sold by the *tabletiers*.
Boxes suitable for royalty and nobility, however, were executed by the most fashionable
box makers. Duvaux's day book records, on 17 December 1750,

M. Ducrolay: Un dessus de boëte d'ancien lacq, à oiseaux

and in October 1752, also to Jean Ducrollay

> *Une boëte de lacq noir & feuillages en or, travaillé partout*

Whether Duvaux had any part in determining the style of the gold frameworks of these and other boxes is impossible to verify.

Still other boxes, especially those of hardstone which they could set themselves, may have been made entirely in the merchants' shops. This is a possible interpretation of an entry of 14 November 1752 in Duvaux's journals:

> *Mme la Marq. de Pompadour: La monture d'une tabatière de sardoine; pour or, façon, émail & taille des cailloux.*

As has been noted, it was contrary to guild regulations for a *marchand mercier* either to manufacture anything himself or to deal with French goldsmiths' work. That these rules were continually violated is evident from the number of times they were restated in the seventeenth and eighteenth centuries, and from the occasional protests of the goldsmiths who felt that the merchants were cutting into their livelihood. (Duvaux, however, as court goldsmith and jeweller, was free from many of the restrictions of his guild and was probably a practising *orfèvre*. He could hardly have sold an all-gold box, as he did to Mme de Pompadour on 4 November 1755, unless he was.)

In addition to composing new boxes, the *marchands merciers* repaired and refurbished old ones. The convenience of the *tabatière à cage* was that its various elements could be altered, substituted or retained as fashion or sentimentality required. This is especially noticeable in boxes decorated with miniature paintings which often differ in date by many years from the gold frames into which they are set (*52*).

The variety of shapes and materials of boxes in current use during the 1740s is suggested by the list of those included in the *corbeille de mariage* in 1745 of the Spanish Infanta, Maria Theresa:

> *une boîte de burgau, à fond d'or*
> *une autre, à coquille*
> *six boîtes d'or, émaillées*
> *une boîte de nacre de perle*
> *une boître de laque en forme de bahut*
> *une autre d'or et nacre, émaillée de grappes de raisin*
> *une boîte de caillou d'Egypte*

The shell shape is unusual at this late date—it is seen about the same time in two boxes by Jean Ducrollay (*37, 38*)—having been supplanted by the oblong (often of slightly curving profile) with a projecting cover rim, rounded corners and *bombé* sides. *Tabatières à cage* were mounted in a fairly standard framework of wavy-ridged cover and foot rims and straight-edged corner mouldings. The box '*en forme de bahut*' is not known from examples in gold; trunk-shaped boxes were, however, popular at the Mennecy porcelain factory. The barrel-shaped box also appears about this time. A gold-mounted mother-of-pearl version is dated

1738–44; the shape, which occurs also in other materials, is seen as late as 1768–9 in an enamelled gold box by J. J. Barrière (*154*).

Decoration in tinted ivory, mother-of-pearl and shell is said to have been introduced to Paris from Germany during the Régence, but French boxes in this technique date only from the 1740s. One dated 1742–3 by Antoine Filassier (Louvre) is appliquéd with chinoiseries in coloured shell and precious stones; chinoiserie and genre scenes also appear on boxes dating between 1748–51 (Louvre) and as late as 1759–60 (formerly Fribourg collection). This type of work also occurs on boxes with architectural (*25*), geometric (*16*) and floral ornament (*23*).

From about 1745 enamelling is the dominant type of decoration on gold boxes. It was at first used naturalistically, as on boxes painted with sprawling bouquets or flower trails (*34*) or with simulated peacock feathers (*37*). This style of all-over decoration is a regular feature of boxes of the 1740s and coincides with the gradual modification of their shapes from the baroque profiles, rounded edges and tiered mouldings of the 1730s to the plain, straight-sided shapes dominant after 1750. Bands of scrolls or foliage which wind around the entire surface of the box occur *c.* 1742–50 in versions executed entirely in gold; in combinations of gold and mother-of-pearl; and of gold enamelled in strong contrasting colours such as the leaf green and orange of a box of 1750 in the Wrightsman collection. Oblong, circular and oval boxes predominated in the 1750s and were constructed with straight sides, sharp edges and without mouldings or thumbpieces to interrupt the surfaces. They were larger, averaging $3\frac{1}{4}$ inches in length. (The largest boxes of this period are usually the most elaborately decorated and were undoubtedly intended for table use rather than for 'wearing'.) Each side of a box was treated as a canvas and was entirely covered by a single decorative subject. From about 1750 to 1754 enamelled scenes were painted *en plein*, that is, directly on the surfaces of the box; the gold backgrounds were chiselled and/or engraved with herringbone, sunburst, latticework or other all-over patterns. Mythological subjects, religious scenes and pastoral and genre scenes in the manner of Boucher occur on these boxes. Several dating 1749–50 are decorated with exotic birds and flowers (a subject again current about 1757) on a bold spirally channelled ground. At least one (*36*) is by Jacques-Malquis Le Quin, who is known chiefly as a maker of *vaisselle* (all the recorded boxes by Le Quin are dated between 1749 and 1751). It is hazardous, however, to attribute similar, or even identical, boxes to the same maker. Fashion demands duplication. That some goldsmiths repeated their work is demonstrable: a circular enamelled box of 1771–2 by Charles Le Bastier in the Louvre is matched by another, made in the same year, in the Wrightsman collection (*160*). A duplicate of the box by Pierre-Claude Pottiers (*191*), also made in 1780–1, is in a private collection. In 1786, according to the *Comptes des Menus-Plaisirs*, Petitjean furnished two '*boîtes d'or, rondes, émaillées en plume de paon*'. Nevertheless, it is equally certain that popular decorative styles were copied by several makers, perhaps from pattern books, perhaps from models which would have been generally known in the closed community of the goldsmiths. Boxes enamelled *en plein* in the early 1750s were made by Ducrollay, Le Quin,

23

Paul Robert and Jean Moynat. The enamellers are mostly anonymous; an example by Ducrollay in the Louvre (*43*) is signed by the unidentified painter Liot.

This pictorial style of decoration was also carried out entirely in gold. Such decoration depended heavily for effect on the textures and colours of the metal, and channelled and matte grounds were widely used. Boxes chiselled with bouquets of flowers silhouetted against sunburst grounds were popular from 1750 to 1757 and comprise much of the work of Jean Moynat and Jean Formey during this period. Ducrollay, Jean Frémin, Charles Le Bastier and Jean George also worked in this style. A pair of almost identical boxes of 1754–5 (Metropolitan Museum, Wrightsman collection), one clearly marked by George (*68*) corresponds to the report by George in 1757 of the loss of a

> *tabatière de chasse en or, dont les 6 faces, gravées en soleil, portent un bouquet de fleurs d'or de couleurs.*

Architectural perspectives and landscapes occur on boxes of the same period (*53*, *55*).

After 1755 the visual interest of these all-gold boxes was considerably enriched by the use of varicoloured gold. A box of '*or de couleur*' made by Daniel Govaers is recorded as early as 1726: although the description undoubtedly does refer to varicoloured gold (as enamelled gold was always so specified) examples of the technique date only from 1754–5; it is first mentioned by Lazare Duvaux in 1755. The practice of alloying gold with other metals was informal, no regulations determining the resulting standards being enforced by the goldsmiths' guild. There were four basic colours: red, green, blue and white. The modern term *quatrecouleur* is something of a convention, however, as three shades of green alone are recorded. In the *Secrets concernant les arts et metiers* (1790) the proportions were given as follows: red gold was the result of three parts pure, or 24 carat, gold alloyed with one of copper; blue or grey gold was produced by the addition of arsenic or steel filings. White gold was basically silver to which varying amounts of gold were added. Green gold was also an alloy of gold and silver: '*vert de pré*' was three parts gold to one of silver, '*beau vert feuille morte*' was eighteen to six, and '*vert d'eau*' was fourteen to ten.

About 1755 miniature painting began to assume an importance in the decoration of gold boxes it was to retain until the Revolution. Miniatures were at first enamelled *en plein*; their importance was emphasised by an increasingly complicated rhythm of panels and borders executed in enamel and vari-coloured gold. The *Encyclopédie* observed:

> *Nous avons vu deux orfèvre bijoutiers, les sieurs Hamelin et Maillé, en 1754, commencer à peindre en émail sur des bijoux d'or, et porter, depuis cet art à un point de perfection.*

Hamelin specialised in flower painting, which enjoyed a particular vogue from 1756 to 1758. Boxes by Ducrollay (1756–7), Jean Formey (1757–8) and Jean Moynat (1757–8) are similarly painted with floral still lifes enframed in chased and enamelled borders. Hamelin's signature appears on a box of 1757–8 by Ducrollay (*84*) who also, in the same year, executed a similar

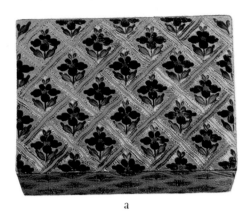

a

b

c

d

II   a) Gold, enamelled. English, 1770-80.

b) Mother-of-pearl, set in a gold frame studded with rubies and diamonds.
German or English, *c.* 1755. *A La Vieille Russie, New York.*

c) Gold, enamelled and set with grisaille miniatures. *Maker* Louis-Phillipe
Demay. French (Paris), 1768-9. Ex coll. Earl of Harewood

d) Gold, with gouache miniatures. Inscribed on the rim *Roucel Orf [evr]e du Roi
à Paris. Maker* Louis Roucel. French (Paris), 1766-7. Ex coll. Earl of Harewood

diamond-studded box enamelled with flowers by the unidentified painter Aubert. Charles Jacques de Mailly (1740–1817) combined flower painting with grisaille allegorical scenes, surrounding the latter with garlands of plump roses, peonies, etc. His signature appears on a box by L. P. Demay of 1766–7 (Louvre); the enamelling on a box of the following year by Louis Gallois is also attributable to Mailly. Other flower painters were Parpette (w. 1755–1806), a painter at Sèvres whose signature appears on a box of 1763–4 (Louvre), and Gerard van Spaendonck (1746–1822).

The vogue for floral miniatures was quickly followed by that for scenes of Flemish peasant life adapted from the paintings from David Teniers the Younger (1610–90). Several boxes of this type are recorded between 1758 and 1760 in the *Comptes des Menus-Plaisirs*; most surviving boxes are dated in the same period, although Teniers subjects are found mounted in *tabatières à cage* dated as late as 1764. None of these miniatures is signed.

Apart from the mainstream of goldsmiths' work of the 1750s may be considered the *œuvre* of two individual makers who are represented by an unusually large number of boxes. The bulk of the work of Jean Ducrollay is encompassed in this decade. He became master in 1734 and is last recorded in 1760/1. His earliest known work is an oval box of 1736–7 chased with scrollwork and gadrooning characteristic of the period (Wrightsman collection). Completely individual is one of 1746–7 (*37*) entirely enamelled to simulate peacock feathers. More conventional boxes by Ducrollay are decorated with genre scenes in shell and ivory (Louvre), pastoral scenes enamelled *en plein* (Louvre), Teniers subjects and miniature paintings. Ducrollay's name occurs several times in the day-books of Lazare Duvaux, for whom he provided gold frames for panels of Japanese lacquer; examples dating 1753–4 and 1754–5, respectively, are in the Metropolitan Museum (*60*) and the Wrightsman collection. The taste for snuff boxes composed of oriental lacquer arose *c*. 1745. Lacquer boxes are cited regularly by Duvaux from 1750; the fashion reached its height in the mid-1760s. The lacquer trade between Japan and Europe (through the agency of the Dutch East India Company) was then at its lowest point, the Japanese having imposed so many restrictions that no profit was to be gained. Duvaux generally refers to '*ancien lacq*', by which he meant seventeenth-century work, as the trade was unrestricted until 1672. Chief among the objects imported into Europe were boxes for writing, incense, etc., in a wide variety of sizes and shapes. A few were apparently mounted without alteration: on 9 March 1751 Duvaux furnished the duchesse de Lauraguais with

> *Une tabatière de lacq, à trois tabacs, la garniture émaillée*

which was perhaps formed of a trefoil-shaped incense box. Mostly, however, the lacquer boxes were cut up, their panels being reset into gold frames conforming to the accepted shapes of *tabatières*.

Contemporary with Ducrollay was Jean George (m. 1752, d. 1765). While his earliest boxes have an elegant simplicity (*57*, *68*), much of his later work possesses a combination of richness and unexpectedness that was equalled by few other goldsmiths in eighteenth-century Paris. The varied techniques and materials of his boxes attest the cultural harmony which enabled several craftsman to create a single object. In addition to miniature paintings, George also composed boxes for plaques of Sèvres porcelain. His name and that of Lazare Duvaux occur frequently in the Sèvres sale books between 1757 and 1760: a box such as that dating 1759–60 set with porcelain plaques of amorini and trophies reserved on a green ground (*91*) corresponds to the '*tabatière, vert, enfants colorés*' sold directly to George in 1760; plaques similarly described were sold to Duvaux who then presumably commissioned goldsmiths to complete the *tabatières*. Other types of work by George are known from contemporary records: in 1764 he advertised the loss of a

> *boîte d'or en baignoire, pour homme, à panneaux d'or vert . . .*

This miniature hip-bath is known only from an earlier example by A. A. Chollet (*86*) but was evidently popular in the early 1760s. Another type of box is the '*Georgette*', which was variously described in the eighteenth century. George himself advertised the loss in 1762 of a '*Georgette, montée en or*', which suggests it was made of a material such as tortoiseshell. But an oblong box made entirely of gold, and another in the shape of a bushel basket, were also described as '*Georgettes*'; the designation may simply have resulted from George's practice of signing his name on the rim of most of his boxes.

The pictorial use of gold virtually disappeared after 1760: *quatrecouleur* work was largely restricted to ornamental panels and borders. Some boxes executed entirely in varicoloured gold were produced until the Revolution but merely imitated the *schema* of enamelled boxes. Between 1760 and 1765 the unified appearance of gold boxes was discarded in favour of a rhythmical combination of decorative elements drawn from the Renaissance-classical vocabulary of pilasters, terms and ox skulls, and meander, husk, Vitruvian scroll and *guilloche* borders. Henceforth the division of the vertical sides of the boxes caused by the cover rim —a separation ignored in the previous decade—was clearly marked by a self-contained border pattern. The walls themselves were punctuated by pilasters or panels of pendent husks, etc. This architectonic style was best served by the oblong boxes with cut corners which occurred sporadically from the mid-1750s but which became common only after 1763. A motif of arcades recurs on plain and enamelled gold boxes *c.* 1763–71. On some examples—a box of 1765–6 by Jean-Joseph Barrière in the Louvre and a similar, oval, one made in the following year by Jean-Baptiste Carnay (*127*)—the design is literal; on others, the arches have been stylised to a high degree of abstraction (*128*). A bold use of enamelling characterises boxes of the same period. As early as *c.* 1758 dark-enamelled borders encircle and connect the separate elements of decoration, recalling Renaissance strapwork ornament and its modifications— based on designs by Jean Bérain (1639–1711)—on Continental gold and silver *c.* 1715–30. Panels and borders of marked contrasting colours occur on a box of 1762–3 enamelled with alternate panels of bright yellow and grass green (*126*); in the box by Carnay painted in pale shades of rose and blue; in a pair of green and grey boxes of 1771–2 by Charles Le Bastier (Louvre, Wrightsman collection). Pale turquoise borders contrast sharply with dark mottled green panels enamelled to simulate malachite, on a box of 1769–70 by J. J. Barrière (144). The imitative possibilities of enamelling were first explored about this time; the *marchand mercier* Grancher advertised in 1775 snuff boxes '*ornées de médaillons, d'agates arborisées factices, plus belles que les naturelles, & supérieures, à tout ce qu'on a fait jusqu'à present dans ce genre*'. An extension of this practice of imitating the brachial markings of dendritic agate is found *c.* 1775 in boxes painted with river scenes and landscapes in pale tones of mauve or sepia, the palette duplicating that of the real stone. Generally, however, enamelling of this type was reserved for imitation of the vividly coloured hardstones, malachite and lapis; it recurs later in the work of A. J. M. Vachette (202).

Two predominant styles of decoration are in evidence from about 1760 until the Revolution. The first, more frequently found on oval boxes (although it occurs on oblong ones, notably in examples by Pierre-François Drais and Charles Le Bastier), is characterised by the division of each side of the box into panels centred by a wreathed medallion. The cover was generally set with an enamelled miniature, or a monogram, the sides with rosettes or flat-chased trophies, etc. Fable subjects, pastoral and hunting scenes and trophies occur on all-gold boxes of the same style. About 1763 this basic scheme was enriched by the addition of garlands or laurel swags which served to link together the separate elements of decoration (158): '*boîtes à guirlandes*' figure in the inventory of Mme de Pompadour's estate drawn up in 1764, and boxes '*à guirlandes et rosettes*' are mentioned regularly in the records of the *Comptes des Menus-Plaisirs* from 1763 to 1772.

Gouache miniatures mounted *à cage* in oblong frames comprise the second major group of gold boxes after 1760. Classical subjects, pastoral scenes after Boucher, river scenes, views of châteaux and *fêtes champêtres* are the subjects found on boxes of the 1760s and 1770s. Chief among the miniaturists in this genre was Louis-Nicolas van Blarenberghe (1716–94). His early career as a marine painter is evidenced by a series of romantic riverscapes dated 1757 mounted *à cage* in a box frame of 1765–6 (Louvre). His later work includes paintings of country houses, such as Bercy and Chanteloup. The latter—the seat of his patron, the duc de Choiseul—was painted by Van Blarenberghe in 1767, the miniatures being set into an earlier box (1750–1). As has been mentioned above the *tabatière à cage* was adjustable to the demands of fashion: this convenience is nowhere more apparent than in boxes set with Van Blarenberghe's miniatures, which rarely correspond in date to their gold frames. As a companion to the Chanteloup box Van Blarenberghe provided miniatures for a box by Louis Roucel in 1770–1, depicting five rooms of the Hotel de Choiseul hung with the duke's large collection of Dutch and Flemish paintings. The clarity and completeness of detail, which has made it possible for Mr F. J. B. Watson to catalogue virtually the entire collection as it then was, is characteristic of Van Blarenberghe. It is an equally important feature of the crowded theatre, festival and pastoral scenes which appear on boxes of the 1770s (184). Van Blarenberghe often signed his paintings, but only with his surname; it is thus difficult to separate his work from that of his son, Henri-Joseph (1741–1826), who painted in a similar style. A miniature of Louis XIV crossing the Rhine, set in a box of 1809–19 (*219*) and signed in capital letters rather than the usual cursive minuscules attributed to Louis Nicolas, is probably by the son (*VII,m*). Landscapes and views of country houses painted as a delicate palette and with an attention to detail similar to that of Van Blarenberghe were painted by Savignac (recorded 1734–52/59), a landscape painter at Sèvres.

Miniatures painted in grisaille began to occur on gold boxes about 1760. Often deliberate simulations of cameos, they were generally referred to as scenes '*en camaieu*'; their popularity —and that of the whole repertoire of classical ornament—coincides with the contemporary interest in Herculaneum and the publications, beginning in 1757, of the comte de Caylus. The earliest recorded grisaille miniatures are those by the unidentified Mlle Duplessis, whose groups of cherubs painted in light tones of sepia occur on a box of 1759–62 by Jean George (*110*); two other boxes made by George in the following year (Louvre, Musées Royaux de Belgique) are painted with similar miniatures which, although unsigned are probably also the work of Mlle Duplessis. Her signature also occurs on a box of 1757–8 painted with Teniers scenes in polychrome (Wrightsman collection). In addition to '*scènes d'enfants*', floral and allegorical subjects were also painted in grisaille. Cameo miniatures enjoyed their greatest vogue during the 1770s. Several are attributable to, and many more demonstrate the influence of, Jacques-Joseph DeGault (*c.* 1738–after 1812). DeGault's early career is unrecorded with the exception of two years (1758–60) spent as a painter at Sèvres; his dated work extends from 1771 to the year III (1794/5). His signature—J. J. DeGault (*VI,n*)—appears on miniatures depicting bacchanalia, or heroic mythological or allegorical scenes. They are distinguished by dramatic composition, the sculptural quality of the figures, and the vivid contrast between the slightly shaded white of these figures and the steel-blue background. Other miniaturists recorded by Maze-Sencier (*Livre des collectionneurs*) as working *en camaieu* are François Lainé (1721–1810), Louis Bertin Parant (1768–1851), Anthelme François Lagrenée (1775–1832) and Charles de Chatillon (w. 1795–1808), the last of whom was also a portraitist.

The period 1760–80 marks the apogee of the Parisian gold box. It is impossible to estimate the number of box-makers active in a given year in Paris; as the goldsmiths' guild was limited to a membership of 300 it is unlikely that there were more than 30 (in 1810, with over 800 goldsmiths practising in Paris, only 17 were listed as makers of gold boxes). The issue is not entirely academic: the very large number of boxes surviving from this period gives evidence both of a strong demand, and of a highly organised system of manufacture. Of the time required to produce a gold box we are given some indication in the record of mastership (1734) of Jean Martel whose *chef d'œuvre*, executed in the presence of Gabriel Gallois, was a gold box completed in six hours.

Numerous examples by individual makers make it possible to estimate personal style as well as to follow the progress of fashion. Charles Le Bastier was received master in 1754, and was still working in 1783. His entire *œuvre* is characterised by classical restraint, a spare use of ornament, and the frequent use of subtle—sometimes contrasting—enamel colours. Enamelled miniatures seldom occur on Le Bastier's boxes. The work of Louis-Philippe Demay (m. 1758, d. 1772) and Jean-Joseph Barrière (m. 1763, w. 1793) is visually more brilliant. Enamelled portraits and allegorical scenes figure prominently in the boxes of these two makers, and are set off by a complex arrangement of chased gold borders and panels enamelled in strong colours. Several of Demay's boxes display a dramatic contrast between gold and enamel; Barrière's work has a certain delicacy and grace. The name of Jean-Marie Tiron (m. 1748, living 1781) occurs in the *Comptes des Menus-Plaisirs* in 1766, when he furnished a box with miniatures set *à cage*, and a varicoloured gold box. Among his varied work may also be included an unusual box of modified shell form of 1766–7 (*108*), and a box of 1763–4 decorated with lacquered panels inlaid with birds in piqué hairwork (Louvre). The fashion for mounting panels of genuine oriental lacquer was at its height *c.* 1765. At the same time there appeared boxes with panels lacquered and decorated in the style of the Japanese work, the decoration being carried out in minute strips of varicoloured gold. The subjects were not so much oriental as generally exotic: a box of 1768–9 by Louis Roucel (Wrightsman collection) is inlaid in this manner with a rhinoceros and palm trees. Other goldsmiths active during the period 1760–80 were Pierre-François Drais (m. 1763, w. 1788), Pierre-François Mathis de Beaulieu (m. 1768, w. 1791) and Nicolas Menière (m. 1758, w. 1776).

The last major innovation in the decoration of gold boxes was engine turning. It was said in 1792 (*Manuel du tourneur*) to have been first used about the middle of the century in the decoration of tortoiseshell boxes. The *Comptes des Menus-Plaisirs* records in 1747 the presentation by Louis XV to his daughter, Mme Adelaïde, of '*Une boîte de chasse à deux tabacs, à gorge d'or, guillochée, vernis par Martin*'. The origin of the term *guilloché* to define machine-engraved line ornament is conjectural; it appears at least to have no relation to the interlaced border pattern generally referred to from at least the end of the seventeenth century as *guilloche* (*114*). Machine engraving was executed on the *tour à guillocher* or rose engine: the work piece revolved in place while the cutter—fitted into a slide or compound rest—traced the desired pattern, dictated by a shaped metal disc or rosette placed against the surface, on the box. A variety of patterns are recorded: the earliest reference to engine-turning in the *Comptes des Menus-Plaisirs*, in 1755, describes a box '*guillochée à étoiles*'; boxes engine-turned '*en osier*' are mentioned in 1782 in the sale catalogue of the collection of the Duc d'Aumont. Engine-turning was most often used to produce wavy lines simulating moiré; the effect of watered silk was reinforced by the practice of overlaying the engraved ground with translucent colours. Ruby, dark blue, dark green, gold, orange, turquoise and powder blue occur during the 1770s. From *c.* 1780 the most commonly used colours were a vivid midnight blue and dark purple. (The latter colour was apparently in use before 1780 as Horace Walpole bought 'a purple snuff-box' on his visit to Paris in 1771.)

The perfection of engine turning *c.* 1768 in effect standardised the decoration of gold boxes which, from now until the Revolution, consisted primarily of translucent-enamelled panels interrupted only on the cover by an enamelled medallion. Leaf-tip borders chased in vari-coloured gold are usual in the 1770s, being replaced *c.* 1780 by an almost universal border pattern of 'pearls' and leaves enamelled in white and green, often on a matte ground. The same decorative scheme was followed even on boxes without engine-turning: panels enamelled in opaque colours—white, mauve, citron yellow—are commonly found on boxes dating *c.* 1775. Mythological and allegorical subjects enamelled on copper or ivory plaques are usually set in the cover medallions of the boxes. Separate gold plaques repoussé with amorini, etc., occur *c.* 1770. A box of this type, with plaques '*ciselés d'après l'antique*', was made by P. F. Drais in that year, the chiselling being the work of Gérard Debèche. Such plaques occur on several boxes by Nicolas Menière of the mid-1770s; the style remained in fashion into the nineteenth century, increasing in importance until the entire cover of a box was given over to a single scene. Late examples of this style of decoration occur in plaques signed by a member of the Kirstein family of Strasbourg.

Enamelled portraits occur occasionally after 1760; those that survive are mostly royal portraits by Louis Marie Sicard (1746–1825) or Pierre Noël-Violet (1749–1819). Sicard was the chief portraitist of Louis XVI. His name appears regularly in the *Comptes des Menus-Plaisirs* from 1780 to 1786; his miniatures are set in boxes by Jean-Etienne Blerzy in Paris and in a box by an unidentified maker in Moscow (*342*).

Portrait miniatures in gouache occur rarely on gold boxes after 1770, being reserved for those made of ivory, tortoiseshell or horn. Gold-rimmed circular composition boxes with lift-off lids, inlaid with gold strips, lined with tortoiseshell and set with a miniature on the cover were popular *c.* 1775. Among the painters whose work is recorded on portrait boxes are François Dumont (1751–1831), miniaturist to Louis XVI; Pierre Adolph Hall (1736–93), who came to Paris from Stockholm in 1760 and was appointed painter to Louis XV; Nicolas André Courtois (w. *c.* 1770–7); Jean-Laurent Mosnier (recorded 1775–88); and Jean-Baptiste-Jacques Augustin (1759–1832), one of the portraitists of Napoleon and Josephine and later miniaturist to Louis XVIII.

In 1781 appeared a pattern of engine turning that was widely used on gold boxes until the Revolution: a horizontally lined background interrupted at regular intervals by small depressed circles, sometimes alternated with rosettes or stars. This basic pattern was used as the sole decoration of plain gold boxes, and also as the 'bed' for *basse taille* enamelling; it was also imitated in opaque enamel colours.

Gold boxes of the 1780s are typified by the work of two masters, Joseph-Etienne Blerzy (m. 1768, w. 1806) and Adrien-Joseph-Maximilien Vachette (m. 1779, d. 1839). Boxes by the former are invariably oval, decorated with a single enamelled medallion on the cover, enamelled engine-turned panels and 'pearl' borders. Several are set with royal portraits, not only of Louis XVI, but of Catherine II of Russia and Joseph II of Austria. These royal boxes are often heavily ornamented with diamonds. Similar work is found on boxes by Charles

Ouizille (m. 1771, w. 1806) and David Lhonorey. The considerable *œuvre* of Vachette displays a thoroughly eclectic taste. Virtually all his pre-Revolutionary boxes are *tabatières à cage*, oblong with cut corners, enclosing plaques of porcelain, agate, enamelled imitations of lapis and malachite, gouache miniatures, tortoiseshell piqué and oriental lacquer. Vachette's work is the only substantial link between boxes of the *ancien régime* and those of the First Empire.

Although their guild survived until 1797, no records concerning goldsmiths and their work are available between 1791 and 1806, when the first list of goldsmiths active in Paris after the Revolution was published (S. P. Douet, *Tableau des symboles de l'orfèvrerie de Paris*). Excepting portrait boxes, virtually no snuff boxes are known from this period. Jean Formey, P. F. M. de Beaulieu, J. J. Barrière and P. N. Pleyard are among those last recorded in the early years of the Revolution. Vachette's boxes made for Napoleon—to whom he was *orfèvre bijoutier*—are in keeping with current fashions, as were his pre-Revolution boxes and his last work, executed for Charles X under the Bourbon Restoration.

Surviving Napoleonic boxes are mostly *boîtes à portrait*, differing from their Bourbon prototypes only in stylistic details. The official snuff box was as essential a part of Napoleon's diplomatic life as it had been of Louis XV's. In 1806 Bernard-Armand Marguerit, jeweller to the Emperor, furnished 100 gold, diamond and portrait boxes; in the following year he supplied another 50, the firm of Nitot et Fils 42 more. These were variously decorated with Napoleon's portrait, or with his or the Empress Josephine's monogram set in diamonds. In 1811 Nitot et Fils furnished 27 snuff boxes 'carrées, longues, à pans coupés ou arrondis, ovales, émaillés'; most were set with Napoleon's portrait or monogram surrounded by diamonds. Portrait boxes of *c.* 1810–15 are generally oblong, with rounded corners; shallow foot rims begin to appear at this time. The covers surrounding the central portrait are chased with rinceaux, the sides and bottom are engine-turned in an increasingly varied combination of geometric patterns. Enamelling occurs rarely at this period; narrow borders of a deep translucent blue appear later, in Restoration boxes. This style of decoration persists with slight modifications through the reigns of Louis XVIII and Charles X. In the earlier period (1814–24), gold-rimmed tortoiseshell boxes are common, their covers being set with a chased gold plaque centred by a portrait medallion (*228*). A number of these boxes are fitted with portraits of Louis XIV and his family, of which some are nineteenth-century copies of miniatures by, or in the style of, Petitot.

Among Napoleon's portraitists are the unidentified painter Gilliard (active 1811), and Jean-Baptiste Isabey (1767–1855), '*peintre dessinateur du cabinet de sa Majesté l'Empereur, des cérémonies et des Relations extérieures*'. Miniaturists who were active during the First Empire and the reigns of Louis XVIII and Charles X are Daniel Saint (1778–1847), a pupil of J. B. J. Augustin, and Saint's pupil Mme Lizinska Mirbel (1796–1849).

About the middle of the nineteenth century snuff boxes in the style of those of the 1760s and 1770s were executed by Alexandre Leferre (w. after 1838). His work is entirely derivative and marks the end of the creative development of the Parisian gold box.

III Other Continental, English and American Gold Boxes

1 *Austrian*

The most conspicuous feature of Austrian boxes is the influence of Parisian style. The dislike of the Empress Maria Theresa for Frederick II of Prussia, the political alliances between Austria and France and, perhaps most important of all, the marriage of Maria Theresa's daughter to the future Louis XVI all contributed to the preference of French fashion over German.

French taste is nowhere more evident than in oval boxes enamelled with Teniers subjects by Philipp Ernst Schindler the Younger (1723–93). Like his father, Philipp Ernst I (1695–1765), Schindler worked for the Meissen porcelain factory (*c.* 1740–50); he moved from there to Vienna where he became chief painter in 1770. Porcelain boxes by the two Schindlers are not known, and a comparison of their styles is impossible. While the 'Teniers' boxes could have been painted by the elder Schindler, there is more reason to attribute them to the son. He was already working as a *Hausmaler* in enamel on copper while at Meissen: Honey notes (*Dresden China*) that J. G. Herold complained of this outside activity. Schindler commonly signed his work with his surname, occasionally adding 'Wien' as well. The boxes with Teniers subjects are closely modelled on Parisian examples of *c.* 1758–60 and are clearly contemporary with them. In addition to his vigorous peasant scenes impeccably painted in bright (but subtle) colours, Schindler added on at least one box (*235*) much smaller medallions enclosing delicate oriental landscapes in grisaille. These provide a stylistic connection between the earlier group and later boxes bearing the same signature painted *en camaieu* with classical heads (*237*) or amorini (formerly Fribourg collection). The makers of Schindler's boxes are not known. Few Austrian boxes are marked at all and their attribution must often rest on external evidence, e.g., a box set with a cameo portrait of Maria Theresa's daughter, Maria Anna (*238*). Thought to be Austrian are a number of boxes dating *c.* 1785–90 enamelled with a scale-and-leaf diaper pattern (*240*). A simplified version occurs in Paris as early as 1763–4 (*112*) and reappears there *c.* 1784.

A number of boxes of varied styles have been called early nineteenth-century Austrian work on the strength of a single mark, a backhanded capital A in a slanted rectangle (*V,m*). This mark, in use in Vienna in 1806–7, was a state tax mark applied to all small work in 20-carat gold for sale in the city at that time. It should not be assumed that boxes struck with this mark are necessarily of Austrian make.

Oblong portrait boxes set with brilliants occur in Vienna from *c.* 1815. Dating *c.* 1835 are cushion-shaped boxes of lobed outline, encrusted with rhinestones; the shape is probably derived from Swiss boxes made for the oriental market a decade earlier.

2 *German*

The manufacture of gold boxes in Germany was comparatively small. It was naturally limited by etiquette, which restricted the privilege of 'wearing' a gold box to the nobility. The large-scale hardstone and porcelain industries diminished the importance of gold boxes still further.

German boxes date only from the middle of the eighteenth century: in 1741 Frederick II, in order to encourage native artists, forbade the importation of French goldsmiths' work. While the motifs utilised in the decoration of German boxes generally coincided with Parisian styles, the boxes are essentially baroque. It may be observed that from the outset they were generally larger than French examples, and that the importance of the country's mineral wealth is apparent in the liberal use of jewelled thumbpieces. To the first half of the period can be assigned oblong boxes with pictorial decoration in carved and tinted mother-of-pearl and ivory superimposed on a plain or engraved gold ground. The technique was native to Germany, occurring on hardstone boxes *c.* 1730. Interest in the style was undoubtedly sustained by its adoption in France in the 1740s; while the Parisian goldsmiths customarily inlaid such decoration, in Germany it was almost always applied. This relief work is associated with Berlin, the provenance of hardstone boxes appliquéd with flowers and insects (*460*); it is probable that many of the gold boxes of this type are also Berlin work. Two similar boxes, executed *c.* 1765–70 in Stettin by the unidentified maker D.B., are the only known marked examples that document the dispersal of the style. That they were executed by the Berlin goldsmith Daniel Baudesson, as has been suggested, is not impossible. Baudesson may have retired to Stettin after working for the court, bringing Berlin fashions with him. Such an assumption at this time, however, is unwise as Baudesson's life remains obscure.

Applied decoration—of mythological subjects, amorini, etc.—also occurs on agate-panelled *tabatières à cage c.* 1745–50.

The Berlin style of raised enamelling (see Chapter IX) is also apparent in a box enamelled with animals in very high relief (*255*).

Oblong and cartouche-shaped boxes ornately chased with allegorical figures and scroll-work surrounding a central medallion were made in Berlin *c.* 1745–50. They were the equivalent of the Parisian *boîte à portrait*, generally being set with a portrait of Frederick II. Two examples in the Hermitage Museum, one with a portrait of the king attributed to Daniel Chodowiecki, the other with a miniature of the Empress Elizabeth, are further enriched with diamond-set scrollwork in a style also popular in Paris at the time. Like most German boxes, these are not marked. The provenance of the entire group can be derived from an example formerly in the Schloss Monbijou (*248*) which was furnished to the king in 1746 by his commissioner Johann Ernst Gotzkowsky.

Also Berlin work is a group of large oblong boxes with allegorical scenes enamelled *en plein* on engraved grounds (*252*). Clearly modelled on French examples, their prototypes can be found in boxes by Jean Moynat and J. M. Le Quin of *c.* 1746–9. The enamelling on two of the Berlin boxes (Louvre, Metropolitan Museum) is signed by Daniel Chodowiecki (1726–1801), who began his career painting enamel snuff boxes, adding in later years the roles of designer, engraver and chief artistic adviser to Frederick II. The Metropolitan box, and another in the same collection, are also inscribed on the rim with the name of Daniel Baudesson, a Huguenot refugee who is recorded as working in Berlin during the second third of the century. A fourth, unsigned, example, undoubtedly the work of Baudesson, is in the Wrightsman collection. Related to this group is a *tabatière à cage* in the Wallace Collection with pastoral scenes and diaper-filled panels (*256*).

Of somewhat later date, *c.* 1760, are boxes with allegorical or mythological subjects applied in layers of carved mother-of-pearl and/or ivory, the resulting illusion of perspective being reinforced by the application of gold details in one or more of the layers. Boxes of this type are invariably cartouche-shaped, a baroque form that was discontinued in Paris by 1740 but that still occurred in England and Germany 20 years after, and in Scandinavia as late as 1775.

Enamelled miniatures *en tableau* occur, although infrequently, on German boxes. Gottfried Chodowiecki (1728–81), brother of Daniel, was, like him, an enameller. His signature appears on the plaques of a *tabatière à cage* in the Louvre (*262*). Boxes dating *c.* 1775 with enamelled scenes and restrained chiselling in the French taste are thought to be German; their refinement is, however, more characteristic of Austrian work of that period.

3 Dutch

Very few gold snuff boxes were made in Holland, where a general absence of luxury and a preference for pipe smoking over snuff taking militated against a large production. The few that have come to notice are of two periods. The first, dating in the middle of the eighteenth century, are oblong (generally with slightly curved sides or corners) and are chased on their covers with classical or allegorical subjects enclosed in scrolled frameworks. Narrow shaped thumbpieces are usual. The sides and bottoms of these boxes are generally left undecorated.

The second group comprises a few boxes datable in the second decade of the nineteenth century: they are shallow, oblong with rounded corner, and are entirely engine-turned.

4 *English*

The earliest mention of gold snuff boxes in England occurs in 1681 with the advertisement of 'a Gold Snuff Box' in the *London Gazette* (28 July). Two notices in the same newspaper the following year are more explicit about the appearance of early English boxes: 'a Gold Snuff-Box weighing about One Ounce, with an Earl's Coronet, and a cipher on the Lid' (20 March 1682) was probably, judging by its weight, no more than two inches in length. A circular gold box is mentioned on 9 September of the same year. Until *c.* 1720 engraved armorials and/or ciphers were the chief decoration of gold boxes which were generally oval, their covers being attached by an external hinge riveted on to the back (*269*). The integral hinge was standard by 1740, although circular boxes were made with lift-off lids.

The practice of combining gold with hardstones occurs as early as 1705 with the mention in the *Daily Courant* (24 February) of 'a large Gold Snuff-Box, with a large blue Onyx stone upon the lid'.

Chased decoration begins to occur *c.* 1720. The *Daily Courant* of 12 August 1718 recorded the loss of 'a large oval Snuff-Box of Gold, embos'd at the Top with the Arms [of] the Cotton Family ...'. Repoussé decoration had been common to English silversmiths' work *c.* 1660–80 and was revived in the eighteenth century under Dutch influence. Embossed heraldic ornament is rare; the closest parallel to the box just cited is perhaps a Dutch silver example with the engraved De Peyster arms surrounded by chased figures (*356*). Allegorical scenes appear on boxes probably made in London *c.* 1720–30 (*272, 273, 275*). Chased in low relief on matte grounds and enclosed within borders punctuated at the corners with scroll and shell motifs, they are unmistakably derived from Parisian silversmiths' work: the hunting scenes on the sides of the box shown in Fig. 274 are very similar to those on a cruet stand of 1718–19 by Nicolas Dandrieux (Musée des Arts Décoratifs, Paris). The English box, which is the only one of the group to bear any identification, is signed by the unknown artist Burel, probably a Huguenot emigrant. Also reflective of French style, but characteristically English in execution, are the borders of these snuff boxes, which parallel those found on salvers made in London *c.* 1719–28, especially those by Paul de Lamerie.

Chased decoration in high relief, of allegorical and classical heroic subjects, was common by 1745; it appears as early as 1741–2 on a gold box signed and dated by G. M. Moser (Wrightsman collection), and on a silver toilet box by Augustin Courtauld in the Hermitage Museum. In London as in Paris there were chisellers who specialised in executing relief decoration for the goldsmiths. Heal (*London Goldsmiths*) records two such artists: Bingant, otherwise unidentified, described *c.* 1751 as a 'gold-chaser'; and George Michael Moser (1704–83). Moser, born in Schaffhausen, began his London career as a chaser of bronze ornaments for a cabinet-maker, and is recorded as a 'gold-chaser' in 1736. His signature and the date 1741 appear on the cover of a large footed box—possibly a jewel box—by the unidentified maker P.R. (Wrightsman collection). Moser continued to work in this medium at least until 1763 when he was described as 'Chaser and Painter in Enamel Colours'. English gold boxes are rarely marked, and the chased boxes of the mid-eighteenth century are so similar to Dutch and German styles as to make positive attribution often tentative. A comparison of Figs. 266 and 282 will explain the difficulty. In general, the English examples tend to be of irregular shape: the elongated pouch shape (*277*) is characteristic of London work *c.* 1749; by 1760 it had been modified into the cartouche, then also current in Germany. In addition, the English boxes are often profusely decorated with C-scrolls and shell motifs on all the surfaces: Dutch examples are more often chased only on their covers. French influence is apparent in a box which, chased with exotic birds against a background of ridged swirls (*284*), is almost a duplicate of work by the Parisian goldsmith J. M. Le Quin, 1749–51 (*36*). Among the few makers recorded in the middle of the century are Henry Miller, and the unidentified P.P., F.H., E.R. (possibly Elias Russel?) and P.R. Heal records Charles Mackenize (d. 1749) as a 'gold snuff-box maker'.

Miniatures occur intermittently from *c.* 1720. Two years earlier the anonymous author of *Pandora's Box, a Satyr against Snuff* observed:

> *Within the Lid the Painter plays his Part,*
> *And with his Pencil proves his matchless Art:*
> *There drawn to Life some Spark or Mistress dwells,*
> *Like Hermits chast and constant in their Cells.*
> *. . . were a strict Inquiry to be made*
> *Through all the Town, and ev'ry Box survey'd,*
> *You'd seldom find the Picture of one Spouse . . .*

Even less innocent, he continued, were the

> *. . . lustful Postures all the Rakes and Fops*
> *Have most obscenely drawn in ev'ry Box*

Few subjects of this type survive. Portrait miniatures occur frequently: their importance as personal documents has led past collectors to insert them in boxes of quite unrelated date or style, e.g., a box of 1737–8 by Jean Ducrollay (*9*) which was fitted at a later date with a portrait of Lady Bagot in the style of John Smart. Miniatures never intended for snuff boxes were also mounted in the eighteenth century. The catalogue of Horace Walpole's collection describes

> *A fine gold escalop shaped* SNUFF BOX, richly enamelled with flowers, on the top is a very fine miniature of James I, by Hilliard, and with a portrait of Queen Elizabeth, also by *Hilliard . . .* the onyx at the bottom of the box is considered perfectly unique

Equally anachronistic, at least in the choice of the subject of the miniature, is the portrait of Mary Queen of Scots set in a gold box of *c.* 1720 (*271*). The miniature is one of several copies made by Bernard Lens (1682–1740) of a portrait (considered at the time to be contemporary with the sitter) then in the possession of the Duke of Hamilton; another, unmounted, version is dated 1720.

Miniaturists in addition to Lens whose work is recorded on English gold boxes are Luke Sullivan (1705–71); Richard Cosway (1740–1821); James Scouler (1740?–1812); George Morland (1763–1804) and Henry Bone (1755–1834). Also among English miniaturists may be included the German John Henry Müntz (*fl.* 1755–75), a protégé of Horace Walpole who commissioned miniatures for a snuff box from him in 1759; and André Rouquet (1701–50) who, although of Swiss birth, spent most of his career (*c.* 1727–53) in London.

In a century when drawing and painting were general accomplishments it is not unlikely that many miniatures were the work of amateurs. George Montagu wrote to Walpole on 18 February 1762:

> I have just seen Lady Kingsland's two pictures of Madame Grammont. One is a small one in water colours in a snuff-box, the eyes very blue and sweet, brown hair, fully-chested, a bust only, a large neck, very French, and full forty.

The *tabatière à cage* was not adopted in England, although in a tradition shared with Germany hardstone boxes were occasionally set in pierced gold frameworks (*286*). A variant of this style may be seen in a gold and agate box *c.* 1760 (*287*): a watch is set on the front panel, while the hinged back conceals a painted moving landscape. It is an early example of the fanciful combinations of goldsmiths' work and automata popularised 1766–73 by James Cox (d. after 1791), an entrepreneur associated with the Swiss firm of Jaquet-Droz and Leschot which provided him with many of the mechanisms for his inventions. Cox worked primarily on a large scale; excepting for one scent bottle, no *bijouterie* of this type of decoration can be attributed to him. The combination of agate, gold cagework and watches was generally reserved in England for large *nécessaires*; its adaptation to snuff boxes is rare.

Enamelled decoration in the French taste, with bouquets, all-over floral or diaper patterns, garlands and classical borders, occurs on English boxes of the 1760s and 1770s. The unbroken diaper pattern also occurs on an all-gold box made by Elias Russel (w. 1755–73) in London, 1761–2 (private collection). Oblong, with high sides, its shape is contemporary with Parisian fashion, while the continuous diagonal pattern recalls work of about 12 years earlier. In addition to the maker's mark, the box bears the signature of the jewellers *Parker and Wakelin* (for John Parker and Edward Wakelin, in partnership *c.* 1760–76) by whom the box was sold. Several dozen jewellers and 'toymen'—dealing not only in gold and silver boxes but also, like the Parisian *marchands merciers*, in those of tortoiseshell, hardstone, porcelain and enamel— are recorded by Heal. It has been suggested that the customary absence of marks on English gold boxes is due to the system of retailing whereby the goldsmith was responsible to the jeweller rather than to his guild. Such a deviation from the usual authority of the guild is improbable, however. Enamelled classical motifs derived from the designs of Robert Adam and Josiah Wedgwood occur *c.* 1775–80. Throughout the period 1760–90 the boxes are commonly oval, becoming shallower and more elongated *c.* 1775; shuttle-shaped boxes appear *c.* 1782. The sharp-edged oblong box with canted corners popular on the Continent scarcely occurs in England. Top-hinged lids occur infrequently during the last quarter of the eighteenth century. Some of the enamelling on these later gold boxes was certainly the work of Geneva-trained artists settled in London. In this category may be placed G. M. Moser who, as we have seen, was described as an enameller as well as a gold-chaser in 1763. It is as an enameller—and also as the first Keeper of the Royal Academy—that Moser is chiefly remembered. However, no signed enamels by him are known and it is impossible to attribute work to him with any certainty. Peter Wirgman (w. 1784–96) and Thomas Pepper (w. 1790–6) are the only two goldsmith-enamellers recorded by Heal in the last years of the century.

By 1800 enamelling had been all but displaced by engine-turned decoration. The rose engine lathe had been developed in Birmingham *c.* 1763, when it was first used by Josiah Wedgwood to decorate ceramics, but it was not applied to goldsmiths' work until the turn of the century. Engine turning is the principal feature of a number of oblong boxes with rounded edges, machine-engraved with an all-over wicker-work design *cf. 296*; the few marked versions are all London work and range in date from 1799 to 1816.

With the commercial development of engine turning, Birmingham became an important centre of manufacture of gold boxes in the nineteenth century. The styles of London and Birmingham from 1810 to 1830 are little different: oblong, with slightly rounded edges, the boxes are generally covered on all surfaces with panels enframing a single machine-engraved pattern. Cast or chased floral thumbpieces occur *c.* 1815; about the same time the sides of the boxes begin to be pinched in (*300*). In London, and to a considerably lesser extent in Birmingham, this basic scheme was often enriched by chased floral or foliage borders around the rims. A wide chased oakleaf-and-acorn border is found on many boxes *c.* 1815; it is an especially characteristic feature of the work of A. J. Strachan. Until recently known only by the initials of his mark, Strachan was clearly the most important box maker in London during the first quarter of the nineteenth century. His many recorded boxes, which date from 1806 to 1823, include 'Freedom' and royal presentation boxes as well as simpler work. An atypical box of 1823, bearing a portrait of George IV as Prince of Wales by Henry Bone (after Lawrence), is further ornamented with diamonds and blue-enamelled borders, in a style clearly imitative of the Parisian *boîtes à portrait* of the same period.

From *c.* 1812 the covers of gold boxes were occasionally set with plaques chased with hunting or other scenes; the fashion continued in favour until *c.* 1840.

Gold box makers active during the first third of the nineteenth century are Jacob Amedroz, David Hennell, Strachan, I.N. (possibly John Northam), William Eley and William Snooke Hall, all working in London; and J. Mackay in Edinburgh.

Outside the mainstream of English goldsmiths' work was the production of 'Freedom' boxes which, beginning early in the eighteenth century, reached its height in the first third of the nineteenth. They were, as their name suggests, boxes made to commemorate the conferring of the Freedom of a city which was inscribed on a scroll enclosed within the box. Of the same dimensions as snuff boxes, they were undoubtedly used as such. Generally oblong, their decoration uniformly consisted of the arms of the city or borough engraved or chased on the cover, the remainder of the boxes being left plain or, from *c.* 1810, being decorated with panels of engine turning. While most gold 'Freedom' boxes bear makers' marks, few of the goldsmiths have been identified. The chief maker of 'Freedom' boxes in the nineteenth century was A. J. Strachan.

5 *American*

In America, gold boxes were not in general use. They are so conspicuously absent from contemporary records that the mention of one in the will of a Mrs Anne Van Horne of New York, in 1772, leads one to suspect that it was English. Of the few American gold boxes that have been recorded only one, engraved with a family coat of arms (*353*) is at all personal in its decoration, and it is likely that even this one was a presentation box of some sort: its recipient was William Dummer, Lieutenant-Governor of Massachusetts from 1716 to 1730.

The remaining American gold boxes are 'Freedom' boxes. Chief among their makers was Charles Le Roux (w. 1713–45), who was the official silversmith of New York City for many years and, from 1720 to 1743, the only New York maker of 'Freedom' boxes. He is represented by a box commissioned in 1735 and presented to Alexander Hamilton, in honour of his defence of the printer John Peter Zenger (Philadelphia Historical Society). Like two later New York 'Freedom' boxes by Samuel Johnson the Le Roux box is oval, with a loose cover, and is engraved with the arms of the city on the cover. Le Roux is recorded as having made other 'Freedom' boxes in 1723 and 1728, but they do not appear to have survived; the same is true of a gold box extending the Freedom of the city of Albany to George Washington, made in that city by Jacob Gerritse Lansing in 1782.

A box of *c.* 1835 (*355*), also a presentation box, gives evidence of the period's ubiquitous fashion for engine-turned decoration.

6 *Scandinavian*

Swedish gold boxes, of which most surviving examples were made in Stockholm, are closely patterned on Parisian models. Cartouche-shaped boxes by Frantz Bergs (w. 1725–77) chased with figure groups, scrolls and gadrooning—parallel examples by Daniel Govaers and Jean Ducrollay in the 1730s. While these are not datable by year, it is apparent from the comparison of other French and Swedish boxes that fashions current in Paris appeared almost immediately in Stockholm (usually retaining their popularity for a longer period than in France): thus, Bergs' early boxes probably date no later than 1740–5.

Oval and oblong boxes enamelled *en plein* against an engraved diaper ground, a style popular in Paris *c.* 1755, appear in Stockholm at least by 1759, as evidenced by an oblong box of that year formerly in the Falk Simon collection. An enamelled *boîte à guirlandes* of 1769 (formerly Simon collection) and a varicoloured gold box with medallions and garlands, *c.* 1770–5 (*308*), both reflect contemporary French fashion. The engine-turned dot-and-line pattern of the 1780s occurs in Stockholm in 1794 in a shallow circular box by Friedrich Fyrwald (w. 1786–1813/14).

So few Danish gold boxes are known that no consecutive account of their manufacture can be offered. The most important box maker in Copenhagen in the eighteenth century was Frederick II Fabritius (1740–1829). To him may be assigned two boxes of diverse style. The first (*310*), a *tabatière à cage* of agate and gold, is thought to have been made by Fabritius (the mark is not entirely clear) in 1767 or 1768 when he started working for his father, Christoffer. Although trained in Paris, Fabritius displays in this box an easy familiarity with English goldsmiths' work, the natural result of a cultural rapport between the two countries dating from the seventeenth century and reinforced in the eighteenth by intermarriage between the two royal houses. More in the French taste is a varicoloured gold box of 1785 by Fabritius, flat-chased with views of Copenhagen bordered by garlands and pilasters (formerly Falk Simon collection). Also of French style are two boxes with enamelled stripes and portrait medallions (*312, 313*) which, on the strength of only partly decipherable marks, may tentatively be considered Danish work.

7 *Swiss*

Among the earliest Swiss gold boxes are a small number of oval boxes, dating *c.* 1770–5, chased in varicoloured gold with medallions, pilasters, garlands, etc. They are the work of the unidentified goldsmith D.M.C.; the technical skill of his boxes and his clear understanding of French style suggest that he may have been trained in Paris.

By 1790 enamelling had emerged as the chief decoration of Swiss boxes. Although it had been equally prominent in the decoration of watch cases *c.* 1680–*c.* 1720, it had been all but abandoned owing to the deterioration of the surfaces exposed to wear. A transparent colourless enamel, developed in Geneva *c.* 1780, served as a protective covering for paintings and made a revival of enamelling practical. From *c.* 1790–1840 Swiss boxes were commonly oblong and very shallow (about $\frac{3}{4}$ in.) and were painted on the cover and occasionally the

III   Comus shell, mounted in enamelled gold. Inscribed on the rim Sageret, Paris.
Maker Barnabé Sageret. French (Paris), 1746-7

bottom, a shallow base rim protecting the latter from wear. The sides were engine-turned or were enamelled in opaque colours; the rounded corners were marked by enamelled pilasters or vases. The subjects of the enamel paintings were most often alpine landscapes, river and pastoral scenes and allegorical subjects. They were frequently reserved against a background enamelled with a geometric pattern in strong contrasting colours, e.g., blue, black and white.

Although largely unmarked, these boxes can be attributed to Geneva, the centre for enamelled watches and jewellery since the seventeenth century. In 1789 there were 77 enamel painters in the city. Most of the box enamellers are anonymous, but the names of three have been recorded: David Etienne Roux (1758–1832), his brother Philippe Samuel Théodore (1756–1805) and their pupil, Jean Louis Richter (1766–1841). Although the Roux brothers specialised in painting landscapes on boxes, their work has not been identified. Several boxes by Richter, representing hunting, pastoral and boating scenes, are in the Musée d'Art et d'Histoire, Geneva, and are notable for their clear colours and meticulous technique. They are signed 'Richter' in cursive script.

Oval boxes of lobed outline occur *c.* 1825. Some examples painted with scattered bouquets and sprays of flowers were probably made for the Turkish market: the enamelling is similar to that found on watches with numerals rendered in their original Arabic form made *c.* 1820–60 at Geneva and La Chaux-de-Fonds. Other boxes of this type, dating *c.* 1830–5, are enamelled with harbour views and seascapes enclosed in wavy-edged reserves. Diamond-studded boxes occur about the same time.

Snuff boxes enclosing musical mechanisms or automata were introduced in the last quarter of the eighteenth century. In January 1775 the *marchand mercier* Grancher advertised (*Mercure de France*)

> Tabatieres & flacons en or de couleur, renfermant un carillon, jouant
> chacun trois airs differens . . . .

These were probably of Swiss manufacture; however, commercial production of musical snuff boxes dates only from *c.* 1810. According to the *Rapport de l'Exposition de l'Industrie genevoise* of 1828 the perfection of musical snuff boxes was the work of Isaac Piguet (b. 1775) in 1802. Interest in the boxes grew rapidly: in 1809 Napoleon ordered several gold and enamel boxes that would play Tyrolean music as gifts for his generals after the Austrian campaign. By 1812 there were 174 craftsmen in Geneva producing musical mechanisms '*tant tabatières que cachets [étuis* for sealing wax]'. Like ordinary Genevan snuff boxes these are commonly oblong, enamelled with a scene on the cover; the mechanism is enclosed in a shallow space in the bottom (which is hinged). Occasionally the boxes are divided into three top-opening compartments: a centre one for snuff, the side ones for the mechanism and a watch, respectively. From 1815 musical snuff boxes began to be made of horn, shell and tin-plate. The principal manufacturer of these boxes in Geneva was the firm of Piguet and Meylan. After 1811 musical snuff boxes were also made at Sainte-Croix.

Also of Genevan origin are singing-bird boxes in which a central medallion on the cover opens with a spring to release a singing bird. Horace Walpole wrote to Mary and Agnes Berry on 5 March 1791:

> A Parisian watch-maker [has] produced the smallest automaton that I suppose was ever created. It was a rich snuff-box, not too large for a woman. On opening the lid, an enamelled bird started up, sat on the rim, turned round, fluttered its wings, and piped in a delightful tone the notes of different birds; particularly the jug-jug of the nightingale. It is the prettiest plaything you ever saw; the price tempting—only five hundred pounds. That economist, the Prince of Wales, could not resist it, and has bought one of those dicky-birds.

The classification of these boxes as *tabatières* is somewhat loose, as generally only a very shallow space (about one-half inch) is left in the bottom of the box as a container. Although Walpole credited the invention of singing-bird boxes to a Parisian, they were at this time manufactured only in Geneva by the firm of Jaquet-Droz and Leschot. The latter wrote to a customer in Berlin, in 1793,

> *Quant à la tabatière à oiseau que vous avez vue, cette pièce mécanique est certainement de notre atelier, j'ai eu l'honneur de vous prévenir il y a plusieurs années, que nous faisions de ces sortes d'ouvrages en mécanique d'oiseau en bijouterie, comme tabatière, flacon, etc.*

He goes on to remark that many of the boxes are engraved as coming from London (where Jaquet-Droz had established a branch in 1783) because of the prevailing opinion that English work was superior. Prior to the Revolution some of the box frames enclosing the mechanisms were made in Paris. Walpole's assumption of the Parisian origin of the Prince of Wales's box may refer to the maker of the box itself: Jean-Etienne Blerzy is known to have executed this type of work.

Among the artists working for Jaquet-Droz and Leschot 1802–13 are Mussard and Doebricht, 'joailliers', and the *bijoutiers* Collard and Martin, who specialised in '*boîtes de tabatières (pour) oiseaux mécaniques*'. The marks of unidentified makers, presumably regular employees of the firm, frequently occur, struck two or three times, on the cases of singing-bird boxes. After *c.* 1820 these boxes were also made in Geneva by Jacob Frisard and the firm of Frères Rochat. A third variety of the Genevan mechanical snuff box, popular from *c.* 1820, is exemplified by Fig. 332, which is fitted with an animated gardening scene. Music mechanisms are generally included in these boxes.

8 Russian

It is somewhat misleading to speak of 'Russian' gold boxes, as most *tabatières* made in Russia in the eighteenth century were the work of foreign craftsmen. The centre of manufacture was St Petersburg, whither western goldsmiths were attracted by Peter the Great as early as

1714. The large number of foreign craftsmen in that city led to the establishment of a foreigners' guild into which, after a period of apprenticeship, the goldsmiths were accepted as masters. Some, like Jean-Charles Blerzy, later became citizens and members of the Russian goldsmiths' guild. Bäcksbacka (*St Petersburgs juvelerare*) records the careers in St Petersburg, between 1714 and 1800, of no less than 234 German goldsmiths, 216 Scandinavian and 43 French (not all of whom, of course, were box makers). Smaller numbers of English, Swiss and central European goldsmiths are also recorded, as is a single Italian, one Bernardi, who combined the roles of jeweller and diplomatic confidant of Catherine II. Sir Charles Hanbury-Williams, then British Ambassador to the Russian court, wrote Catherine in 1756 (26 November),

> I must tell you that I have a snuff-box, set in brilliants, which is a kind of nick-nack that I do not care for. I had given it to Bernardi to exchange for me for some sort of aigrette for my daughter. He told me that the snuff-box would please you. . . .

In reconstructing the prevailing taste in gold boxes at the time of this letter we may keep in mind the heavily chased, diamond-studded boxes of Berlin origin of which examples dating *c.* 1750–5, inset with enamel portraits of Frederick the Great and the Empress Elizabeth, are in the Hermitage Museum. It may safely be assumed that the style was duplicated in St Petersburg. The lavish use of diamonds is characteristic of Russian-made boxes: jewelled thumbpieces and borders are common; occasionally the entire decoration of a box is carried out in diamonds, as on one set with a jewelled flower basket by the Geneva-born goldsmith Jérémie Pauzié (w. Russia 1740–64, d. 1779). Pauzié's boxes are the earliest recorded by Foelkersam (*Starye Gody*, 1907). Of cartouche, circular and shaped oblong form, they are decorated in relief with scrollwork and/or floral decoration often set against engraved diaper grounds in a manner common to Parisian work *c.* 1735–50. Several are further ornamented with the monogram of the Empress Elizabeth and can probably be dated before 1745; despite the geographical and cultural distances between France and Russia, decorative styles current in Paris quickly appeared in St Petersburg and Moscow.

It appears that not until *c.* 1770 was there any considerable production of gold boxes in Russia. The influence of French taste is conspicuous until *c.* 1800, reinforced by the presence of such French goldsmiths as Jean-Jacques Duc (w. 1770–85), Jean-Pierre Ador (w. 1770–85), François Seguin (w. 1779–85), Nicolas Pierre St Beuve (w. 1787–93), Jacques-François Metrot (w. 1789–92), Pierre Théremin (w. 1793–1801), Jean-Charles Blerzy (w. 1794–1811), François-Claude Théremin (w. 1795–1801) and Antoine Nicolas (w. 1798–1831). Of these, the most prominent was Ador. Of oval, circular or oblong form, his boxes generally combine chased borders and secondary ornamentation in the French taste with miniatures. Little information concerning the painters of gold boxes is available. The few miniatures that have been identified are western. That some were specially commissioned is apparent from a *tabatière à cage* by Ador presented by the Empress to Gregory Orloff. This box (now in the

Smithsonian Institution) is set with paintings of the events leading to Catherine's accession signed by the unrecorded artist Kaestner (who may have been related to the Dresden miniaturist Carl August Kästner [*fl.* 1797–1822]). Of a later date are a Moscow box set with a portrait of Louis XVI by Sicard (*342*); a circular box *c.* 1800 by Otto Samuel Keibel (w. 1797–1810) set with pastoral scene probably by Louis-Nicolas van Blarenberghe (Metropolitan Museum); a box *c.* 1820 by an unidentified Moscow maker with a portrait of a woman by Karl Christian Kanz (1758–*c.* 1818) (Metropolitan Museum); and a box of *c.* 1820–30 with a portrait signed with the unidentified initial *B* (*347*). Some of these miniatures may have been transposed from Parisian boxes. Names of Russian miniaturists do not appear to be recorded.

French influence is characteristic of gold boxes made during the last quarter of the eighteenth century, even those by goldsmiths of German origin. Circular and oval boxes are common; oblong boxes, sometimes with canted corners, occur *c.* 1800. Johann Gottlieb Scharff (w. 1772–1808) is represented in the Hermitage Museum by ten boxes, of which a circular one, set with a miniature of a borzoi encircled by a succession of diamond borders and a diamond-studded floral diaper background, may be considered characteristic. A rare instance of enamelled decoration occurs on another box by Scharff decorated with flower sprays (Foelkersam, 1907). Enamelling is also the principal feature of a box of 1800 (*344*) which is similar to work by Benjamin Gottlieb Lincke (1776–1829) recorded by Foelkersam. Other box makers of German extraction active in the last quarter of the century include Johann Balthasar Gass (w. 1760–93), Christian Gottlieb Göbell (w. 1760–80), Johann Christian Kayser (w. 1773–1801), Alexander Lang who was born in St Petersburg (w. 1773–77), and Hieronymus Friedrich Teschner (w. 1786–95).

A conglomerate style of decoration, in which chased representational subjects are combined with a variety of geometric ground and border patterns, occurs in boxes by Jean-François-Xavier Bouddé (w. 1769–after 1789), a native of Hamburg, and Joseph Friedrich Kolb (w. 1806–24).

Shallow oblong *boîtes à portrait* chased with *rinceaux* are common during the reign of Alexander I (1801–25), whose often-encountered portrait appears not only on Russian boxes but on Parisian ones of earlier date (*112*). Oblong portrait boxes bordered with large brilliants occur *c.* 1830 and are found, with slight variations in outline, as late as 1853.

9 *Spanish and Italian*

Despite the historical pre-eminence of Spain in the consumption and manufacture of snuff, the production of boxes in any material appears to have been wholly insignificant. Only one example of goldsmith's work can be offered here (*348*), and its attribution must rest largely on supposition.

In Italy, gold snuff boxes are mentioned in literature as early as 1636, in *La Tabaccheide* by

Francesco Zucchi. As in Spain, however, almost no examples are known. Two stylistically related boxes dating in the third quarter of the eighteenth century (*349, 350*), while reflective of contemporary Parisian styles, are undoubtedly Italian. The miniatures on the earlier of the two depict Turkish lion-hunting scenes, a favourite subject in Venetian decorative arts throughout the eighteenth century.

A shallow oblong Neapolitan box of 1827 (private collection) is, like virtually all European boxes of the period, decorated with engine-turned panels enclosed within foliate borders. Two Roman nineteenth-century boxes recorded by Bulgari (*Argentieri gemmari e orafi*) are composed primarily of hardstone: an oval lapis box by Giovanni Andrea Mascelli (m. 1826, d. 1870) is mounted with engraved gold rims in eighteenth-century taste; an oblong grey stone box with canted corners, by Girolamo Menazzi (m. 1801, d. 1835), is set on the cover with a mosaic hunting scene and is similar to work seen in France and England *c.* 1815–20.

IV Silver Boxes

1 Dutch

Little information is available concerning Dutch silver snuff boxes, which were over-shadowed throughout the eighteenth century by the more popular tobacco boxes. Despite what appears to have been only a minor production, their stylistic influence is apparent in England and America (especially New York State); it is in this light that the few examples included here may perhaps best be considered. Few of the makers of Dutch boxes have been recorded; none of those illustrated here can be attributed. Fredericks (*Dutch Silver*) records an oval box, engraved with scrollwork and portraits of Luther and Hus, by the Amsterdam silversmith Willem Wobbe (w. 1730–53). There appears to have been no overlap in Holland (any more than in England) between the makers of snuff and tobacco boxes.

2 English

Comparatively few English silver boxes dating before 1730 are known. A picture of their early development and variety must depend largely on written descriptions of the period, especially those in the London newspapers. Silver (like gold) boxes are first mentioned in 1681, and from that year until the turn of the century probably differed little from tobacco boxes. The traditional distinction between the two—that tobacco boxes were made with loose covers while snuff box lids were hinged—is evidently not entirely valid, as the *London Gazette* of 25 January 1683 described, as if it were unusual, 'an Oval Silver Tobacco Box (without a Spring)'. The chief distinctions between snuff and tobacco boxes in the seventeenth century were the smaller size of the former and the customary gilding of their interiors to prevent discoloration. Both types of boxes were commonly oval and were decorated only on their covers with engraved heraldic ornament. The *London Gazette* of 19 September 1692 described

> a Silver Snuff-Box Guilt on the inside, and the top of it is Engraven a Cypher
> with the Garter round it, and a Dukes Coronet.

This type of work survives chiefly in tobacco boxes of the period, of which one of 1699–1700, engraved with the Blakiston arms (*363*), may be considered characteristic. Engraved subject decoration is recorded as early as 1697 (*The Post Boy*, 11 February) on

a silver Gilt Snuff-box with a Cypher on the bottom; and on the top two
Death's Heads with a flower between them, and written above *Memento Mori*,
and underneath *All Flesh is Grass*.

An oblong box with cut corners illustrated by Jackson (*English Plate*, II) is engraved with a
similar type of decoration and is probably a snuff box of about the same period.

The shapes of boxes are occasionally mentioned in early records: oval boxes were the most
usual, retaining their popularity until the last quarter of the eighteenth century. Shell- and
cartouche-shaped boxes occur intermittently *c.* 1710–40. Octagonal boxes, which were
mentioned as a novelty in Holland as early as 1665 by Karel van Mander, were fashionable in
silver from *c.* 1705: an example is mentioned in London in that year; Jackson (*English Goldsmiths*) records examples of 1704–5 (by Ishmael Bone) and 1710–11 (Hezekial Mountfort).
The shape persisted, in one medium or another, as late as 1735 (*435*). On 11 August 1709 the
Daily Courant advertised a double box in the form of a boat, a shape not known in silver but
seen in other materials (*436*). (A late eighteenth-century semicircular double box (*372*) is
clearly a refinement of this shape.) Two months earlier (9 June), the same newspaper described
an oval silver box 'with a double Lid, both opening with the same Joint, and the Picture of a
Woman between'. The popularity of illicit miniatures, of which this appears to be one, has
already been mentioned (Chapter I); they, and mirror-lined lids—which are mentioned in
1718—were evidently combined with silver as well as gold boxes. A silver box in the shape
of a book, one that has generally been identified only with the last quarter of the century,
is mentioned in 1711 by Addison in the *Spectator* (12 April).

Dating from *c.* 1715 to as late as 1742 are small oblong boxes with canted corners, their lids
being hinged on the top near one short end (a placement of the hinge characteristic of
English silversmiths' work—later imitated in America—until the early nineteenth century).
A single engraved band of stylised scrollwork along the hinge and/or front edge is the customary sole ornament of these boxes.

Engraving—chiefly armorials and ciphers and, from the middle of the eighteenth century,
monograms—remained the usual decorative feature of English silver boxes. Chased decoration occurs briefly *c.* 1745 on cartouche-shaped boxes imitative of current goldsmiths' work;
the technique was inappropriate for the softer metal, however, and in general the thematic
variations of goldsmiths' work did not affect the independent stylistic development of silver
boxes, which were essentially personal and unpretentious. An exception can be found in the
description, in the *Daily Courant* of 29 September 1709, of

> a Silver Snuff-Box, on the Lid a Locket compos'd of 10 Garnetts, in the middle
> an old-fashioned Chrystal under which was 2 Angels supporting a Crown over
> a Cypher, at each corner of the Box on the same side was set 4 Escalope Shells
> at the Tail of each Escalope with [sic] four Stones.

Such an elaborate setting of silver is rare, although by the last decade of the seventeenth
century it was usual to combine silver with other materials, especially shell, mother-of-pearl

or agate (a practice which occasionally makes attribution difficult, as such boxes were exempt—at least in England—from the regulations concerning marking and were made on the Continent and in America as well as England). A silver-lidded shell box 'that shuts with a good spring' is mentioned as early as 1697 (*The Post Boy*, 28 August): the popularity of shell boxes, generally cut and fitted with smooth silver lids engraved with a monogram, lasted until the end of the following century (*369*). An example by Hester Bateman (private collection) is one of the few recorded English silver snuff boxes by a silversmith whose primary work was of a different nature (viz., tableware). Jackson records silver boxes dating before 1740 by Philip Robinson (ent. 1715), John Bromley, Thomas Folkingham, Edward Feline and Père Pilleau (all ent. 1720), Edward Dymond (ent. 1722), Johnathan Newton (1718), George Brome and Robert Williams (1726), Benjamin Blakely (1738), George Boothby, Abimilech de Oliveyra and Louis Laroche (all 1739) and the unidentified BE (on a box of 1727-8). Henry Le Grand is recorded in 1726 as a 'silver snuff-box maker', indicating an established system of specialisation by material that appears to have been strictly observed until the nineteenth century. A. J. Strachan is known to have made silver (*373*) as well as gold boxes; examples in both metals by the unidentified Birmingham makers I.L., W.A. have also been noted.

Relatively few all-silver boxes of the second half of the eighteenth century are known. An oblong example inscribed with the name of the unrecorded goldsmith John Derussat and the date 1756 (*365*) is engraved with an allegorical subject in a style analogous to work on Dutch silver tobacco boxes of the period. Engraved decoration is cited by Jackson on boxes, mostly oblong in shape, made in the 1750s by Thomas Beere (ent. 1751), Robert Cox (ent. 1752), Thomas Towman (1753), Simon Le Sage (1754), Constantine Teulings (1755) and Tompson Davis (1757). It is worth noting that no makers of snuff boxes are recorded by Jackson between 1768 and 1788, and almost no examples have been recorded for this period which coincided with the competitive manufacture of enamel boxes in Staffordshire (see Chapter IX).

In the nineteenth century Birmingham was the centre for the production of silver boxes as it was for gold. Oblong boxes with incurvate walls and engine-turned panels were universal; after *c.* 1820 they ranged in size from large table boxes about 3½ inches in length to small ones of about two inches. By *c.* 1830 these latter were commonly ornamented on the cover with views of castles, abbeys, etc., cast in very high relief; several hundred different views are known to exist. Thumbpieces were usual, varying from narrow shaped flanges to heavy cast floral ridges. The most active box makers in Birmingham were Samuel Pemberton (boxes of 1784–1813), John Shaw (1795–1809), Nathaniel Mills (1826–50) and Edward Smith (1833–52). Other makers were Matthew Linwood (1789–1806), T. Simpson & Son (1811–12), Ledsam, Vale & Wheeler (1825–6), Thomas Shaw (1825–6) and John Bettridge (1829–30), and the unrecorded ER, most of whose work is dated 1835.

Sheffield Plate

The manufacture of silver-plated snuff boxes was a natural outgrowth of a box-making industry which had been active in Sheffield, under the aegis of the Cutlers' Company, since 1680. Snuff boxes were among the first wares to be made in Sheffield plate. The earliest examples, dating about 1755–60, were circular, small—averaging two inches in diameter—and were generally chased or die-struck on their covers and bases with rococo scrollwork. The covers were separable and the interiors were unplated. Circular plated boxes of the same period were also made with lids, and sometimes bases, of wood, enamel, tortoiseshell or horn.

With increased assurance in the working of the plated copper came an increased variety in the shape and decoration of snuff boxes. Those made during the last quarter of the eighteenth century were generally made with hinged covers, and their interiors were tinned or gilded. Oval and rectangular boxes were made, a variation of the latter shape apparently peculiar to Sheffield plate being the pinched oblong.

The production of plated boxes on a commercial scale was already over in Sheffield by 1775, although the Sheffield City Museum possesses examples dating as late as 1847. The silver-plating industry shifted to Birmingham, where Matthew Boulton had begun manufacturing plated wares in 1762, to be followed by a number of other manufacturers in 1770. Despite his role as a 'toy-maker', Boulton is not known to have made any snuff boxes in silver plate.

3 American

It is natural that in the first half of the eighteenth century the production of silver snuff boxes in America should have been limited to those areas with active commercial contacts with Europe, namely Boston and New York. The established habit of snuff taking among English and Dutch government officials and merchants provided a demand that did not become more general until *c.* 1760. While there were active communities of silversmiths in New Jersey, Maryland, Virginia and the Carolinas, virtually no boxes can be traced to these states. One of the few southern goldsmiths to emphasise the manufacture of 'all sorts of small work in Gold or Silver, particularly Snuff boxes' was Lewis Janvier (w. South Carolina *c.* 1735–40) but work of this nature by him is not known. In large part, the work of the American jewellers and silversmiths, versatile counterparts of the London 'toy-men', consisted in the importation of silver and plated boxes and the mounting of hardstones, shells, and enamel and papier-mâché boxes in silver rims which are rarely marked, thus making attribution all but impossible. (In 1806, the Albany silversmith Joseph Warford advertised for sale not only the usual complement of table silver, watches, snuff and tobacco boxes, but soap, pencils, camels' hair brushes, cotton suspenders and shaving powder: the inventory of his merchandise may recall that of the early Parisian *marchands merciers*.)

In America, the silver snuff box was from the beginning something of a luxury item and it is notable that many of the early boxes are by the most prominent silversmiths of their day, such as John Coney and Jacob Hurd of Boston, Peter Van Dyck of New York City and Joseph Richardson of Philadelphia. There appears to have been insufficient demand for more than an occasional silversmith (such as the Albany maker A.C.) to specialise in box making.

The earliest American silver boxes are two by John Coney (1655–1722) and clearly reflect the style then current in Europe for both snuff and tobacco boxes. They are both oval, with loose covers: hinged snuff boxes, although they occur by 1730, became usual only in the last quarter of the eighteenth century. The earlier of the two Boston boxes (Mabel Brady Garvan collection, Yale University) is engraved with the date 1701 and the Jeffries arms; the later (*383*), dating *c.* 1720, bears the arms of Wentworth. (It should be emphasised that the dating of American silver boxes is highly speculative, as no system of date letters was in existence and boxes are struck only with a maker's mark. Even the presence of an engraved name or monogram cannot be relied upon as a guide to dating: it has of course always been common practice to add initials to an earlier piece of silver; in addition, the custom of bequeathing money for commemorative silver is frequently evident from American wills. Thus in 1772 a David Jones, of Fort Neck, Queens, left his daughter £100 'to be laid out in utensils of silver, and marked with my name'.) The carefulness of the engraving and the accuracy of the heraldry is to be expected on boxes made for first-generation English families, among whom heraldry was always highly respected. The Wentworth armorial, which is in a style observable in England *c.* 1680–1710, was probably copied from a bookplate. Differencing in the arms excepted, it is very similar to one with the arms of Wentworth of Raby, dated 1698. The allied crafts of silversmithing and engraving are well recorded in the career of Paul Revere, whose signature on four armorial bookplates has been noted. Even more active as an engraver was the silversmith Nathaniel Hurd (1730–77) who announced in the *Boston Gazette* of 28 April 1760 that

> he continues to do all Sorts of Goldsmiths Work. Likewise engraves in Gold, Silver, Copper, Brass and Steel, in the neatest Manner, and at reasonable Rates.

Fifty-five armorial bookplates, 40 of them signed, are ascribed to Hurd, as are another 15 engravings of varied subjects. For the most part, however, the engraving on silversmiths' work was executed by specialists such as Francis Garden who solicited work in 1745 (*Boston Evening Post*, 4 March) engraving 'Coats-of-Arms, Crests or Cyphers on Gold, Silver, Pewter or Copper'.

John Coney's boxes are typical of those made in New York and New England as late as the 1760s. Generally oval, they are engraved only on the cover; an almost invariable feature of the decoration is a highly stylised husk border framing a central design. Apparently original to Albany, among silversmiths of Dutch extraction, is a vigorously engraved floriated quatrefoil motif which frequently recurs in the work of the unidentified A.C., and which is also seen in New York City (*387*). Similar work occurs on a box by William Whittemore of New Hampshire (*390*), while more sophisticated variants occur in Newport, Rhode Island (*384, 385*).

Chased decoration on American boxes is rare. The somewhat crudely wrought scene on an unmarked box of *c.* 1720 (*378*), while possibly Dutch, is more likely to have been the work of a local silversmith working in a prescribed, unfamiliar technique. The style of the box may be compared with an advertisement in the *Boston Gazette* of 3/10 September 1722:

> Lost on Tuesday . . . an oval Silver Snuff Box, the Cover Gilt, inside and out, and the Rivell of the heathen gods in raised work on the Cover.

Chased decoration in the English taste was current in the middle of the eighteenth century. In 1759 (25 January) the Philadelphia silversmith John Leacock announced in the *Pennsylvania Gazette* that he had just imported from London 'chased snuff boxes, gilt the inside'. A cartouche-shaped box, inscribed 1752, by the Boston silversmith Thomas Dane (1724–96; Hammerslough collection) is in the style of boxes made in Paris and London *c.* 1735–40. Another, of 1757, made in Philadelphia by Joseph Richardson (*394*), is unusually elegant for American work, and the chasing may indeed be from the hand of an English or Continental craftsman. In this connection it may be noted that in 1769 *The New-York Gazette and the Weekly Mercury* (31 July) printed an announcement by the silversmith Daniel Fueter—who had emigrated from London *c.* 1763—that

> Mr John Anthony Beau, Chaiser, from Geneva, works with him; where Chaising in general, viz. Snuff Boxes, Watch Cases, &c. &c. is done in the best and cheapest Manner.

Michael De Bruls, who advertised 'Curious Chasing or other Raised Work, in general on Gold and Silver Watch-Cases, Snuff Boxes, &c.' (*The New-York Gazette or the Weekly Post-Boy*, 19 December 1757), would also appear to have emigrated from the Continent.

By 1770 the pervasiveness of English taste is evident in the appearance, all along the Eastern seaboard, of oval snuff boxes with top-hinged lids, and of silver-mounted shell boxes. Decoration was generally confined to a border on the cover, occasionally repeated on the sides, and an unframed monogram engraved in a characteristically loose, open style. Armorial decoration does not occur on American boxes after *c.* 1730. After *c.* 1785 bright-cut decoration, which had appeared in England only a few years before, largely supplanted engraving which was confined to monograms and inscriptions.

In addition to cowrie and other native sea shells, tortoiseshell was popularly combined with silver for snuff boxes. It is likely that many of these boxes in use in America, such as the 'turtle shell snuff box set in silver' bequeathed in 1785 by one Joseph Wright of Flushing, New York, were imported from England: they are often included among the wares received by the silversmiths. An example by Peter Van Dyck of New York (*624*) is one of the few marked American boxes of this type.

4 *Canadian*

It is probable that the earliest silver snuff boxes in use in Canada were those brought over by French officials and settlers, and that their style was imitated by the Canadian silver-smiths, themselves *émigrés* or first-generation Canadians. Unfortunately, no French-Canadian snuff box is known to have survived, and the rare mention of a box, such as the '*tabatière d'argent*' offered as a prize in a lottery in Montreal in 1730, does nothing to suggest either their popularity or style.

The bulk of extant Canadian silver dates after the Treaty of Paris of 1763 in which the territory was ceded to England. While much of the large-scale silver (ewers, bowls) continued to reflect French fashions, snuff boxes are almost entirely derived from English prototypes. This is especially noticeable in the work of Laurent Amiot (1764–1839), who reputedly worked in Paris from 1784 to 1786. While his *vaisselle* is closely patterned on French models, the plain oblong snuff boxes bearing his mark, with their flat, slightly projecting thumbpieces, are English-inspired. Other features borrowed from England by the Canadian silversmiths are top-hinged lids and, from *c.* 1825, oblong boxes with incurvate walls. Decoration of the boxes was generally confined to engraved monograms or inscriptions; repoussé figural decoration such as that on a box by James Godfrey Hanna (1780–1851) (*410*) is rare.

Other Quebec silversmiths by whom snuff boxes are recorded are Peter Arnoldi (b. 1769, living 1792), Henri Polonceau (w. 1796–1824), and Etienne Plantade (w. 1806–21).

5 *French*

There is almost no information, either in the form of documents or of actual examples, concerning the manufacture of silver snuff boxes in France before *c.* 1730. The only record of seventeenth-century Parisian boxes is that, recorded by Nocq, of the seizure by the wardens of the Paris guild in 1681 of five silver *tabatières* from the shop of Pierre Reversé (m. 1661). Silver snuff boxes with spring hinges are mentioned by Furetière in 1694. A group of small shell-shaped boxes with chased figure groups, datable within the first quarter of the eighteenth century, were considered to be French when they were published in the catalogue of the Falk Simon collection. Although possibly of provincial origin they are unmarked, a circumstance most unusual in French metalwork, and are probably not French. Many of the boxes that were presumably made prior to 1709 were undoubtedly destroyed in that year when Louis XIV, who needed cash to carry on his war in Flanders, ordered that all plate be turned in to the mints to be melted down. In the main, the edict affected table ware: Saint-Simon reports that opposition to the order was based on a general distaste for eating off pewter, but that '*Tout ce qu'il y eut de grand a de considérable se mit en huit jours à la faïence*'.

Restrictions on the manufacture and use of silver occur as late as 1720 in a declaration of the Regent, designed to prevent the manufacture of luxury goods, which forbade the production of single silver pieces without written permission. The force of this decree in relation to silver snuff boxes (which, of course, were not single pieces but were raised from several sheets of metal) cannot be fairly estimated, but the climate of repression undoubtedly accounts in part for the absence of boxes at this period.

There appears to have been little demand for silver boxes in Paris; they do not figure in the large private collections of the eighteenth century, e.g. the Duchesse d'Orléans (1723), Mme de Pompadour (1764), the Prince de Conti (1777) and the Duc d'Aumont (1782). The few boxes that have been recorded are conspicuous for their duplication of styles currently fashionable on gold boxes: several *tabatières à cage* by Antoine Daroux are set with plaques of brightly tinted carved and inlaid mother-of-pearl (*418*). Also by Daroux are two oblong boxes with slightly waisted sides, one chased with pastoral subjects (*417*), the other with an all-over leaf trail pattern (*416*). Shell-shaped boxes chased with genre and pastoral scenes occur *c.* 1735–43. The decoration of a box of 1737–8 (*415*) is comparable to that on gold boxes of the same period by Ducrollay and Govaers. Like many Parisian boxes it is entirely gilded in an obvious attempt to reproduce, however fleetingly, the impression of 20-carat gold. The implications of this practice became apparent in 1765 when the issue was raised as to whether silver-gilt snuff boxes were or were not deceptive; the Paris Court of the Mint decided (2 December 1765) in the negative, partly on the basis of an earlier judgment of the king that

> *une branche de commerce qui dépend totalement du goût des acheteurs & changemens introduits pour l'usage, ne soit point restreint.*

By the same decree goldsmiths were permitted to manufacture silver boxes decorated in varicoloured gold and hinged with gold. This appears to have been merely a formal acceptance of an established practice: several boxes in this technique by Charles Le Bastier (who is exceptional in having made boxes in both gold and silver), dating between 1760 and 1765, are known (*421*). And in 1763 the goldsmith Jean Duché lost an oval box of silver hinged with gold.

Parisian goldsmiths who are presumed on the basis of contemporary records to have made silver snuff boxes, but whose work is not known, include Claude Bertin (m. 1698/9, living 1715) whose shop in 1702 was at the sign of the '*Tabatière royale*'; Etienne Pollet (m. 1715, d. 1756); Claude Coppin (m. 1725, d. between 1752 and 1762); Claude Boyer (m. 1738, not listed 1752); Edme-Toussaint Le Vacher (recorded 1733–9); Louis Charmoy (m. 1759, living 1789); Antoine Nicolas (m. 1773, living 1831?); Antoine Tigé (m. 1775, living 1793).

A number of goldsmiths working in the small towns within the Generality of Paris are recorded as having executed silver snuff boxes as their *chef d'œuvre*. They are: François-Martin Langlois (m. 1758 in Provins); Pierre-François Roussel (m. 1766, Senlis); Jean-Etienne Vairlet (m. 1769, Beauvais); Jean-Pierre Briand (m. 1769, Meaux); Jean-Alexandre Besnard

(m. 1770, St-Germain-en-Laye); Charles-Thomas Coutellier (m. 1772, Vernon); Louis-André Balthazar Jullien (m. 1772, Melun); Jean Langlois (m. 1774, Compiègne); Louis-Joseph Prevot (m. 1787, Bray-sur-Seine).

The manufacture of silver snuff boxes was undoubtedly much greater in the provinces than at Paris. As early as 1714 a dispute arose between the goldsmiths and the *marchands merciers* of Lille over the sale of silver *tabatières*. At that time an informal agreement was reached whereby the merchants were to continue to sell silver and silver-mounted boxes, provided the weight of the metal did not exceed one ounce. The issue was revived in 1735 when the goldsmiths, accusing three *merciers* of violating this agreement, confiscated 77 silver boxes from their shops. After prolonged litigation the question appears to have been settled in 1739 in favour of the goldsmiths. Among the boxes at issue was one of shuttle shape, an unusually early occurrence of a form that did not become general until *c.* 1775. An oblong box made in Lille probably in 1740, engraved with strapwork and chinoiseries (*412*), indicates a stylistic independence of Paris.

Undoubtedly many provincial boxes have been retained as heirlooms in private collections and have, by their personal nature, escaped general notice.

A breakdown in national styles after the Revolution is apparent in French boxes, which from *c.* 1800 are commonly decorated with panels of engine turning. Bright-cut engraving occurs infrequently at the beginning of the nineteenth century. Few nineteenth-century French silver boxes are known; in 1804 only ten of the 804 goldsmiths working in Paris were listed as makers of silver boxes.

6 Scandinavian

Only the sketchiest view of Scandinavian silver boxes is possible at the present time, when photographs of many examples in Denmark and Sweden have not yet been made available. The few Swedish examples shown here are markedly influenced by French styles, especially that (*425*) which borrows the sunburst motif popular in Paris *c.* 1755 and which is contemporary with it. Changes in fashion are less impulsive in provincial centres, and it may be gathered from boxes formerly in the Falk Simon collection that cartouche-shaped boxes flat-chased with figural subjects were made as late as 1776 in cities outside Stockholm (e.g., one of that year by Jonas Aspelin of Ystad). From the same collection, dating in the 1780s and 1790s, are a number of shallow oval boxes with loose covers; all are similarly engraved on their covers with a garland-hung rosette, in a simplified imitation of Parisian work *c.* 1770.

7 Russian

Russian silver boxes dating before *c.* 1780 are uncommon; the peak period of their manufacture came only after 1825. A few early boxes exhibited in London in 1935 were commemorative of the reigns of Peter the Great (made after his death) and Catherine II and were set with medallic portraits or allegories.

Chased ornament on Russian boxes is almost unknown; niello is the characteristic form of decoration from *c.* 1780 to *c.* 1860. In this technique the subject is engraved on the silver with a burin, the lines being filled with a powder composed of silver, lead, copper and sulphur which is then fixed by heat. Representational scenes were the most usual: landscapes, pastoral subjects, figure groups, views of cities, churches, castles all occur on boxes made in Moscow and St Petersburg. Only slightly less popular were boxes nielloed with maps and city plans. Several examples bearing maps of the province of Vologda, east of Leningrad, were shown in 1935; ranging in date from 1793 to 1822 all were probably (and one certainly) made in the capital city of Vologda. Boxes with a plan of St Petersburg and with maps of Siberia (*431*) have also been noted.

Russian silver boxes are commonly gilded on the inside, and often on the outside as well. Eighteenth-century examples vary considerably in shape, circular ones predominating. In the nineteenth century virtually all are rectangular.

V Marking Gold and Silver Boxes

The marking of boxes in eighteenth-century Europe was essentially the same whether the material was gold or silver. Only in France was *orfèvrerie* marked systematically: the complete absence of marks on a gold or silver box is generally a safe indication that it is not French.

There are customarily at least four marks to be found on Parisian gold boxes: the maker's, the warden's and the two marks of the tax collector (*fermier*). They were struck in a particular sequence which is reflected in their size, location and condition. By a royal edict of 1679 goldsmiths were required to mark with their personal mark each section of a work as soon as it had been roughed out. Each piece was then registered at the office of the *fermier*, who added his charge mark; it was then assayed and stamped with the *poinçon de la maison commune* by the warden of the guild. Thus, a cluster of three large marks will usually be found inside the cover, bottom, at least one wall and, occasionally, on the insetting rim, of a gold box. When the box was completed it was returned to the *fermier* for payment of tax upon which a fourth, discharge, mark was struck, releasing the piece for sale. This last mark, in order not to deface the decoration, was always struck on the insetting rim of the box and was considerably smaller than the others. Because of this sequence the maker's, warden's and charge marks are often difficult to decipher, having been stretched, hammered and sometimes cut off in the course of finishing the piece. (Although goldsmiths were supposed to strike their marks again if they became illegible while working a piece it is obvious they rarely did so.) The discharge mark, by contrast, is always perfectly clear.

The form of the Parisian goldsmith's mark, as established by 1540, consisted of a crowned fleur-de-lis designating Paris, the initials of the goldsmith and a personal device, and a small dot on either side of the fleur-de-lis. These two *grains de remède* symbolised the tolerance of two grains permitted in the standard of silver which was 11 *deniers* 12 *grains* (the equivalent of 928/1000 silver). From 1721 the standard of gold was 20 carats (843/1000 gold) with a variation of $\frac{1}{4}$ carat allowed. The goldsmith used the same mark on gold or silver work, but often registered two punches of different size to accommodate small pieces.

The warden's mark was in the form of a crowned letter in a cycle of the alphabet that included all letters, excepting J, U and W. The letter U, however, was used once only, in 1783–4. The cycle which, with few exceptions, was renewed in mid-July each year, continued without interruption until 1784. From that year until 1789 the warden's mark was altered to the crowned letter P accompanied by the last two digits of the year. The form of the letter struck on gold boxes was italic; silver boxes were marked with a roman capital letter.

The farmers, who were appointed by the king's council of state for an average term of seven years, registered two sets of charge and discharge marks at the outset of their terms. The first was for use on large pieces of silver and is mentioned here because the charge mark occasionally appears on gold boxes, presumably having been punched in error. (Its appearance on boxes of questionable authenticity is a useful indication of forgery.) The charge mark was in the form of a capital letter A, the letter which designated the Paris mint, and varied in style from one farmer to the next. The large discharge mark was in the form of some representational object, e.g., the head of a bird or animal. The second set of tax marks was intended for use on gold and small silver objects. Both the charge and discharge marks in this set were representational. In place of the discharge mark registered by a given farmer, another mark often appears on gold boxes. In 1733 an edict required that work intended for export be marked with a special discharge mark. While the symbol is not mentioned it is apparently the mark of a cow (*V, l*) which was in use until 1775. Its frequent occurrence bears witness to the extent of the distribution of Parisian work in the eighteenth century. After 1775 the symbol changed with each farmer.

In addition to these four, other marks are often found on the rims of gold boxes. Some are eighteenth-century countermarks: at the beginning of his term it was the *fermier*'s responsibility to visit each goldsmith, examine the wares in his shop and, if they were properly marked, to add a countermark of his own. Countermarks were also struck on pieces that came up for resale. Of the same size and nature as discharge marks, they can easily be mistaken for them. Two variants of a nineteenth-century mark also commonly occur on earlier gold boxes. In the form of a small eagle's head, it was a restricted warranty mark, i.e., a confirmation of the minimum standard of the gold attested by the touchstone method of assaying rather than an exact determination of the standard using the cupel. It was enclosed within a single outline from 1838 to 1847 and within a double one from 1847 to the present.

Under the guild and tax-farming systems of the *ancien régime* the marks for gold and silver differed in appearance from one community to the next, although their nature was the same as those in use in Paris.

The goldsmiths' guild was the only one to survive the Revolution; although abolished with all the *corporations* in March 1791 it was reinstated the same month and continued in existence until 1797. The tax marks registered in 1789 remained in use until late 1791 or early 1792. There are few records, and even fewer boxes, to document the marks in service between 1791/2 and 1797 when new regulations governing *orfèvrerie* were established.

The functions of the maker's, assayer's (warden's) and tax collector's marks were retained after the Revolution, but in considerably altered form. Goldsmiths' marks were required to be enclosed in a lozenge; the initials and device of the marker were retained as were, officially, the *grains de remède*, although they seldom occur. The crowned fleur-de-lis was of course forbidden. This form of maker's mark was decreed in 1797 and 1798, but there are indications that it was in use before this date. By the decree of 1798 the State, which assumed the responsibilities formerly allotted to the guilds and tax farmers, authorised assay and tax marks each consisting of an invariable symbol used throughout France. Three standards of gold were henceforth permitted: 920/1000, 840/1000 and 750/1000. Gold boxes were made of second or third standard gold, the standard being indicated in the assay mark by the numeral 2 or 3. The same symbol was used for gold and silver. The symbol of the assay mark was altered in 1809, 1819 and 1838, thus making it virtually impossible to date nineteenth-century French boxes with the precision afforded by the pre-Revolution yearly cycle of the alphabet. The old charge and discharge marks were combined into a single excise mark of representational design; the mint was indicated by numerals, 85 designating Paris. In 1838 the assay and excise marks were combined in a single mark which has remained in use.

It is a unique characteristic of pre-Revolution French marks that the outline of the punch conforms closely to that of the letters and symbols (marks of this type registered in London at the end of the seventeenth century are invariably those of Huguenot *émigrés*), while all marks in use elsewhere in Europe and in America—and in France itself after 1798—were enclosed in reserves of arbitrary outline.

In addition to the marks required by the guild and the State, Parisian gold boxes are frequently inscribed on their front rims with the name of a goldsmith. Mostly these are the names of the makers of the boxes: Daniel Govaers, Jean Ducrollay, Jean George, Joseph Vallayer, Jean Formey, Charles Ouizille and A. J. M. Vachette commonly identified their work with their signature as well as their punch. In many cases, however, the inscribed names are not those of the makers of the boxes. Boxes inscribed *Du Petit Dunkerque* remind us of the role of the *marchands merciers* in the retailing of goldsmiths' work. It is unfortunately not possible to identify by such overt means boxes sold by most of the Parisian merchants such as Duvaux, Madame du Lac, Jabac and Poirier. Gold boxes were also sold through the jewellers and goldsmiths in the service of the Court. The signature of Pierre-André Jacquemin (m. 1751, d. 1773) appears on a box by Jean Ducrollay (*38*); Jacquemin was one of the chief *fournisseurs* of the king in the 1750s. A box by an unidentified maker in the Louvre is signed by Charles-Barnabé Sageret, a *fournisseur* whose name appears in the *Comptes des Menus-Plaisirs* in the 1770s.

Still other boxes bear the signature of goldsmiths whose own work is well known. Barnabé Sageret, his son Charles-Barnabé, Jean-Baptiste Beckers, J. F. Garand and Jean Formey evidently maintained large shops from which they occasionally sold the work of their colleagues. Garand's name occurs on boxes by Jean Formey and Charles Le Bastier; a box by Mathieu Coiny is signed by Beckers. That the arrangement was informal is apparent from the fact that boxes by a single goldsmith are variously inscribed: some boxes by Ducrollay are signed with his own name while others are signed by Jacquemin or Constant (*80*).

In England as in France the marking of silver boxes was strictly observed. English gold boxes, however, are rarely marked. Officially they were struck with the maker's mark, the date letter and the standard and town marks. The first consisted of the goldsmith's initials without additional symbols. (During the so-called high standard period, 1697–1719, it was altered to include the first two letters of his surname.) The date letter included all letters of the alphabet excepting J, V, W, X, Y, Z in a cycle that ran from the 30th of May; the style of the lettering was changed each year. The standard mark used in London until 1798 for 22-carat gold was the lion passant; the same mark was also used for sterling (925/1000) silver. A second standard of gold, of 18 carats, was authorised in 1798, being designated by the mark of a crown with the numerals 18. In addition to these, a crowned leopard's head serving as the town mark was also required. A fifth mark, in the form of a sovereign's head, occurs after 1784 and is the equivalent of the Parisian discharge mark. The regular absence of marks on eighteenth-century English gold boxes has not been satisfactorily explained.

As Birmingham was the centre of production of silver boxes after *c.* 1780, the marks in use in that city may also be mentioned. The Birmingham assay office was established only in 1773. The lion passant and, after 1784, the sovereign's head occur. The town mark was in the form of an anchor. The cycle of the alphabet included all letters, but J was omitted in alternate cycles.

The marking of German, Swiss, Dutch and Scandinavian gold and silver boxes is so irregular as to make any systematised account impossible. In attempting to identify their marks, recourse to the monographs included in the bibliography is suggested.

American boxes are customarily marked only with the goldsmith's punch, which is often struck two or three times. Until *c.* 1730, it generally comprised the initials of the maker; after that date the surname was more usual. No official mark, representing either a guild or state system of regulation, was ever in use except in Baltimore from 1814 to 1830. Tested examples of silver have shown that the English sterling standard was observed.

VI Brass, Copper and Other Base-Metal Boxes

Base-metal boxes appear to have become popular, first in Holland and England, towards the end of the seventeenth century. A Dutch brass box of the turn of the century in the Museo di Palazzo Venezia (*434*) is engraved with a biblical scene and foliate borders in a style common to Dutch silver boxes as late as 1740. A similar box, probably of Dutch workmanship, is described in the *London Gazette* of 22 February 1692:

> a Brass Snuff Box gilt with Gold, Engraven on the Lid with the Story of Joseph and Potiphar's Wife, on the inside, with other figures on the bottom and Lid.

Oval and polygonal boxes of brass and copper, engraved with biblical—or, more rarely, pastoral or peasant—scenes, continued to be made in Holland until about 1750. After that date, rectangular boxes predominated and stamped decoration of a topical nature largely replaced engraving. This style of decoration is common to both snuff and tobacco boxes. The latter, although characteristically of an elongated oblong form, occasionally repeated the various shapes of the snuff boxes and, like these, had hinged covers; they are distinguished by their greater size (at least four inches). The Dutch type of tobacco box occurs in Germany in the second half of the eighteenth century; it is probable that snuff boxes were also made.

The earliest record of the manufacture of base-metal boxes in England is in Sheffield. In 1680 the Cutlers' Company established a Storehouse into which the masters of the guild deposited their wares to be sold at fixed rates. For an undetermined reason, tobacco boxes (which were not among the goods normally manufactured by the cutlers) were placed on sale in 1681, and snuff boxes shortly thereafter. According to the historian of the company, R. E. Leader, they were made of iron, some being fitted with horn lids.

Also dating from the seventeenth century in England are brass boxes. The London *Post Boy* of 29 October 1698 advertised

> a Princes-Mettle[1]-Snuff-Box, double gilt with Gold, with an Agget in the middle, with a Figure in the middle of the Agget like a Duck.

A boat-shaped brass box in the collections of Colonial Williamsburg (*436*) probably dates within the first half of the eighteenth century when that shape, recorded as early as 1709, was current.

---

[1] Prince's metal: a variety of brass composed of approximately 65 per cent. copper and 35 per cent. zinc, credited to Prince Rupert.

By 1747 the production of base-metal boxes had so expanded that the *General Description of All Trades*, published in that year, included among its professions

> Birmingham Hard-ware-men, Or Dealers in *London, Sheffield,* and *Birmingham*
> Ware . . . so called because they principally deal in . . . all sorts of Tools, smaller
> Utensils, and Toys, in Iron, Steel, Brass, &c. made at *London,* and the great
> trading Towns of *Birmingham* . . . and *Sheffield.*

Production on such an industrial scale is scarcely suggested by the few known examples of brass and copper snuff boxes. Most have probably long since deteriorated, as the alloys were often of indifferent quality. Those that survive, having no pretensions to more than family or local interest, have not come to general attention. The Sheffield Box Trade (as it was termed by the Cutlers' Company) reached its height in 1749, but the expense of maintaining a business independent of the regular cutlers' trade proved too great and it was abandoned in 1756.

English brass boxes of the second half of the eighteenth century are generally modelled on oblong and oval silver boxes; they are rarely ornamented with more than the name of the owner. An unusual bow-fronted box in the Metropolitan Museum (*439*) is certainly based on a shape that occurs among South Staffordshire enamel boxes in the last quarter of the eighteenth century; the allusion to steam power, then being developed nearby at Birmingham by James Watt and Matthew Boulton, suggests the provenance of the box. Brass and copper boxes of a purely local style, dating about 1790–1840, are attributed to the watchmaking town of Prescot (Lancashire). Of oval, shuttle and oblong shape, they are characterised by hinged covers which are fastened by combination locks operated by dial plates or revolving knobs. Also thought to be Lancastrian, of the second half of the eighteenth century, are brass-plated wood boxes of a variety of shapes, their covers set with small circular openings covered by swivel plates (a style that recurs in boxes carved entirely of wood). The use of wood as a filling between two layers of metal is recorded elsewhere about the same time. In 1766 (10 March) Horace Walpole wrote to Lady Hervey from Paris that

> I sent your Ladyship Lady Albemarle's box . . . . It is lined with wood
> between the two golds, as the price and necessary size would not admit
> metal enough without, to leave it of any solidity.

Copper snuff boxes of the quality of goldsmiths' work are said by d'Allemagne (*Accessoires du costume*) to have been made in Paris in the middle of the eighteenth century by a jeweller whose name is not recorded; they were known as *boîtes à Pomponne* after the *hôtel* in which they were made. Among the topical boxes popular during the Revolution and First Empire was a copper version of Napoleon's tricorne.

The hardness of steel made it a suitable material for the duplication of the precise chiselling on gold boxes; steel 'toys' were made in England and on the Continent from the end of the seventeenth century. Steel is mentioned in America as early as 1711 when the Boston *News-Letter* (10/17 December) recorded the loss of a snuff box 'almost Square, the bottom and sides are of Silver, and the top Steel, the Inside wash'd with Gold'. A number of German steel boxes in the Musée Le Secq de Tournelles are imitative of styles current among the Paris goldsmiths about 1740–55 (*437, 438*). A plain octagonal box at Colonial Williamsburg, and a very similar one dated 1735 (*435*) were perhaps made at Birmingham or Sheffield. Cut-steel jewellery was one of the chief productions of Matthew Boulton's Soho factory during the period of Boulton's partnership with James Fothergill (1762–81). Snuff boxes of this provenance are not known to exist; that they were made is suggested by a visitor to Milan in 1790 who remarked that faceted steel boxes for sale in that city 'can be had better and cheaper at Birmingham'.

Steel boxes of an undetermined style, whose novelty lay in their finish, were advertised in Paris in 1775 by the *marchand mercier* Grancher.

From about 1775 pewter was the most commonly used base metal for snuff boxes. Its popularity was not restricted to the lower classes: Fanny Burney was shocked to discover that Sir Joshua Reynolds carried a 'vile and shabby tin' box along with his customary gold one. And Mrs Piozzi, visiting a nobleman in Genoa in 1784, was offered snuff from 'dirty little tin boxes'. No marked pewter snuff boxes have been recorded. The majority of surviving examples are oblong or oval and frequently show traces of gilding inside. Those with simple engraved monograms and borders are probably of English and American origin. (The manufacture of base-metal boxes in America seems to have been entirely insignificant. They are only rarely mentioned among the wares of tinsmiths, who as a rule worked also in copper and brass.) A number of early nineteenth-century boxes with stamped diaper, scroll or conventional flower ornament on their covers are probably Continental. Pewter boxes certainly of English provenance are those in the form of books, high-heeled shoes and pistols (*443*), dating from about the last decade of the eighteenth century into the middle of the nineteenth. Also characteristically English, dating about 1820, are oblong boxes with rounded edges and slightly concave lids (*444*), which parallel goldsmiths' work of the same date.

Snuff boxes of pinchbeck (90 per cent. copper, 10 per cent. zinc) and Britannia metal (an alloy of tin, antimony and copper commercialised about 1787) were made in England at the end of the eighteenth century.

VII Hardstone Boxes

Metal boxes set with hardstones on their covers were in use in England from the last years of the seventeenth century. The stones were usually varieties of agate of which small deposits were scattered throughout England and Scotland. Silver boxes set with 'Scotch pebbles' or 'Egyptian pebbles' are occasionally cited in American newspapers until about 1775: the former term is perhaps a reference to cairngorm, a brownish rock crystal native to Scotland; the latter—the *caillou d'Egypte* of the French—is another name for Egyptian jasper.

Boxes carved entirely of hardstone did not become common until about 1720 (although Francesco Zucchi, in 1636, speaks of snuff boxes of rock crystal). The stones were found in commercial quantities only in Germany—Bohemia and Silesia being the chief sources of the quartz family of stones commonly used for carving boxes. These include colourless quartz (rock crystal) itself, and the several kinds of chalcedony: agate, aventurine, carnelian, jasper, bloodstone, puddingstone, heliotrope, onyx, petrified wood and chrysoprase. In addition to the quartzes, copper minerals such as lapis lazuli and malachite were often used (especially in France). So, during the first half of the eighteenth century, was amber, which was still generally believed to be a mineral and was carved as such (although its softness— $2\frac{1}{2}$ on the Mohs scale in contrast to the 7 of quartz—made it unsuitable for objects subject to abrasion; virtually no amber boxes survive today). The unexplained origin of the amber deposits along the Baltic coast, the traditional associations of the material with superstition and magic, and the strict regulation of the supply by the Prussian state which held the amber monopoly, all contributed to making Pope's Sir Plume and his contemporaries 'of amber snuff box justly vain'. A sudden decline in its popularity as a material for boxes coincides with the recognition by Linnaeus and Lomonosov in the 1750s that amber was not a semi-precious stone at all but a vegetable product, a fossil resin of the extinct tree *Pinus succinifer*.

Boxes carved from a single stone, the rims mounted in silver or gold, were especially common in Germany and England throughout the eighteenth century. In addition to those of circular and shell form, basket-shaped boxes are characteristic of German work about 1740. Fantasy boxes in the shape of reclining animals, sphinxes, etc.—their necks often encircled with an enamelled collar inscribed in faulty French—appear to be entirely English work of about 1760. The origin of these is perhaps to be found in boxes such as that mentioned on 19 April 1757 in the day-book of the Parisian *marchand mercier* Lazare Duvaux:

> Mme la Marq. de Pompadour . . . *La garniture en or à gorge & charnière d'un petit chat de lacq, formant une tabatière* . . .

In France, simple boxes of this type were in evidence during the Régence: of the 67 snuff boxes listed in the 1723 inventory of the Duchesse d'Orléans, 20 were hardstone. They were carved from jaspar, agate, lapis lazuli, rock crystal, aventurine and amber. They were mostly shell-shaped—although oblong, circular and even trefoil-shaped boxes are mentioned. They were mounted in plain or enamelled gold rims; the stone itself of one jasper box is described as being enamelled with stars. These boxes were possibly all German; stone-bodied boxes of French workmanship are said to have been introduced only in 1736, by the *marchand mercier* Joaguet: a number of elegantly shaped boxes of bloodstone, lapis and agate—some with carved decoration—are all dated within the period 1736–44 (*480, 481*).

An early German variation of this basic design was the application to the covers of elaborate mythological or oriental scenes executed, about 1730–45, in ivory and mother-of-pearl, some pieces of which were tinted in pale shades of pink, green and blue. From about the middle of the century this appliqué work was executed in gold. One of the few marked boxes of this type, by the unidentified Viennese maker I.W.S. (*458*), is dated 1774 and is among the last examples of this genre.

Relief decoration executed entirely in hardstone occurs on boxes probably all made in Berlin about 1740–60. The bodies of the boxes were usually of milky quartz; applied to their covers, and occasionally the sides, were sprays of flowers and fruit in a variety of coloured stones (*460, 462, 463*).

From about 1740 to 1765, stone boxes mounted *à cage* were popular in Germany and England. The stone bodies of the boxes were entirely encased in an openwork gold frame in a manner recalling the pierced watch cases of northern Europe of the second half of the seventeenth century. The recurring motifs of hounds and birds placed in a densely scrolled framework which leaves little of the stone visible (*451*) is characteristic of German work about 1740–60. It was succeeded by a more graceful, less confining, use of the gold, and the appearance of mythological subjects (*453*). English boxes of the same type are generally made of agate set in a simple asymmetrical framework of C-scrolls, sometimes hung with garlands. In France this type of cagework appears to have been little used, despite the facts that the *marchands merciers* had been granted exclusive right to buy, sell and cut hardstones, and that they themselves popularised the technique of fitting gold box frames with plaques of other materials. One of the few known French boxes executed in the German cagework style is a Paris box of 1740–1 by Jean-Louis La Cour in the Louvre. Gold boxes set with panels of stone appear to be more typical of French work. Seventeen hardstone boxes are mentioned in the inventory of Madame de Pompadour's possessions drawn up after her death in 1764. Of malachite, lapis, jasper, petrified wood and agate, they are described as being mounted *à cage* in varicoloured or enamelled gold rims. One of these, '*Une boeste de chasse, de malaquitte, à pans coupés* [with canted corners], *garniture en or de coulleur*' corresponds stylistically to boxes dating as early as 1743–4 (*482, 483*). The style reappears in the decade before the Revolution in boxes by Charles Ouizille and A. J. M. Vachette (*203, 485*), but by then it had become common practice to simulate strongly marked or coloured stones—such as moss agate, lapis and malachite—in enamel colours. Vachette himself successfully duplicated lapis and malachite in boxes in the Metropolitan Museum and formerly in the Fribourg collection (*202, 204*).

The most extravagant hardstone boxes were produced in Berlin under the patronage of Frederick II, and were probably all intended by him as diplomatic presents. They are almost all of chrysoprase, a pale green variety of chalcedony which had been mined at Koseinitz, in Silesia, as early as the fourteenth century. (The economic importance of the Silesian mines was a factor in Frederick's decision to annex the state. His exploitation of the chrysoprase mines, which had been rediscovered in 1740, dates from his conquest of the following year.) The boxes are of modified shell or rectangular form, and are larger than average, measuring about $3\frac{1}{4}$ by 4 in. The cover rims are heavily encrusted with precious stones, and small diamonds are often used in the subject decoration, in the style current among Parisian gold-smiths in the 1740s. Applied to all the surfaces are elaborate architectural, floral, chinoiserie or pastoral compositions worked in thin sheets of gold glued to the box at a few hollowed-out points in the stone. This basic decoration was occasionally supplemented by enamel paintings, such as that of the Three Graces by Daniel Chodowiecki on a box formerly in the Schloss Monbijou, or of Diana at the Bath by John William George Kruger. Kruger, a Londoner by birth who worked in Berlin from 1755 to 1768 at Frederick's invitation, was also responsible for the design of many of the boxes.

During the last quarter of the eighteenth century mosaic hardstone boxes were executed at Dresden. The technique of mounting the stones in gold cloisons (*zellenmosaik*) was per-fected by Heinrich Taddel (master 1739, died *c.* 1794), Inspector of the Green Vaults, the repository of Saxon royal treasures; it is first noted in 1769 on a box by Taddel inlaid with rustic scenes and a console table by his pupil, Johann Christian Neuber (1736–1808), with whose name such work is commonly associated. Received master goldsmith in 1762, Neuber was appointed court jeweller some time before 1775, a post he held until 1805. His earliest known snuff box is dated 1770; the bulk of his work was encompassed within the period 1770–88, in which latter year financial difficulties forced him to hold a lottery. No mark is recorded for Neuber, who inscribed some of his boxes '*Neuber à Dresde*'. These are usually oval or circular, with a formal concentric or radiating pattern of hardstones (mostly varieties of agate) on all sides; the centre of the cover is generally set with a portrait miniature or a jewelled or mosaic floral ornament encircled by a border of pearls or inlaid flowers. Neuber did not use hardstones for pictorial decoration, as did Taddel; one box, in a private collection, is decorated with chinoiseries in carved mother-of-pearl superimposed on the usual geometric ground pattern. Neuber, who rented several quarries, was interested in the exact identification of the stones he used, and to this purpose often provided a little booklet with his boxes in which the stones, distinguished by numbers engraved on the cloisons, were described for the purchaser (*472*). Mrs Piozzi, visiting Vienna in 1786, described a box probably by Neuber,

> consisting of various gems, none bigger than a barley-corn, each of prodigious
> value, and the workmanship of more, every square being inlaid so neatly, and

no precious stone repeated, though the number is no less than one hundred and eighty-three; a false bottom besides of gold, opening with a spring touch, and discovering a written catalogue of the jewels in the finest hand-writing, and the smallest possible.

A contemporary of Neuber's, the Court lapidary Christian Gottlieb Stiehl (*c.* 1708–92), also executed mosaic stone boxes. His reputation was placed above that of Neuber in 1782 when Johann August Lehninger, in his *Description de la ville de Dresde*, praised

> *La Fabrique de Tabatières, composées de pierres précieuses, représentant toute sorte de figures en bas-relief très artistement travaillées chez Biehl* [*sic*]. . . . *Ce célèbre lapidaire qui est unique dans son art, envoie quantité de ses ouvrages en France & d'autres pays étrangers.*

Zellenmosaik enjoyed a minor fashion in Paris about 1785. In Italy, Florence was the centre for work in inlaid stones and is perhaps the provenance of an early nineteenth-century box in the Royal Scottish Museum (*486*).

Hardstone boxes are rarely marked. In England, a regulation of 1739 specifically exempted from taxation (and thus assaying and marking) 'snuff box rims, whereof tops or bottoms are made of shell, or stone'; and in France the goldsmiths had been permitted since 1679 to leave unmarked any pieces of gold or silver that would be defaced by the punches. The marking of German stone boxes appears to have been similarly optional.

VIII Porcelain Boxes

Snuff boxes of Meissen porcelain were manufactured in vast quantities from about 1735 to 1765, a period roughly coincident with the directorship (1733–56) of Count Heinrich von Brühl, who himself possessed over 700 (gold) boxes and who can be assumed to have been naturally sympathetic to the production of such *Galanterien*.

The shapes of the boxes were for the most part adapted from gold and silver models or, as in the instance of the basket-shaped boxes which came into favour about 1755, from examples in hardstone. Shell- or cartouche-shaped boxes predominated until about 1755. They differed from their metallic prototypes in being rather high; this permitted painted decoration on the sides as well as on the two surfaces of the cover. Painted scenes were generally enclosed within lobed medallions reserved against solid-coloured grounds. Chinoiseries and occasional landscape or hunting scenes occur, but clearly the most popular decoration was shipping scenes, a subject probably originated by the landscape painter Johann Georg Heintze (*fl.* 1720–49) and continued by Christian Friedrich Herold (1700–79), with whose name such paintings are generally associated. Herold came to Meissen in 1726 from Berlin, where he had been an enamel painter in the shop of Alexander Fromery. There his work consisted chiefly of painted and relief-gilded decoration, a style which he intended to introduce at Meissen, submitting a sample of gold relief on porcelain for approval in 1739. However, no boxes by Herold in this technique are known to have been made at Meissen. There, although he is known to have painted both battle and genre scenes, his speciality was a scene of merchants, barrels of cargo and ships which occurs with innumerable and subtle variations. The subject appears frequently, painted by different hands, not only on Meissen porcelain boxes, but on those of other German, and even Italian and Russian factories. A variant form of composition portrayed groups of Europeans and Orientals promenading on the quay of an eastern port city whose profusion of classical and onion-domed buildings rise in the distance. Such a scene was possibly allusive to the thriving trade (primarily in coffee-cups) between Meissen and Turkey.

A greater variety in the shapes and decoration of Meissen boxes occurs about 1755, when barrel-, trefoil- and basket-shaped boxes and cane handles with snuff compartments begin to appear. A vogue for pug dogs is noticeable in shaped boxes with figures of the animal modelled on the covers (495). More usual, however, were the simple rectangular boxes painted with landscapes, mythological scenes, pastoral and Italian Comedy subjects, and sprays or bouquets of flowers. In this group may also be placed a distinctive group of boxes painted with scenes of Saxon mining attributed to Bonaventura Gottlieb Häuer (1710–82), painter at Meissen from 1724. The coloured grounds of the earlier period were no longer used, the boxes being glazed a clear white and the paintings often being enclosed within a lightly moulded framework of rococo scrolls.

Production at Meissen was interrupted at the beginning of the Seven Years War with the occupation of Dresden—and the factory itself—by Prussian troops; it was resumed in 1757 under the patronage of Frederick the Great, who ordered large amounts of porcelain to be made for his personal account, including snuff boxes—he, like Count Brühl, being addicted to the collection of them. At the end of the war the Emperor turned his attention to the porcelain factory at Berlin, and Meissen returned to Saxon state control. For a few years, production was sustained: no less than 11 varieties of snuff box are described in a price list of 1765. Those decorated with flowers inside and out were the cheapest, at six to nine thalers. Then followed boxes painted with flowers and 'mosaic' (scale or diaper) borders, boxes with flowers inside and garlands outside; with flowers on the outside, and figures of landscapes inside the lid; boxes with pastoral or genre scenes on the outside and, most expensive of all (76–88 thalers), boxes with figures or views on the outside and 'miniature histories' inside the lid.

By the date of this list, however, rival factories both in Germany and abroad were eroding Meissen's virtual monopoly of the porcelain industry, and the factory rapidly declined. From about 1765 porcelain snuff boxes were manufactured in Germany on a large scale only at Kelsterbach in Hesse-Darmstadt (1761–8). These were commonly shell-shaped and were rather heavily painted with mythological, hunting or genre scenes enclosed in scrolled reserves. Floral boxes, some with moulded basketweave grounds, were executed in imitation of Meissen or Mennecy work. A box cover in the Grossherzoglichen Privatsammlungen, Darmstadt, is painted with a shipping scene in the style of C. F. Herold reserved against a bold fish-scale ground pattern. Also from Kelsterbach are a number of plain white (unfinished?) boxes with moulded grounds or scrollwork.

Snuff boxes of Ludwigsburg, Nymphenburg and Berlin porcelain, dating in the 1760s and 1770s, generally reflect the styles current in Paris. A Nymphenburg price list of 1767 mentions gold-mounted oval and square boxes, for men or women or *à chasse*, painted with flowers or landscapes, at 5 florins apiece. Boxes painted with portraits and landscapes sold for 10 to 50 florins (approximately the price of an entire coffee service). Characteristic of the factory are oval boxes modelled with pilasters and garlands and, on the cover, a portrait medallion, in the style of Paris gold boxes of about 1765–70. Rectangular double boxes, the lids hinged on the ends, appear in Berlin and Ludwigsburg about 1770. Snuff boxes decorated with inlaid gold and mother-of-pearl were executed at Frankenthal during the Seven Years War by Johann Martin Heinrici (1711–86) who had until that time been a painter at Meissen.

A considerable amount of factory-produced German porcelain was painted by independent artists—*Hausmaler*—who are for the most part anonymous. Painters whose work on snuff boxes is known include Johann Andreas Bechdolff (*fl.* 1758–*c.* 1770) of Ellwangen, who painted boxes with views of that city and/or saints; and the otherwise unrecorded Viennese artist 'Winceslaus Chudy 1758' whose signature appears on a box painted with cloudborne putti.

A few snuff boxes can be ascribed to the Viennese porcelain factory, made during the proprietorship of Claud du Paquier (1719–44); they are of interest for the variety of their shapes. An unusually large box (5 inches) modelled in the form of an open hand—the cover hinged at the wrist—was formerly in the Blohm collection. A small octagonal box is in the collection of Judge Irwin Untermyer; a larger oblong box with bombé sides is owned by Mr R. Thornton Wilson. The decoration of all three pieces includes the intricate but transparent strapwork (*Laub- und Bandelwerk*) introduced about 1725–35, and gaming motives— dice, playing cards and, on the bottom of the Wilson box, a chessboard—popular with many of the German factories in the 1740s. Black monochrome painting (*Schwarzlot*) was introduced at Vienna in the 1730s by Jakob Helchis (*fl.* 1730–49) who is known to have painted snuff boxes.

The earliest French porcelain snuff boxes are those made at Saint-Cloud. An advertisement of 1731, describing the wares offered by the Paris branch of the factory, included '*Tabatières de toutes sortes de contours, garnies & non garnies*'. These would have been shell-shaped or circular boxes, rather small, painted—sometimes on a coloured ground—with boldly outlined Chinese figures and landscapes. Honey notes that silver-mounted examples of this type range from 1723 to 1738/9. About 1725 appeared boxes with raised gilded decoration painted over with translucent colours in a manner first practised extensively in Berlin by the artist-enamellers C. F. Herold and C. K. Hunger. Although the Saint-Cloud factory survived until 1766, no snuff boxes appear to have been made after about 1750; none is mentioned in the inventory drawn up in the last year of the existence of the factory.

Boxes with painted floral decoration, some modelled in the form of a high-heeled shoe, were made at Chantilly about 1740–50; the shoe form reappears slightly later at Mennecy, where a variety of snuff boxes were made in the third quarter of the eighteenth century. Examples set in marked silver rims are dated in the *fermiers'* terms of 1744–50, 1750–6 and 1756–62. It has been suggested by Honey that some boxes traditionally ascribed to the Mennecy factory may have been made at Crépy-le-Valois where a factory specialising in 'toys' was started in 1762 by a Mennecy modeller, L. F. Gaignepain. Mennecy boxes are typically moulded with an all-over basketweave or waffle pattern and are sparingly painted, generally on a white ground, with flower sprays. This basic decoration—in addition to occurring on the usual oval and oblong examples—is also found on boxes in the shape of miniature commodes, on those in the form of a heart or basket, and on trunk-shaped boxes. An approximate date of the last may be estimated from a notice in 1764 that a gold snuff box of the same shape was in the shop of the widow of the goldsmith Guillaume Jacob.

Snuff boxes made entirely of Vincennes (*536*) or Sèvres porcelain are rare. A few are mentioned in the day-book of Lazare Duvaux, who was instrumental in the establishment of the porcelain factory under royal patronage. In 1755 he furnished the king with several gold-mounted boxes, one of which is described as a '*tabatière, forme de boëte*', by which is presumably meant a rectangular box rather than one of the shell form which was just going out of fashion in both metalwork and porcelain. Oval and oblong boxes of 'porcelaine de France' painted with figures and animals occur in Duvaux's records for 1757 and 1758. It appears to have been more usual, however, for the factory to furnish painted plaques for mounting in *tabatières à cage*. In 1755 the factory sale book lists '*Deux plaques de tabatières, enfants colorés*'; again, in 1757, '*A Duvaux. Tabatière en six plaques, enfants colorés*' and in 1758, to Duvaux again, a '*Tabatière enfants colorés*'. A box in the Louvre by Jean George, 1758–9, set with six Sèvres plaques of putti and trophies of the arts, may be taken as representative of this type which appears several times in the factory records until 1760. In this last year plaques painted with Teniers subjects, birds and animals were supplied. After 1760 snuff boxes figure insignificantly in the factory accounts and virtually not at all in the large collections of boxes formed by such amateurs as Gaignat, the Prince de Conti and the duc d'Aumont. The chief productions at Sèvres were tablewares and—after the Revolution—sculpture. A single box is recorded among the presents given by Napoleon in 1814: gold-mounted, it was set with a portrait of Marie-Louise by Isabey. An oval hard-paste porcelain box painted with miniatures reserved on a striped ground is in the Musées Royaux d'Art et d'Histoire, Brussels. Probably made at Sèvres in imitation of a style current among Parisian goldsmiths *c.* 1775, its mounts are dated 1838–46.

In Italy snuff boxes were made at Doccia, Venice (Cozzi factory) and Naples (Capodimonte). Examples from the first two factories, which are rare, appear to have been in the style prevalent during the mid-1760s, with painted pastoral scenes and floral ornamentation. Peculiar to Capodimonte are the snuff boxes 'imitating sea shells' which are first mentioned in 1743. They were modelled in high relief with small shells, snails and other *frutti di mare* gilded and painted in bright colours. The interiors of the lids were painted with portraits or mythological scenes. Although none is signed, it is probable that some were the work of Giovanni Caselli, principal painter of the factory, who is recorded as having done some of the gilding on the exteriors of the boxes. The moulds of the shell boxes were the work of Giuseppe Gricci, chief modeller at the factory. Capodimonte boxes painted with chinoiseries are first mentioned in 1745–7.

In 1759 the personnel and apparatus of the factory were transferred to Madrid and re-established in the gardens of the Buen Retiro palace by Charles III upon his succeeding to the Spanish throne. Although Gricci was among those who went to Madrid he evidently did not pursue the sculptural style of snuff boxes; the few boxes attributable to Buen Retiro are plain rectangular boxes lightly painted with landscapes or figures.

Snuff boxes made at the Imperial Porcelain Factory in St Petersburg reflect the styles initiated at Meissen, some of which would have been introduced by the founder of the factory, Christoph Konrad Hunger (Hunger was an itinerant arcanist—one professing to hold the secret of the composition of porcelain—who is first recorded at Meissen, and then at Vienna, about 1717.) 'Envelope' boxes were especially fashionable *c.* 1753–64. Favoured by the Empress Elizabeth as New Year's presents, those made for her in the last years of her reign were traditionally inscribed in cyrillic letters on the cover *Her Imperial Majesty Elizabeth Petrovna Autocrat of all Russia Empress the Most Gracious.* French inscriptions occur on many other envelope boxes. The 'seals' on the bottoms of the boxes were 'impressed' with the Moscow arms, family arms or, occasionally, classical figures. The insides of the lids were sometimes painted with genre scenes or were further inscribed with a letter. 'Fantasy' boxes in such shapes as drums and fruit also occur at St Petersburg (*559*).

Porcelain snuff boxes were not made in England in any quantity. Only the Chelsea factory produced 'toys', but limited its wares in this line to scent flasks, cane handles and bonbonnières: snuff boxes are nowhere mentioned in the price lists or sale catalogue of the factory. While it seems curious that so popular an object as the snuff box should not have been made in porcelain, it must be remembered that enamel boxes were already being manufactured on an industrial scale in South Staffordshire and that production in a second medium was presumably considered unprofitable. A few circular earthenware boxes with screw lids were made in England in the second half of the eighteenth century. Although these are not demonstrably snuff boxes, an example is offered here (*566*) as it is of reasonable size and as its screw lid suggests the necessity of preventing snuff from spilling or drying out. Almost certainly a snuff box is the earthenware box in the form of a shoe (*565*), a model which appears frequently, in all media, in the 1760s. About the middle of the eighteenth century, according to Eliza Meteyard, Thomas Whieldon manufactured small oval snuff boxes painted with flowers on a white ground, first independently and later (1751–2) in partnership with Josiah Wedgwood. Wedgwood's continued interest in the production of such 'toys' is evident from a letter of 1766 (8 and 10 November) to Thomas Bentley: in discussing the terms of their proposed partnership, he includes snuff boxes among the 'articles to begin the work'. And twenty years later (18 December 1783), the sculptor John Flaxman submitted a bill to Wedgwood for

> Grinding the Edges of 6 Snuff-boxes for the Spanish Ambassador   15s.

Despite this contemporary evidence, snuff boxes composed entirely of any of Wedgwood's ceramic materials are not known to exist. Jasper plaques—e.g., Flaxman's *Muses Watering Pegasus in Helicon* (*294*)—were set, *c.* 1786–95, in snuff boxes of gold- or steel-mounted tortoiseshell.

Porcelain boxes of all the European factories were commonly mounted with silver (often gilded) or copper-gilt rims. Gold mounts are found on Meissen boxes, but no gold-rimmed French examples are known. With the exception of some dated French examples, the mounts are always unmarked.

IX Enamel Boxes

The manufacture of enamelled copper snuff boxes first flourished on the Continent in the first half of the eighteenth century. Development of the technique was a practical, economical solution to the problem of imitating the much-admired Chinese porcelain which was just beginning to be duplicated successfully—but expensively—at Meissen. The advantages of the method were that boxes could be made cheaply and in quantity of a base metal (copper, which was plentiful in Germany and England), given their base coat of white enamel, and then left blank to be decorated quickly to suit the demands of the market or of an individual purchaser. An account of enamel boxes is necessarily related to examples in porcelain: the decoration of the cheaper wares was frequently imitative of porcelain styles, often, in fact, being executed by painters who worked in both media. This can be seen in a group of Danish boxes (581, 583, 585) painted by Josias Brecheisen, who was a painter at Copenhagen, first at the Fournier porcelain factory (1757–c. 1760), then, until 1763, at the Royal Factory; and in German boxes painted by C. F. Herold (570) and J. A. Bechdolff. It is likely that much of the decoration of German enamel boxes—and, perhaps, some of the English—was executed by independent painters who, possessing their own muffle-kilns, were in a position to work in either technique.

The chief centre of production during the first half of the eighteenth century was the Berlin shop founded by Pierre Fromery and continued by his son Alexander, whence originated a technique of gilded relief decoration combined with enamel-painted details. The style is exemplified by the work of C. F. Herold, whose association with the Fromery workshop is attested by a snuff box lid of 1739 (formerly in the collection of Lady Bessborough) signed by Herold and Alexander Fromery. Although by this date Herold had been established at Meissen as a porcelain-painter for 13 years, he continued to paint on enamel at least until 1763, when he justified this practice to the factory authorities on the grounds that the two types of work were not in competition. How long Herold continued to work with relief decoration is not known. His signed work (570) is characterised by central figures executed in gilded relief placed against a painted background. The resulting impression is not unlike that of flat-chased gold and silver boxes of the second quarter of the century. A decorative variation of the Fromery style, consisting of a delicate combination of ribbons, flower trails and incidental figures executed in gold relief overpainted in translucent enamel colours and set on a plain ground, is found on Meissen porcelain decorated by Conrad Hunger c. 1717. Enamel boxes attributable to Hunger are not known to exist; there are, however, examples decorated by followers of his style. Relief decoration similar to that associated with the Fromery workshop was employed in France on Saint-Cloud porcelain; a variation occurs on an enamel box dated 1744–50 (579), a rare example of French enamel work.

With the increasing success of the German porcelain factories, the decoration of enamel boxes became either imitative or purely topical. In the former category belongs a group of small oblong boxes, dating in the late 1740s, painted in a somewhat Cubist manner with playing cards, in the style of Du Paquier porcelain of five to ten years earlier. Variations of this occur on boxes dating as late as 1757 in which the playing cards are altered to letters, sometimes combined with sheets of music. Mention may also be made here of boxes in the form of envelopes popular from *c.* 1745-65. Their origin is perhaps to be found in France, in boxes of Mennecy porcelain; their popularity is evident from examples in German, Russian, Danish and English enamel (*581, 617*). With the Seven Years War (1757-63) the German enamellers turned almost entirely to propaganda. There are two types of boxes characteristic of this period. The first, which appears to have been made at Berlin and Dresden, is painted on the cover with a battle plan, of which those of Leuthen and Rossbach are the most commonly encountered. Mr John Hayward has emphasised (*Apollo*, 1945) the speed with which these boxes were produced in his account of one dated within a week of the battle of Leuthen on 5 December 1757. The other type of box bears a gilt profile portrait of Frederick the Great on the cover surrounded by wreathed inscriptions of his victories (the list of which varies according to the date of the box). The insides of the covers, the vertical sides and bottoms are generally painted with Frederick's monogram, trophies and adulatory phrases, in French, to the King. In this same period can be placed a very few boxes with rather mannered *scènes galantes* painted by Frederick's chief designer and engraver, Daniel Chodowiecki.

The source and distribution throughout Germany of copper blanks for enamelling has not been determined. Provincial *Hausmaler* whose work on enamel boxes is known include Carl Ferdinand von Wolfsburg (1693-1764) at Breslau, who specialised in crowded bacchic scenes in the style of his master, J. Bottengruber; and Johann Andreas Bechdolff (w. 1758-*c.* 1770) of Ellwangen, who painted views of that town and figures of saints. A provincial freshness also characterises the work of the anonymous painter of a group of boxes decorated with biblical scenes (*576*).

A small group of Viennese boxes, recorded by John Hayward (*Freunde der Schweizer Keramik*, 1950), are signed CAvZ; the initials are thought to be those of Anton von Zirnfeld (although the C remains unaccounted for), who, having begun his career at Doccia, worked at the Vienna porcelain factory from *c.* 1754. Vigorously, and somewhat naïvely, painted with military figures placed against sketchy backgrounds, the boxes undoubtedly allude to the Seven Years War.

By 1770 commercial manufacture of enamelled copper boxes in Germany was rendered obsolete by porcelain, which was widely and cheaply available. Production on a considerably larger scale, however, was flourishing in England, where porcelain never attained the availability it had in Germany.

The history of English snuff boxes officially begins with the establishment of York House,

73

at Battersea, on the south side of the Thames, in 1753. There is evidence, however, that enamelled snuff boxes were made for some time before that. A. J. Toppin (*English Ceramic Circle*, IV, 1932) notes the existence—between 1709 and 1757—of over 300 apprentices to toymen, enamellers, japanners and snuff-box makers in Birmingham, London and several South Staffordshire towns. Among the masters working before the founding of Battersea was Joseph Allen (w. London, 1742–54), 'Snuff box maker and Enameller'. The commercial feasibility of enamelling on copper was probably suggested to the English by examples of German work; skill in the technique itself, however, very likely derives from the familiarity of the English—from the end of the seventeenth century—with watch cases enamelled in Geneva. The precise connection between the Swiss and English enamellers has not been determined. However, several of the former (including André Rouquet and Theodore Gardelle) worked in London for part of their careers; and Mr Toppin has pointed out elsewhere (*English Ceramic Circle*, IX, 1946) that the Geneva-born enameller Anthony Tregent, whose signature appears on an enamel box of 1759 (Schreiber collection), was living at Battersea in 1752.

The York House factory was established in 1753 by Stephen Theodore Jansson (d. 1776), a wealthy merchant-stationer, and two associates: Henry Delamain (d. 1757) and John Brooks (*c.* 1710–after 1756). The former, who had just given up the proprietorship of an unsuccessful pottery works in Dublin, appears to have been the business manager at Battersea. To Brooks, a designer and engraver, belongs the credit for the characteristic feature of English enamels, transfer-printed decoration. Briefly, the process involves covering an engraved copperplate with a special ink (printer's ink) that sinks into the engraved lines and can be wiped off the remaining surface. A piece of paper is placed on the copperplate and pressed with it in a hand roller, the inked lines being transferred to the paper. The paper is then fitted to the enamelled surface to be decorated and placed in a muffle-kiln until the design has again been transferred, and fused, on to the enamel, and the paper has burnt away.

Jansson's factory was active for less than three years: in 1756 he was declared bankrupt, and an auction was held of the stock, which included 'snuff-boxes of all sizes, of a great variety of patterns . . . mostly mounted in metal, double gilt'. Among the early Battersea boxes are those of circular and shell form; most of the later printed boxes are oblong. In the first group are boxes entirely painted on a white ground (the only coloured ground known to have been used at Battersea was yellow), with rural or Italianate landscapes, pastoral or genre scenes on the cover and flower sprays on the sides. On a few boxes scenic decoration is carried out on all surfaces of the box. Boxes in the second group were printed in a pale shade of red, purple, sepia or blue. Transfer printing in black was developed only after the demise of York House, and then chiefly for use on porcelain. (Robert Hancock (1730–1817), to whom the perfection of black-printing is attributed, is thought to have been a pupil of Brooks and to have worked at Battersea.) The chief subjects were printed on the two surfaces of the cover, extending to the edges without a border; the sides were printed with unrelated stock vignettes of amorini, etc., or with scrolled panels enclosing latticework.

Many of the designs used on Battersea boxes were designed by the artists active at York House. To Brooks have been attributed the portraits of Maria Gunning, Countess Coventry (*588*); Lionel Sackville, Duke of Dorset; and Sir Robert and Horace Walpole. Allegorical scenes of Great Britain are the work of the Dublin-born designer and engraver James Gwim (w. by 1723, d. 1769; his name has been variously spelt Gwinn, Gwin, Gwym), whose signature appears on an enamel printed with 'Britannia Encouraging the Linen Manufacture in Ireland'. Related scenes—'Britain presenting Coins to Science and the Arts', and 'Paris presenting the Apple to Hibernia' (Schreiber collection)—are also by Gwim. The most prolific designer, and the chief engraver, at Battersea was Simon-François Ravenet (1706–74), a Parisian who is thought to have emigrated to London about 1746, where he first worked for Hogarth. Although he engraved the work of other artists (e.g., Gwim's 'Linen Manufacture' which is inscribed 'Drawn by Gwin [*sic*], engraved by Ravenet for ye Battersea Manuf're . . .') most of the subjects ascribed to him are probably his own. Ravenet's signature has been noted on a plaque with a portrait of George II. Other subjects considered to be by Ravenet are portraits of Frederick Louis, Prince of Wales, George III as Prince of Wales, and Peter the Great; religious scenes (the Crucifixion, the Holy Family); mythological scenes (Europa and the Bull, Apollo and Daphne, Venus and Triton, Laocoön and the Wooden Horse); and genre scenes such as the Punch Party and the Fortune Teller (Schreiber collection, nos. 49, 50). In addition to these Ravenet is credited with the design of the secondary vignettes repeated on the sides of many boxes. Another painter whose residence—and presumed employment—at Battersea is recorded in 1753 is Charles Fenn, who specialised in scenes of water-birds. These are not known on boxes from the Battersea period, but occur on later South Staffordshire boxes copied from engravings of Fenn's designs published in Robert Sayer's *The Ladies Amusement* (1759/60) and in two (untraced) drawing books of his own.

The stylistic traditions of York House were continued for a short period after 1756. They are evident in a group of boxes printed in black with almanacs (for the years 1758, 1759 and 1760); with songs and musical instruments (probably inspired by similar German enamel boxes); and a box of 1761 commemorating the marriage of George III and Queen Charlotte. The provenance of at least the first group is suggested by an almanac box of 1759 in the Schreiber collection (no. 339) signed by Anthony Tregent, then working in London, whose earlier residence at Battersea has been mentioned. Also in this group are two boxes (Schreiber collection, nos. 345, 346) black-printed with hunting and genre scenes and, on the sides, vignettes in Ravenet's style. Monochrome boxes do not occur after this date, the prints being overpainted in bright colours which conceal the lines.

From about 1760 to 1800 Staffordshire boxes have a consistency of style that tends to elude specific dating. They are generally oblong, with rounded corners, slightly convex lids, and straight or *bombé* sides. Metal foot rims are rarely used, but are occasionally simulated by a row of gilt dots painted around the bottom edge of the box. The boxes are painted on the cover and sides in a shade of one of three colours: rose, turquoise (in tones ranging from sky-blue to pea-green) or midnight blue (shading to purple). Reserved against this ground are printed and painted scenes. The undersides of the boxes are usually left white and are sparsely decorated with a formal raised pattern with occasional details in gilt.

Several subjects occur frequently on Staffordshire boxes: *Pensent-ils au raisin?* after a painting of 1747 by Boucher; *L'Après Dîner* after Nicolas Lancret; and *La Partie Carrée* after Watteau (all of which are also known on boxes from the Battersea period). Others were adapted from the title vignettes in song books (*604*), or reflected contemporary events such as boxes with a portrait of John Wilkes (*603*) or of Frederick II of Prussia. It is probable that most of the engravings used as sources for box paintings were to be found in the many drawing books published in the second half of the century: 291 were advertised in 1762 by Robert Sayer. Two in particular, *The Ladies Amusement* (published by Sayer in 1759/60) and *The Artist's Vade Mecum* (also published by Sayer, in 1762, and repeating many of the plates from the earlier volume) served as source books for enamel painters. They included a few illustrations of genre, pastoral and ornamental subjects after Continental artists (Van Loo, Bloemaert, Pillement), but consisted chiefly of architectural landscapes, *scènes galantes* and genre scenes by contemporary English artists such as Charles Fenn and Robert Hancock. Among the subjects recurring frequently on Staffordshire enamels are a scene of a lady and two gentlemen fishing; a couple walking in a park; and a bullfinch perched on an overturned basket of fruit, engraved by Hancock, who may have been familiar with a similar subject on Meissen porcelain (*500*). Also by Hancock is *The Tea Party*, one of the most popular subjects and one that appears not only on enamel boxes, but on Worcester, Bow and Chinese export porcelain. From other sources come such subjects as two ladies and a gentleman fishing in a park, after an engraving by William Woollett (1735–85), and a view of the Thames near Twickenham (*608*).

The secondary decoration of Staffordshire boxes falls into two main groups. The first, and probably earlier, is that in which the printed and painted scenes are enclosed in reserves framed by asymmetrical panels filled with a variety of diaper patterns in a style common to German porcelain and enamels c. 1720–50 (*602*). In the second and later group these small panels disappear and the entire ground of the box is enamelled with a diaper pattern, the reserves being framed by gilded rococo scrolls (*612*). A third, smaller group is characterised by the undulating profile of the oblong boxes and the use of a white ground overlaid with raised gilded scrollwork and flower sprays (*606*).

While records provide the names of a few enamellers active in Staffordshire and Birmingham, it is not possible to associate any of these with specific styles of enamelling. The most considerable factory at Bilston was that established in 1748 by the toymaker and enameller Benjamin Bickley (d. 1776). In 1770, according to the Birmingham *Directory*, Isaac Smith,

Perrey & Sons, Thomas Knowles and John Buckley were practising as box enamellers; 11 years later the widow of Benjamin Bickley was described as a maker of enamel boxes: to her have been attributed boxes painted with bouquets on a mesh-patterned rose-pink ground (*615*). In Birmingham, the firm of Boulton and Fothergill evidently experimented with enamelling, as Boulton mentions work in this medium in a letter to Robert Adam in 1770. Boulton can be presumed to have been a major supplier of the copper blanks and of copper and pinchbeck mounts for the boxes, and probably to have enamelled them as well, although this has not been determined.

Among the several discernible styles of enamel painting, two are especially noticeable. A small group of boxes is painted with flower and fruit still lifes in subtly shaded colours on a luminous steel-grey ground (*612*). Another, much larger group is characterised by the painter's use of colour to define forms, of vivid contrasts between light and shade, and the almost invariable presence of sheep (*616*). Other personal styles are apparent in the painting of the bouquets of flowers on the sides of the boxes.

English enamel boxes were mounted in gilded copper or in copper alloys such as pinchbeck and bath metal. The copper came chiefly from the Ecton Hill Copper Mine in Staffordshire, the mounts being manufactured locally at Bilston, Wolverhampton and Birmingham.

X Lacquered and Varnished Boxes

Experiments in varnishing or lacquering were begun in England and Holland as early as the first quarter of the seventeenth century. Interest in the technique was aroused by the gold-painted black screens being imported from Japan and dispersed throughout Europe by the Dutch East India Company. Because of her restrictive trade policies, Japan allowed little of such work to leave the country, and as the European demand always outran the supply various imitations were developed.

In his *Usefulness of Experimental Philosophy* (1671), Robert Boyle—who himself experimented with making varnish, using a formula described by Jan van Linschoten in his *Itinerario* (1596)—remarked that 'I am credibly informed, that the art of making . . . varnished wares is now begun to be a trade at *Paris*, and I doubt not but it will before long be so in *London* too'. The word 'japan' entered the English language in 1688 as a term synonymous with black varnish or lacquer applied to wood. In the course of the following century it was extended to include a varnish of any ground colour applied over wood, papier-mâché, metal or even leather: an advertisement in *The New-York Gazette and the Weekly Mercury*, 8 July 1771, sought the recovery of 'a leather japan'd snuff box, with a Scotch peble set in silver on the top'. By 1800 'japan' had shifted meaning once again to refer exclusively to varnished metalwork.

In 1688 John Stalker and George Parker published the first English manual on the subject, *A Treatise of Japanning, Varnishing and Guilding*. Their recipe for 'Black Varnishing or Japan' —which remained essentially the same through the eighteenth century—called for six layers of seed-lac (a preliminary state of shellac) and lamp black mixed; another six layers of seed-lac and turpentine mixed with just enough lamp black for colouring, a space of 12 hours to elapse between the third and fourth coats; and 12 layers of seed-lac tinged with lamp black, 12 hours again being required between the sixth and seventh layers. Five or six days after this the object was polished with water and tripoli. The result was 'as glossy, and beautiful a Black, as ever was wrought by an English hand, and to all appearance . . . no way inferior to the Indian'. This process differed from the Japanese originals—called Indian by Stalker and Parker as Bombay was the port of transhipment—in having as its basic ingredient shellac, a resinous secretion of the coccid insect, dissolved in alcohol and combined with opaque paint; while the foundation of Japanese lacquer is the sap from the tree *Rhus vernicifera*.

Stalker and Parker did not mention snuff boxes, but illustrate designs appropriate to patch- and powder-boxes; as both the custom of snuff taking and the technique of varnishing were brand new, it is probable that some varnished wood snuff boxes were made in the last years of the seventeenth century. The first commercially successful application of lacquering to the manufacture of snuff boxes came only after 1720 in Wales under the direction of Major John

78

Hanbury at his family ironworks in Pontypool. The lacquer used by Hanbury had been developed shortly before by the independent japanner Thomas Allgood (d. 1716) who obtained the opaque black ground colour by combining raw linseed oil, asphaltums, umber and thinning, and fixing the mixture to an iron body—which at Pontypool was tinned—by stoving it at about 300–350 degrees for a few hours. Black was the only colour to be used at first. A deep crimson was developed by about 1741, the approximate date of the earliest recorded Pontypool snuff box. The third major ground colour was tortoiseshell, which is mentioned for the first time only in 1756, but which was being used at least by 1749 (*680*). The decoration of Pontypool boxes was largely personal, consisting of the name of the owner of the box, the date, and sometimes the name of his house, painted in gold. These inscriptions were occasionally supplemented by portraits or landscapes. Chinoiseries (*682*) were evidently popular, for the traveller Richard Pococke wrote in 1756, when he visited Pontypool, that the boxes were adorned 'with Chinese landscapes and figures in gold only, and not with colouring as at Birmingham'. It might be supposed that Pontypool wares enjoyed a strictly local reputation, but this is apparently not the case. The historian of the factory, W. D. John, states that of the 'many thousands of snuff boxes of all shapes and sizes' produced at Pontypool 'a large proportion' were exported to Holland. They were presumably shipped undecorated and painted locally on the Continent.

The Pontypool works existed alone until 1763, when a family dispute caused members of the Allgood family to establish a rival japan factory seven miles away at Usk. Prior to 1800 the wares of the two factories are virtually indistinguishable. Pontypool survived until 1822, the Usk factory until 1862.

Pontypool japanning was quickly imitated at Birmingham under the direction of John Taylor (1711–75), a journeyman cabinet-maker who turned to the manufacture of lacquered snuff boxes about 1738. To him, wrote the Birmingham historian William Hutton in 1781, 'we owe . . . the japanned and gilt snuff boxes' as well as the 'painted' ones. He was rivalled by John Baskerville, who turned from teaching to japanning snuff boxes about the same time. Baskerville advertised mahogany, black and tortoiseshell japan, and is thought to be the first japanner to have decorated his wares with polychrome paintings, a feature which—we have seen from Pococke—distinguished Birmingham work in the middle of the century. Lacquered metal snuff boxes were probably not made much after 1750 when they began to be replaced in popularity by those of papier-mâché. Taylor was again the originator of this industry; Hutton records that in his factory 'one servant earned three pounds ten shillings per week, by painting [snuff boxes] at a farthing each'. Commercial production of papier-mâché boxes, however, did not get under way until the last quarter of the eighteenth century, following the granting of a patent in 1772 to Henry Clay of Birmingham. Hitherto, papier-mâché had been no more than paper mashed in water, the dried pulp being moulded into the desired shape. By Clay's process, layers of paper—rather like thick, rough-textured blotting paper—were pasted on a wood or metal core, each layer being polished smooth with a pumice stone. Snuff boxes thus formed were lacquered black inside and out and painted. They were generally circular and relatively large, averaging four inches in diameter. Given their size, and the fact that the covers were separate and tended to fit loosely, the boxes were undoubtedly intended only for table use. The subjects with which the lids were painted ranged from genre and pastoral scenes in the French taste to animal scenes and portraits after contemporary English artists and classical subjects copied from Italian paintings. They were painted by the anonymous artists working in the several Birmingham factories (including that of the versatile Matthew Boulton) as well as by the independent japanners who are presumed to have painted on papier-mâché as well as on metal. One artist is commonly associated with Birmingham papier-mâché boxes: Samuel Raven (1775–1847), who was both a painter and (in 1843) a tobacconist. He was a competent workman who, according to one of his apprentices, never designed subjects for box lids but always copied from engravings. Among the subjects painted by Raven were Lawrence's portrait of George IV (*688*), landscapes after Joseph Vernet and genre scenes after Wilkie ('Blind Man's Buff', 'Rent Day', 'The Cut Finger'). He commonly signed his work with his name in red inside the lid, often adding the names of his patrons, the Duke of Sussex and Prince Leopold of Saxe-Coburg. The relative scarcity of Raven's work, and of papier-mâché boxes in general, can be attributed to deterioration: the flaking of the varnish was a serious problem and one that was seldom overcome. Most surviving boxes are in poor condition.

After about 1815 hand-painted snuff boxes were largely supplanted by those decorated with coloured engravings pasted on and varnished. Many of the engravings were of French and American provenance, attesting to the large export trade carried on by the Birmingham manufacturers. Papier-mâché boxes in use in eighteenth-century America appear from newspaper advertisements to have been entirely imported from England. Two notices, however, suggest the possible existence of local manufactories. As early as 1740 a John Waghorne advertised in the *Boston Gazette* that he had lately received

> a fresh parcel of materials for the new Method of Japanning, which was Invented in France, for the Amusement and Benefit of the Ladies, and is now practised by most of the Quality and Gentry in Great-Britain, with the greatest Satisfaction

and proposed to establish a school. Fifteen years later, *The New-York Gazette and the Weekly Post* (16 June 1755) announced that

> John Julius Sorge. Very much noted among the nobility in Germany, for diverse curious Experiments, lately arrived in this City, hereby gives Notice that he . . . Makes all Sorts of Japan-Work, of divers fine Colours, to that Degree, that none heretofore hath ever exceeded him in that Art. . . .

American engravings appearing on Birmingham boxes include portraits of Washington (1801) and of Lafayette (1824–5); of Isaac Hull and Commodore William Bainbridge after portraits by Gilbert Stuart; and views of New York from a series of engravings published in 1831 after drawings by Thomas Burton.

The only production of papier-mâché that matched the English in both quantity and style was that of the German Stobwasser family. Early attempts at lacquering had been made in Brunswick by Johann Christoph Lesieur (d. 1739) who moved there from Hanover in 1717 and, in 1759, by Johann Ernst Abraham Weinziener. Georg Siegmund Stobwasser (d. 1776) was the first to make a commercial success of lacquered papier-mâché. In 1763 he was permitted by Duke Karl I to settle in Brunswick, and in 1769 he was granted exclusive rights of manufacture of japanned furniture, snuff boxes, tea trays, etc. In 1780 the factory produced 589 sugar-, tobacco,- snuff-, powder- and pomade boxes. The Stobwasser boxes are virtually identical with their English counterparts: they are large, circular, shallow and are lacquered an opaque black. They were usually well painted in bright colours with copies of Italian, Dutch, Spanish and French paintings and even, in the nineteenth century, paintings by such English artists as Lawrence and Wilkie. Topical portraits and subjects also occur, and during the Revolution and First Empire portraits of Napoleon and scenes from his career were popular.

Stobwasser boxes are commonly signed on the inside of the lid, the successive forms of the signature being: *Stobwassers Fabrik*; *Stobwasser's/Fabrik/Braunschweig*; *Stobwassers'che Fabrik in Braunschweig*; *Fabrique de Stobwasser a Brunsvic*; *Stobwasser'sche Fabrik/Meyer & Wried/in/ Braunschweig* (after 1832).

Boyle had been quite right in remarking that in 1671 the French were already experimenting with imitations of oriental lacquer. Such work appears to have been restricted to furniture; *carton vernis* snuff boxes (as they were always called, the term 'papier-mâché' being an English invention) were not made until shortly before 1750. The basic material, layers of paper pressed over a wooden core, was essentially the same as that used in England and Germany. The varnish, however, was closer to the Japanese in being also composed of a tree resin, in this instance gum copal from Brazil. It was mixed with linseed oil and turpentine to form a clear varnish that was then covered with up to 40 successive layers of the same basic formula to which, at the later stages, various pigments were added. Like the English lacquer, *vernis Martin* was dried by heat rather than in moist air as in Japan.

A patent for this process was obtained in 1730 by Guillaume Martin (d. 1749), one of four sons of a tailor, who is first recorded five years earlier in the *Comptes des Menus-Plaisirs*. Together with the patent, Martin was also granted the title of *vernisseur du roi*, an honour later shared by his brothers Etienne-Simon and Robert. In 1744 the patent was renewed for 20 years in the name of Guillaume and Etienne-Simon (d. 1770). Four years later they and the remaining two brothers, Robert (1706–65) and Julien (d. 1752), and their four sons, were operating three factories in Paris (faubourg Saint-Martin, rue Saint-Denis and rue Sainte Magloire), with the privileged title of Manufacture Royale. Far from imitating either the colours or patterns of the oriental lacquer, *vernis Martin* snuff boxes paralleled contemporary goldsmiths' work. Those datable in the 1750s are painted—like their enamelled gold counterparts—*en plein*, that is with pastoral or genre scenes 'floating' on the background. Crimson and dark green, sometimes overlaid with a gold waffle or other diaper pattern, were frequently used as the ground colours of these boxes. Black is rarely found as a ground colour, although Lazare Duvaux furnished several boxes (probably not by Martin, as the customary attribution is missing) '*du vernis noir, à bouquet émaillé*' in 1751 and 1752.

As the Martins never signed their work it is impossible to distinguish their boxes from those of the half-dozen other *peintres-vernisseurs* working in Paris about the same time. Chief among these was one Gosse (d. 1766), who in 1759 announced his invention of a black varnish: '*il est employé avec succes pour les tabatières de carton*'. Other competitors were the *tabletiers*: until 1749 the process of manufacturing and decorating *carton vernis* had been the exclusive right of the painters. In that year, however, the privilege was extended to the *tabletiers* and was reaffirmed in 1753 over the protests of Robert Martin.

Vernis Martin snuff boxes evidently enjoyed their greatest popularity in the 20 years after the patent renewal in 1744. '*Tabatières de Martin*' occur frequently in the day-books of Lazare Duvaux, especially in 1748 and 1749; most of the dated boxes—those set in marked gold mounts—fall within the tax-farming period 1762–8. The Martins' factory in the faubourg Saint-Martin was still in existence in 1785, but only a few boxes of this late date survive.

Topical themes absorbed the decorators of *carton vernis* boxes during the Revolution. The timeliness of the motifs is emphasised by the Russian traveller N. M. Karamzin, who attended a debate in the National Assembly in June 1790 during which the Abbé Maury sprang from his seat to defend Catholicism as the national religion. 'The day after the debates', wrote Karamzin, 'paper snuff boxes *à l'Abbé Maury* appeared in the shops. When you opened the lid, out jumped an abbé.' Boxes bearing Napoleon's portrait or commemorating his battles, and boxes with portraits of Napoleon and Marie-Louise are among the papier-mâché boxes popular during the First Empire.

In Italy, in the first half of the eighteenth century, the centre of the lacquering industry was at Venice. There the basic material was stucco, which was painted in tempera colours and finished with a gum copal varnish. While the Venetian school of lacquering is chiefly identified with furniture, smaller items such as toilet sets and snuff boxes were also made.

In 1760 the Turin Società della Fabbrica in Lavori di Cartone vernicato was granted a monopoly of the manufacture of papier-mâché wares. This privilege was occasioned by a clandestine traffic in foreign-made snuff boxes; henceforth this trade was prohibited, and any imported boxes were to be confiscated.

One probable centre for the manufacture of papier-mâché boxes is Spa, near Liège, where in 1756 Mrs Margaret Steuart Calderwood noted that 'the whole imployment of the inhabitants is making and japaning toillet boxes, and things of that kind'.

XI Tortoiseshell, Ivory and Horn Boxes

Snuff boxes of ivory and horn are mentioned in *La Tabaccheide* published in Ascoli in 1636; horn was considered by its author, Francesco Zucchi, to be the most desirable material of all for snuff boxes. The early and lasting popularity of the materials is certainly due in part to their ready availability and cheapness. Horn could be obtained from local butchers, although in England the general demand for the material, especially for use in making lanterns, was so great that by the end of the seventeenth century the supply from neighbouring towns to London was exhausted and horn had to be obtained thereafter from America. Ivory was imported by the Dutch East India Company in commercial quantities in the seventeenth century from India (to which it had been transhipped from Africa) and from Siam. By the end of the century tortoiseshell—obtained from the hawksbill turtle native to Asian tropical waters—also began to be imported.

Examples of seventeenth-century horn and ivory boxes are not known to survive. The notice of a horn tobacco box in the *London Gazette* of 13 October 1684 indicates the treatment of the material at that time:

> a Horn Tobacco Box, the Lip tipped with Silver, Scalloped . . .

The chief characteristic shared by horn, ivory and tortoiseshell was their malleability. When softened, they could be easily shaped and impressed or inlaid with decoration. Methods of working the three materials are described in the *Secrets concernant les arts et métiers* (1790). The procedure most recommended for softening ivory was to steep it in mustard until it became pliable; another method was to soak it for three or four days in a solution of saltpetre and white wine. Horn and tortoiseshell were softened more quickly in boiling water to which a little olive oil had been added. This could be done in either of two ways: the preferred method was to cut a piece of the material and place it between the two halves of a copper mould that was then plunged into the water, the two halves of the mould being pressed together as soon as the material was viable. An iron weight was laid on top and the whole apparatus was then removed to dry. Alternatively the tortoiseshell could be immersed in the water until it was soft and then removed, fitted into the mould and pressed. The disadvantage of this latter method lay in the fact that horn and shell cooled so quickly that there was little time to work them once they had been removed from the water.

From the end of the seventeenth century tortoiseshell was popularly decorated in *pique* work in which the design was inlaid in strips and/or pinpoints of gold or silver. At the same period the technique is also recorded (especially in Italy) on mother-of-pearl, leather and ivory; it was rarely applied to horn. As described in the *Encyclopédie*, a small hole or groove was made in the tortoiseshell; the blow of the hammer heated the shell so that the point or strip of metal could be inserted; when the shell cooled it closed around the metal piece and held it fast.

Piqué is thought to have originated at the end of the sixteenth century in Naples, species of sea turtle being native to the Mediterranean. Havard (*Dictionnaire de l'ameublement*) cites a ewer bearing the signature of the unrecorded artist Laurenti as the earliest example of *piqué* work. It appeared simultaneously in England, France and northern Europe *c.* 1700. The *London Gazette* of 20 July 1699 records 'a large Gold Snuff-Box, the outside like Tortoiseshell with Gold Studs, and the inside solid Gold'. The following year mention is made of a 'round Tortoise-shell Gold studded Snuff-Box with a Gold Joint . . . with a Plate of Gold within . . .'. Similar descriptions in the London newspapers throughout the first quarter of the century suggest that *piqué point* was the usual form of the technique. Most boxes from this early period, however, are decorated with stripwork (*piqué posé*), commonly with variant forms of palmettes and strapwork characteristic of the ornament designs of Jean Bérain. No marked boxes of this type are recorded, and it is thus difficult to separate by country stylistic elements that were common throughout Europe until *c.* 1740. Those boxes in which the strapwork is supplemented by grotesque figures and animals are assuredly Dutch and German (*622*). The plainer, less involuted examples are probably English. Pictorial decoration occurs *c.* 1715; its dependence on metallic prototypes is indicated by an oblong box illustrated by Dent (*Piqué . . .*, pl. V) decorated with a scene from an unidentified legend surrounded by ornate diapered and scroll borders and palmettes. It is an almost exact parallel to two gold boxes of the same period (*272, 275*) which, although unmarked, are perhaps English work: the scheme of decoration can be found in the work of Huguenot refugees in London. French *piqué* boxes *c.* 1720–30 are commonly inlaid in *piqué point* with heraldic, floral and purely ornamental motifs. Thereafter, *piqué point* rarely occurs by itself, the genre, pastoral and allegorical subjects being carried out chiefly in stripwork. The shapes of these tortoiseshell boxes are adapted from those of gold and silver, the shell or cartouche form predominating *c.* 1730–50. The workmanship of *piqué* boxes is generally vigorous and lacking in refinement, qualities that point to provincial manufacture. A more delicate style of *piqué* work is found in Paris in the third quarter of the eighteenth century. Small spherical boxes with rococo ornament traced in *foules points d'or* are mentioned in the day-book of the *marchand mercier* Lazare Duvaux from 1749. Usually described as '*boîtes à ballons*' they are undoubtedly identical in shape and use to the gold '*tabatière en oignon*' mentioned by Duvaux in 1749 (9 July). *Piqué* decoration executed in hair-thin strips of gold and silver occurs on Parisian gold boxes of the mid-1760s, lacquer sometimes being substituted for tortoiseshell as the ground material.

A group of oblong boxes dating *c.* 1750–60, often shaped with undulating sides, *piqué* with a profusion of scrolls and diaper-filled panels are attributed to Naples, where 'the manufactory of tortoise-shell, which they inlay curiously with gold, for snuff-boxes' was a standard tourist attraction in the eighteenth century. Ivory boxes of a slightly earlier date, *piqué* with chinoiseries, are in the Ca' Rezzonico, Venice, and the Museo della Floridiana, Naples.

Towards the end of the eighteenth century in France and England *piqué* boxes became increasingly imitative of goldsmiths' work. Dent illustrates several examples, undoubtedly Parisian, that duplicate the familiar star-and-dot pattern of the 1780s (*194*); variations of this occur on French horn boxes *c.* 1790–1800. In England, gold boxes chiselled to simulate basketry were popular *c.* 1800 and were imitated in tortoiseshell. *Piqué* decoration in eighteenth-century taste occurs *c.* 1810 on boxes by the Parisian goldsmith A. J. M. Vachette (*639, 640*).

The pliancy of horn, ivory and tortoiseshell made them suitable materials for moulded, or pressed, ornament. Boxes decorated in this manner first came into prominence in England with the work of John Obrisset, the son of an ivory carver who emigrated from Dieppe to London. Although not recorded as a member of any London guild, Obrisset signed his name to boxes of horn and tortoiseshell; his initials also appear on the silver appliqués of a box in the British Museum. Described in 1691 (the earliest record of his life) as a 'graveur', Obrisset was perhaps a die-cutter whose boxes were made by independent artisans. It was a common violation of guild regulations for craftsmen to work independently in several related materials.

Obrisset specialised in portraits of the English monarchs from Charles I to George II. These were either profile busts or full-length equestrian figures. Some were copied from medallic portraits, e.g., James II after John Roettiers, and Queen Anne after John Croker. Among other Obrisset subjects are four variants of a box with the name and arms of Sir Francis Drake executed in 1712 (*647*), and bacchic and religious scenes (British Museum). The same subjects occasionally occur in both horn and tortoiseshell. Obrisset's boxes are generally of horn, oval, from $2\frac{3}{4}$ to $3\frac{1}{2}$ in. in width and decorated only on the cover. The rims are unmounted, the covers being attached by means of a flanged silver hinge riveted to one of the long sides. Obrisset signed much of his work, the most common form of his signature being the monogram OB, sometimes surmounted by a heraldic label, frequently with the addition of the date. He occasionally signed his name in full, adding the place and date as well.

A number of Obrisset's royal portraits were struck as plaques; single plaques, and occasionally two of different date, have sometimes been incorporated into snuff boxes at a later date.

Pressed horn and tortoiseshell boxes were made in England and on the Continent well into the nineteenth century. Hunting and genre scenes, floral and geometric patterns occur. Virtually all these boxes are anonymous. In England the horn industry was confined almost exclusively to London, where all such boxes can be presumed to have been made. The name F. Baker on a late eighteenth-century box with masonic emblems and the initials S.L. on a box pressed with a bacchic subject are the only two signatures recorded on English pressed horn boxes. In France, snuff boxes of tortoiseshell impressed with topical subjects were current throughout the Empire and Restoration: portraits of Marat, Napoleon, Benjamin Constant; masonic devices; Bourbon emblems (*660*) were impressed on boxes of tortoiseshell, ivory and papier-mâché.

About 1750 engine turning was first applied to tortoiseshell both in Paris and London, where as early as 1749 a John Jackson was executing engine-turned portraits on wood. In Birmingham the firm of Boulton and Fothergill was manufacturing tortoiseshell snuff boxes by 1767 when James Watt first visited the factory. Engine turning is certain to have been a feature of their decoration, as it was Boulton who provided Josiah Wedgwood with a lathe suitable for machine-engraving pottery *c.* 1763. 'Soon after my connection with Mr B', Watt continues in his memoir of Boulton, 'he declined . . . the tortoise shell boxes.' And in 1768 the Parisian *tabletier* Compigné offered for sale tortoiseshell snuff boxes '*ornées de desseins, executées au tour en écaille & en or*'. By the end of the eighteenth century circular horn and shell boxes, unmounted, with pressed subjects on their covers and engine-turned ornament on the undersides were common.

Of the three materials—tortoiseshell, horn and ivory—the first appears to have lent itself most favourably to experimental treatment. Compigné announced in 1768 that

> *il a inventé de nouvelles boîtes d'écaille transparente, imitant les effets des minéraux & des pétrifications.*

In 1775, the Parisian *marchand mercier* Grancher advertised a variety of tortoiseshell snuff boxes, including those lined with transparent leather; boxes 'representant le *bonheur de la France*', set with gold portrait medallions of Henri IV and Louis XVI; and '*nouvelles taba-tières, dites éternelles, rondes, en écaille, couvertes en requin. . . .*'

Boxes of carved ivory were uncommon in the eighteenth century. A few Parisian examples of the 1760s are imitative of contemporary goldsmiths' work: a circular ivory box with '*galons découpés, guirlandes & doublures d'or*' and enamelled landscapes on the cover was sold from the Gaignat collection in 1768. The decoration of a nineteenth-century box—an allegorical figure of Asia (*655*)—also has its parallel in gold, in a box by G. R. Morel with a figure of America (*223*), by which it can be dated *c.* 1810.

In addition to serving as primary materials, tortoiseshell and ivory were widely used throughout the eighteenth and early nineteenth century as frameworks for snuff boxes set with portraits and other miniatures. Horn was rarely used in this manner, but occurs at the end of the eighteenth century. Among the snuff boxes in the collection of the duchesse d'Orléans in 1723 were an ivory *boîte à portrait* and a painted box '*d'yvoire de Venise*'. Ivory boxes with marine views and landscapes figure in the collection of the Prince de Conti (1777); a number of tortoiseshell boxes set with portraits by Pierre Adolph Hall and mythological subjects by Jacques Charlier were sold from the collection of the duc d'Aumont in 1782. This type of box became popular in France in the few years immediately following the

Revolution, when the dissolution of the goldsmiths' guild and the general democratisation of taste made gold boxes inappropriate. They are usually circular, with unmounted lift-off lids. From *c.* 1810–20 oblong tortoiseshell boxes with rounded corners and plain gold rims were set on the cover with chased gold plaques enclosing portrait medallions (*225, 228*).

Tortoiseshell was popularly used in America, frequently in the form of plaques set in silver frames, as on an example by the New York silversmith Peter Van Dyck (*624*). Boxes made entirely of tortoiseshell in use in America appear from the newspaper announcements of goldsmiths and jewellers to have been imported from England.

XII Wood Boxes

The earliest snuff box was said by the anonymous author of *Whipping Tom* (1722) to have been 'a wooden Box in the shape of a Pear'. Seventeenth-century examples of such boxes are not known to exist, but the type survives in snuff flasks made in Scandinavia in the following century, of both pear and circular shape (Pinto collection). The bulk of wooden snuff boxes date only from the end of the eighteenth century and are generally of only local or topical interest. Exceptions to this can be found in a group of French and English boxes in the Pinto collection: among the former is a well-carved box (*689*) of a shape common to gold and porcelain boxes about 1745–65. Two oval boxes, one with a top-hinged lid, are characteristic of English work of the last quarter of the eighteenth century. The radiating fan design inlaid in one is adapted from one which occurs in marquetry *c.* 1775; the other is closely patterned on silver boxes of about 1775. Despite their large size—$4\frac{5}{8}$ and 5 in., respectively—they are certainly, from their style and elegance, snuff rather than tobacco boxes. Snuff boxes of an undetermined style, assumed by d'Allemagne (*Accessories du costume*) to have been made of elm, were introduced in 1764 by a *tabletier* of Grenoble named Bouron and were called after his name (*bouronnes*).

The most prominent English folk boxes were made at Mauchline, Scotland, in the first half of the nineteenth century. They were oblong, large—4 to 5 in. in length—and commonly made of elm, plane or pine. The covers were attached by means of an integral hinge carved and fitted with a precision equal to that found on Parisian gold boxes. The interiors were sometimes lined with foil. Popular scenes and verses were incised or painted in black on the covers (*701*); coloured decoration was rarely used, although some boxes are entirely painted with tartans.

A type of wooden box, whose shape may be surmised from its name, the 'Lawrence Kirk', was devised early in the nineteenth century at Alyth (Perth) by a James Sandy; it was evidently so much admired, according to Benson Hill, that examples 'were bought and transmitted by Scottish noblemen, as cadeaux to the royal family'.

Wood—like horn, ivory and tortoiseshell—could be softened and moulded by heat. Pressed wood boxes are first mentioned in 1770 in Paris by a *tabletier* named Compigné at whose shop in the rue Greneta one could purchase, in that year, a box impressed with *La Partie de Chasse de Henri IV*. Boxes commemorating the accession of Louis XVI, and the deaths in 1778 of Voltaire and Rousseau (*690*), were also made in the eighteenth century (boxes showing other scenes from the life of Henri IV are nineteenth-century work), but their general popularity, to judge from known examples, came only after the Revolution and lasted until shortly after the Restoration. The subjects pressed on their covers were mostly allusive to contemporary events, reflecting royalist or revolutionary sentiment. Boxes with portraits of Louis XVI, Louis XVIII, Louis Philippe and Charles X co-existed with others depicting the battles of Austerlitz or Jena, or scenes of Napoleon in Egypt. Among the less partisan subjects were portraits (e.g., Layafette, Joan of Arc, Frederick the Great); biblical, mythological and allegorical scenes (Telemachus, Flora, Susannah and the Elders); masonic emblems; genre scenes ('Teniers' and pastoral subjects); and such purely topical subjects as the life and craniological guides of Dr Joseph Gall (*694*). Also occurring on pressed boxes are reversible portrait heads in which—in a tradition going back to the satiric medals of mid-sixteenth-century Germany—a seemingly normal portrait becomes, when turned upside down, a grotesque or animal head. Always circular, averaging three inches in diameter, these boxes are made of birch, maple or pearwood. The covers are separable and the interiors commonly lined with tortoiseshell. Only the covers are decorated; the titles of the scenes are generally included *in exergue*. Two boxes, impressed with the portraits of Pope Pius VII and Louis XVI, respectively, are signed by the otherwise unrecorded artist 'Ramly 1796'; no other artists working in this medium have been recorded.

Wood seems to have been the most popular material for fantasy boxes. Of these, the most recurrent are those in the form of shoes or books, shapes common to virtually all materials on the Continent and in England at least from the second half of the eighteenth century. A number of examples in the Pinto collection are mostly mid-nineteenth century, but a high-heeled shoe with a turned-up toe is probably contemporary with similar porcelain shoes dating about 1760–5. Snuff boxes carved to represent pistols (a form known also in pewter), hands, ships, various types of headgear (including Napoleon's tricorne, which was also reproduced in copper and *vernis Martin*) and bellows were made in the nineteenth century. Also included in this category of memorabilia are the 'relic' boxes, carved from the wood of a particular tree, ship or even building. The London Cutlers' Company was presented in 1838 with a box made from a piece of oak from old London Bridge; even as early as the turn of the seventeenth century the French traveller F. M. Misson took exception to the improbable number of snuff boxes said to have been carved from the Boscobel oak. Another type of souvenir box, popular during the first quarter of the nineteenth century, was in the shape of a coffin. Some of these were clearly intended as *mementi mori*: Benson Hill recalled seeing, shortly after Nelson's funeral in 1806, an oak snuff box 'covered with velvet and ornaments' in exact imitation of the Admiral's coffin.

Dating from *c.* 1830 is the development, at Tunbridge Wells, of simulated mosaic wooden trinkets, including snuff boxes. The technique was a mechanically produced variant of marquetry that was known at Tunbridge by 1697: Celia Fiennes, visiting the spa in that year, observed that there were 'all sorts of curious wooden ware, which this place is noted for the delicate neate and thin ware of wood both white and Lignum vitæ wood'. Tunbridge was surrounded by plentiful and varied timber, beech and sycamore being commonly used as ground materials. Tunbridge-made snuff boxes of the eighteenth century do not appear to be known today, but that they were made may be presumed, if we take into account Defoe's description of the ritual of a young lady's taking the waters at Bath in 1724:

> the musick plays you into the bath, and the women that tend you, present you with a little floating wooden dish, like a bason; in which the lady puts a handkerchief, and a nosegay, of late the snuff-box is added, and some patches. . . .

Such floating toilet sets, of which wood was an essential material, must certainly have been made in Tunbridge.

The mosaic-patterned wood snuff boxes referred to today as Tunbridge Ware (a term which was also in use at the beginning of the nineteenth century to designate the earlier marquetry) were produced by gluing together sticks of varied woods to form large blocks that were then turned on a lathe. This method was known as stickwork or 'inlaid turnery'. Snuff boxes so made are included in the catalogue of *Tiffin's Guide to Folkestone* in 1851, the year in which, thanks to the Great Exhibition, Tunbridge Ware achieved its greatest prominence. It continued to be produced until the end of the nineteenth century.

XIII The Elusive and the Rare

Of the less common—even improbable—materials of which snuff boxes were made something should be said, as they co-existed with more splendid ones on an almost equal footing. Sir Joshua Reynolds, we have seen (p. 62), carried a gold box and a pewter one at the same time. And Horace Walpole's collection of 25 boxes included some of such varied materials as gold, enamel, papier-mâché, Meissen porcelain, lapis lazuli, ivory, granite and 'red and white plaister from the Piscine Miràbili at Rome'. Many snuff boxes of unusual, and seemingly incongruous, composition can be accounted for as by-products of tourism and souvenir-hunting. 'I will not trouble you', Walpole wrote to George Montagu in 1761 as the latter was setting out for Ireland, 'for a snuff box . . . made out of a bit of the Giant's Causey'. But if that geological monument was secure, another was not: Dr John Moore, visiting Naples in 1790, wrote that the 'chief articles manufactured here at present, are silk stockings, soap, snuff-boxes of tortoise shell, and of the lava of Mount Vesuvius'. An example of the latter (702) attests their popularity nearly 30 years later. In Spain, boxes were made of rock salt, of which quarries were worked at Cardona, north-west of Barcelona. An anonymous English visitor to that town in 1808 noted that the material was used 'like our Derbyshire spar, for candlesticks, snuff-boxes, and other trinkets'. Examples of these do not appear to have survived; nor have those of perhaps the most bizarre material of all: coal. As early as 1697, Celia Fiennes observed that near Wolseley, Nottinghamshire,

> they have the mines of the fine sort of Coale, that is hard and will be pollish'd like black marble, for salts or boxes or such like, the only difference it will not bear the fire as marble does else it resembles it very much. . . .

and snuff boxes of coal are specifically mentioned in 1719 in *Snuff, A Poem*, by James Arbuckle. Boxes of cannel coal (which was in durability the opposite of the soft coal now called by the same name) continued to attract attention at least until 1766, in which year Walpole 'ordered some snuff-boxes of coal to be sent to Madame de Guerchy [wife of the French Ambassador to England], which she had desired'.

Among boxes of more plausible materials, but which are seldom met with, may be mentioned those of *verre églomisé*, straw and leather. The first of these is known from a few covers and one entire box (703); all were probably made in Holland or Germany where the technique of painting on the back of the glass and fixing it with a clear varnish (a layer of gold leaf was sometimes interposed) was especially popular in the eighteenth century.

Straw-covered snuff boxes were made in France from the middle of the eighteenth century. In 1759 one Chervain, a Parisian merchant, advertised '*tabatières et plusieurs autres boîtes doublées de paille, où sont exécutées toutes sortes de sujets chinois, flamands, et français, incrustées en bas relief'*. They were generally round; the tinted straw was glued either directly on to the surface of the box—which might be made of wood, papier-mâché or tortoiseshell—or to a piece of paper which in turn was applied to the box. The straw was then trimmed to obtain the decoration. Armorials, floral decoration and Flemish peasant scenes occur in roughly the same styles, and at the same time, as they do in metalwork. In the nineteenth century, boxes with portraits of Louis XVIII and Charles X appear after the Restoration. Straw work was carried on in Italy, Germany and Switzerland in the eighteenth century, and it is probable that snuff boxes were among the wares manufactured in those countries. Snuff boxes entirely woven of straw are among the folk crafts of Sweden in the nineteenth century.

Although leather was used as a secondary material for snuff boxes by 1775 (see p. 86), boxes composed entirely of leather were introduced, in Edinburgh, only about 1780. They were quickly imitated in London where they are first described in an advertisement (1785) of the bookseller and printer, John Wenman:

> Those Gentlemen who are curious in Leather Snuff Boxes, are hereby respect-
> fully informed, that at Wenman's Original Shop, No. 144 [Fleet Street] . . .
> there is now on sale the largest and most beautiful collection of Leather Snuff
> Boxes that ever were offered to the Publick. They are London made, and
> finished in a superior style to those that are usually sold about town. They may
> be had, either plain or mounted, with gold or silver joints, and beautifully
> bordered with gold, and lined either in the usual manner [a reference which
> cannot be explained], or with tortoise-shell or silver, gilt or plain, and orna-
> mented with a great variety of haire-work, and beautiful enamels; where may
> be had, Clarke of Edinburgh's Transparent Leather Boxes . . .

The wide choice of styles offered by Mr Wenman indicates a demand for this type of box which would not otherwise be suspected. Related to these are snuff boxes formed of minia-ture books. Bound in leather, they were constructed in two ways: one type was fitted with a double-hinged binding, one section of which fastened the book, the other a small metal-lined snuff box at the back of the book. Alternatively, the centre section of the book was simply cut out altogether, the cavity being metal-lined. Such boxes, whose attraction must lie in their curiosity, appear to have been an English invention of the early nineteenth century. It may be observed that the artificial ingenuity of their design is inversely proportionate to snuff taking which was by then waning in popularity. They represent a last effort to prolong the natural decline of a once lively and universal habit.

Laurent Pécheux (Italian, 1729–1821). Portrait of Maria Luisa of Parma (1751–1819), wife of Charles IV of Spain. *The Metropolitan Museum of Art*. Maria Luisa holds a gold *tabatière à cage*, c. 1765, set with gouache miniatures of pastoral subjects. Inside the lid is a portrait presumed to be that of her husband.

1 Gold. *Maker* Jacques-Michel Lemaire (m. 1721, d. 1776). Paris, 1723–4. *The Walters Art Gallery, Baltimore.* **2, 3** Gold, with enamel miniatures by Jean-Baptiste Massé (1687–1767). On the cover, '*La Finette*' after Watteau; inside, a detail from '*La Danse dans un Pavillon*' after Lancret. *Maker* Louis Mailly (m. 1723, d. 1738/9). Paris, 1723–6. *Wartski, London.* **4, 5** Gold, studded with diamonds and emeralds. Inside, portrait of Louis XV by an unknown artist. *Maker* Daniel Govaers (w. 1725–36). Paris, 1726–7. *Musée du Louvre, Paris.* **6** Gold, set with plaques of carved mother-of-pearl. *Maker* Daniel Govaers. Engraved *Gouers AParis.* Paris, c. 1730. *Private collection.* **7** Gold, studded with diamonds and rubies. *Maker* Daniel Govaers. Paris, c. 1730. *Staatliche Kunstsammlungen, Dresden.* Recorded in the inventory of the *Grünes Gewölbe* in 1733. **8** Gold. *Maker* Daniel Govaers. Engraved *Gouers AParis.* Paris, c. 1730. *Musée Cognacq-Jay, Paris.* The box also bears the warden's letter for 1755–6, presumably added at the time of some repair.

9 Gold. Inside the cover is a portrait miniature, added at a later date, of Elizabeth Louisa, Lady Bagot (married 1760), in the style of John Smart (1741–1809). *Maker* Jean Ducrollay (m. 1734, w. 1760/1). Paris, 1737–8. *Mr and Mrs Charles B. Wrightsman.* **10** Gold, studded with diamonds and rubies. *Maker* Daniel Govaers. Engraved *Gouers AParis*. Paris, 1733–4. *The Metropolitan Museum of Art.* **11** Gold, chased and enamelled, the bloodstone cover set with an enamel miniature. *Maker* Gabriel Gallois (m. 1714, w. 1754). Paris, 1737–8. Ex coll. A. Chester Beatty. **12** Gold. Paris, 1736–7. *A La Vieille Russie, New York.* **13** Gold. *Maker* probably Jacques Brillant (or Briant; m. 1722, d. 1747). Paris, 1739–40. *The Metropolitan Museum of Art.* **14** Gold. Paris, 1736–7 or 1738–9. *The Metropolitan Museum of Art.* **15** Gold and mother-of-pearl. *Makers* Jean Ducrollay and Jacques-Toussaint Lemire (m. 1714, w. 1757). Paris, 1739–40. *The Metropolitan Museum of Art.* **16** Gold and tinted mother-of-pearl. *Maker* Claude-Auguste Prévost (m. 1714, d. 1759). Paris, *c.* 1740–5.

17, 18 Varicoloured gold, with diamond thumbpiece. Inside the cover, portrait of Christian VII of Denmark (1766–1808) by Christian Hoyer (1741–1804). *Maker* Jean-François Breton (m. 1737, w. 1791). Paris, 1743–4. *Musée du Louvre, Paris.* **19** Gold double box. *Maker* Charles-François Croze (m. 1712, living 1754). Paris, 1742–3. *Private collection.* **20** Gold. *Maker* probably Thomas-Louis Lévesque (m. 1720, w. 1748). Paris, 1744–5. *The Metropolitan Museum of Art.* **21** Gold. Paris, 1749–50. *The Metropolitan Museum of Art.* **22** Gold and mother-of-pearl. Possibly French, *c.* 1745. *Private collection.* **23** Gold, set with plaques of green-tinted mother-of-pearl; cloisonné decoration in shell and hardstones. *Maker* possibly Michel de Lassus (m. 1718, d. 1772). Paris, 1744–50. Ex coll. René Fribourg.

24 Gold, with applied decoration in mother-of-pearl and precious stones. *Maker* Antoine Filassier (m. 1704, d. before 1748). Paris, 1742–3. *Musée du Louvre, Paris.* **25** Gold, with plaques of mother-of-pearl, shell and carnelian. *Maker* Jean Gaillard (m. 1695, w. 1754). Paris, 1744–5. *Musée du Louvre, Paris.* **26** Gold, mother-of-pearl and coral. Paris, 1743–4. *Musée Cognacq-Jay, Paris.* **27** Gold, mother-of-pearl and coral. *Maker* L.P.(?). Paris, 1747–8. *Musée Cognacq-Jay, Paris.* **28** Gold, the decoration overlaid in tinted mother-of-pearl with details in varicoloured gold. *Maker* Claude de Villers (m. 1718, d. 1755). Paris, 1750. *A La Vieille Russie, New York.* A matching box—which differs only in the substitution of a plain for an engraved background—is in the Metropolitan Museum. Made by Villers in the same year, it is further inscribed *Vallayer a Paris.* Joseph Vallayer worked from 1750 to 1770. **29** Gold, ivory and tinted mother-of-pearl. *Maker* possibly Michel de Lassus. Paris, 1749–50. *The Metropolitan Museum of Art.* **30** Gold, enamelled. *Maker* Pierre-François Delafons (m. 1732, d. 1787). Paris, 1747–9. *Musée du Louvre, Paris.*

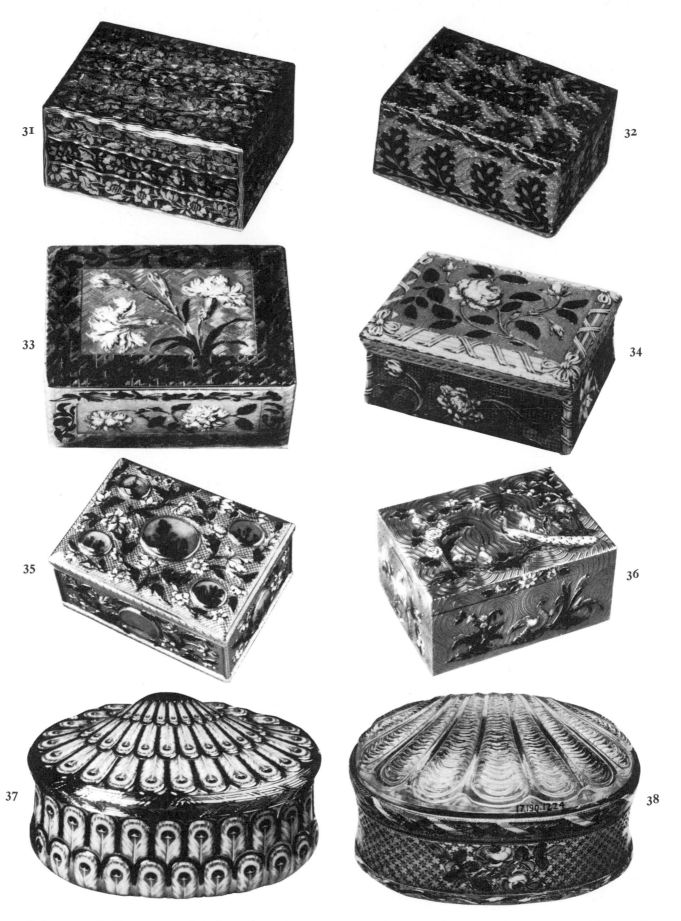

31 Gold, enamelled in orange and dark green. Paris, 1750–1. *Mr and Mrs Charles B. Wrightsman.*   **32** Gold, enamelled in royal blue. *Maker* Michel-Robert Hallé or Hallet (m. 1737, d. 1754). Paris, 1749–50. *Mr and Mrs Charles B. Wrightsman.*
33 Gold, enamelled. *Maker* Jean Moynat (m. 1745, d. 1761). Paris, 1749–50. Ex coll. René Fribourg.   **34** Gold, enamelled. *Maker* Jean Moynat. Paris, 1747–9. *The Metropolitan Museum of Art.*   **35** Gold, enamelled and set with medallions of moss agate. *Maker* Jean Ducrollay, Paris, 1750–1. *Musée du Louvre, Paris.*   **36** Gold, enamelled. *Maker* Jacques Malquis Le Quin (m. 1735, w. 1790). Paris, 1749–50. *Musée du Louvre, Paris.*   **37** Gold, enamelled. *Maker* Jean Ducrollay. Paris, 1743–4. *The Wallace Collection, London.*   **38** Gold, enamelled. The cover is of carved rock crystal. *Maker* Jean Ducrollay. Paris, 1750–6. *The Metropolitan Museum of Art.*

39, 40 Gold, studded with diamonds, emeralds and rubies. *Maker* F.S.C. (or G). Paris, 1750. *The Metropolitan Museum of Art.*
41 Gold, enamelled. *Maker* Jean Frémin (m. 1738, d. 1786). Paris, 1756–7. *Mr and Mrs Charles B. Wrightsman.* **42** Gold, enamelled. *Maker* Jean-François Breton. Paris, 1746–7. *The Wallace Collection, London.* **43** Gold, enamelled. The scene on the cover is signed *Liot. Maker* Jean Ducrollay. Paris, 1753–4. *Musée du Louvre, Paris.* **44** Gold, enamelled. *Maker* Guillaume Loir (m. 1716, d. 1758). Paris, 1753–4. *The Metropolitan Museum of Art.* **45** Gold, enamelled. Paris, 1754–5. Ex coll. Mannheim. *Musée Cognacq-Jay, Paris.* **46** Gold, enamelled. Paris, 1754–5. *The Henry E. Huntington Library and Art Gallery, San Marino, California.*

47 Gold, enamelled. The scene on the cover is signed *LeSueur*. Inside the cover, a portrait of the Marquis of Granby after Reynolds. Paris, 1750–1 or 1752–3. *Victoria and Albert Museum, London.*   **48** Gold, enamelled. *Maker* possibly Joseph Vallayer (m. 1750, d. 1770). Paris, 1750–1. *The Metropolitan Museum of Art.*   **49** Gold, enamelled. *Maker* Jean-François Garand (m. 1748, d. 1778). Paris, 1751–2. *The Metropolitan Museum of Art.*   **50** Varicoloured gold. Paris, 1755–6. Ex coll. A. Chester Beatty.   **51** Gold and mother-of-pearl. Probably Paris, *c.* 1750–5. *Musée Cognacq-Jay, Paris.*   **52** Gold, set with gouache miniatures by Louis-Nicolas van Blarenberghe (1716–94) of the château of Chanteloup. The miniature on the cover is signed and dated *van Blarenberghe 1767. Maker* P.R.(?). Paris, 1750. *Mr and Mrs Charles B. Wrightsman.* The box bears a defaced maker's mark, of which only the first letter, P, is legible.

53 Varicoloured gold. *Maker* Jean Moynat. Paris, 1754–5. *The Metropolitan Museum of Art.* **54** Varicoloured gold. Paris, 1758–9. *The Metropolitan Museum of Art.* **55** Varicoloured gold. *Maker* Charles Le Bastier. Engraved *Garand A Paris* on the rim. Paris, 1760–1. *The Metropolitan Museum of Art.* **56** Gold and mother-of-pearl. *Maker* Charles Le Bastier. Paris, 1754–5 or 1755–6. *Mr and Mrs Charles B. Wrightsman.* **57** Gold. *Maker* Jean George (m. 1752, d. 1765). Paris, 1755–6. *California Palace of the Legion of Honor, San Francisco.* **58** Gold. *Maker* Louis Michelin (m. 1751, w. 1781). Paris, 1752–3. *The Metropolitan Museum of Art.* **59** Gold, enamelled. *Maker* Jean Ducrollay. Paris, 1749–50. *The Metropolitan Museum of Art.* **60** Gold, enamelled; set with plaques of dull vermilion and gold Japanese lacquer. *Maker* Jean Ducrollay. Paris, 1753–4. *The Metropolitan Museum of Art.*

61 Gold, enamelled. *Maker* Jean Moynat. Paris, 1752–3. *Antique Porcelain Company, New York.* **62** Gold, enamelled. *Maker* Noel Hardivilliers (m. 1729, d. 1779). Paris, 1753–4. *Musée du Louvre, Paris.* **63** Gold, enamelled. *Maker* Noel Hardivilliers. Paris, 1754–5. *Rijksmuseum, Amsterdam.* **64** Varicoloured gold. *Maker* Jean Formey (m. 1754, w. Fontainebleau 1791). Paris, 1756–62. *The Bowes Museum, Barnard Castle.* **65** Varicoloured gold. *Maker* probably Jean Formey. Paris, 1757–8. *The Wallace Collection, London.* **66** Gold. *Maker* Jean Moynat. Paris, 1758–9. *Museum of Fine Arts, Boston.* **67** Varicoloured gold. Paris, 1754–5. *The Metropolitan Museum of Art.* **68** Varicoloured gold. *Maker* Jean George. Paris, 1754–5. *The Metropolitan Museum of Art.*

69 Gold. *Maker* Jean Moynat. Paris, 1750–1. *The Metropolitan Museum of Art.* **70** Gold. Paris, 1758–9. *A La Vieille Cité, Paris.* **71, 72, 73** Gold and lacquer. *Maker* François-Thomas Germain (m. 1748, d. 1791). Paris, 1755–6. *Mrs Harvey A. Firestone, Jr.* **74, 75** Gold and lapis lazuli. Paris, 1756–7. *Madame H. Collin du Bocage, Paris.*

76

76, 77, 78 Gold, set with diamond and emerald thumbpiece. *Maker* Jean George. Paris, 1758–9. *The Walters Art Gallery, Baltimore.* **79** Gold, chased and enamelled and set with enamel plaques. *Maker* Jean George. Paris, 1757–8. *The Metropolitan Museum of Art.* **80** Gold, with enamel miniatures. *Maker* Jean Ducrollay. Paris, 1757–8. *The Metropolitan Museum of Art.* **81** Gold, with enamel miniatures. Paris, 1757–8. *The Henry E. Huntington Library and Art Gallery, San Marino, California.* **82** Gold, with enamel miniatures. *Maker* J. B. B. Paris, 1755–6. *The Henry E. Huntington Library and Art Gallery, San Marino, California.*

77

78

79

80

81

82

83 Gold, enamelled. *Maker* Jean Formey. Paris, 1757–8. *Mr and Mrs Charles B. Wrightsman.* 84 Gold, studded with diamonds and set with enamel plaques. The miniature on the cover is signed and dated *Hamelin 1758* on both sides. *Maker* Jean Ducrollay. Paris, 1757–8. Ex coll. C. T. H. Hawkins. *The Taft Museum, Cincinnati.* A spring catch releases the gold lining of the cover, revealing a secret compartment. According to the *Encyclopédie*, Hamelin (who is unidentified) perfected the art of enamelling on goldsmiths' work; his first miniatures appeared in 1754. 85 Gold, enamelled. *Maker* Jean Moynat. Paris, 1758–9. *Musée du Louvre, Paris.* 86 Gold, enamelled. *Maker* Aymé-Antoine Chollet (m. 1756, living 1791). Paris, 1756–7. *The Wallace Collection, London.* 87 Gold, enamelled. *Maker* Paul Robert (m. 1747, d. 1779). Paris, 1758–9. *The Metropolitan Museum of Art.* 88 Gold, enamelled. *Maker* Mathieu Coiny (m. 1755, w. 1788). Engraved *Beckers A Paris* on the rim. Paris, 1759–60. *The Metropolitan Museum of Art.* 89 Varicoloured gold set with diamonds and emeralds. *Maker* Dominique-François Poitreau (m. 1757, w. 1781). Paris, 1759–60. *Musée du Louvre, Paris.* 90 Varicoloured gold. *Maker* Jean Formey. Paris, 1759–60. Engraved *Garand à Paris* on the rim. *Musée du Louvre, Paris.*

91 Gold, set with Sèvres porcelain plaques. *Maker* Jean George. Paris, 1758–60. *Musée du Louvre, Paris.* **92** Gold, set with Sèvres porcelain plaques depicting *Les Chasses de Louis XV*, after cartoons by Jean-Baptiste Oudry, *c.* 1745–8, for a series of Gobelins tapestries. No maker's mark. Engraved on the rim, *George AParis.* Paris, 1756–62. *The Henry E. Huntington Library and Art Gallery, San Marino, California.* Despite the similarities between this box and the preceding one the two are certainly the work of different craftsmen: one presumably George himself, the other a journeyman in his shop. **93** Gold, with enamel paintings by F. Bourgoin (*fl.* 1762–8). *Maker* Jean Ducrollay. Paris, 1759–60. *Rijksmuseum, Amsterdam.* **94** Varicoloured gold. *Maker* Jean-Charles-Simphorien Dubos (m. 1748, w. 1781). Paris, 1760–1. *The Metropolitan Museum of Art.* **95** Varicoloured gold. *Maker* Jean Frémin. Paris, 1763–4. *The Metropolitan Museum of Art.* **96** Gold, set with enamel miniatures. Unmarked. Paris, *c.* 1760–5. *The Henry E. Huntington Library and Art Gallery, San Marino, California.* **97** Gold, with enamelled medallions. *Maker* Jean Formey. Paris, 1762–3. *A La Vieille Russie, New York.* **98** Varicoloured gold. *Maker* Paul Robert. Paris, 1762–3. *The Metropolitan Museum of Art.*

99 Varicoloured gold. Paris, 1762–3. *The Metropolitan Museum of Art.* 100 Varicoloured gold. *Maker* Charles Le Bastier. Paris, 1762–3. *Musée du Louvre, Paris.* 101 Mother-of-pearl and gold. *Maker* possibly Jacques-Michel Lemaire (m. 1721, d. 1776). Paris, 1762–3. *The Metropolitan Museum of Art.* 102 Gold, with gouache miniatures attributed to Lioux de Savignac (*fl.* third quarter of the eighteenth century). Paris, 1762–3. 103, 104 Gold. *Maker* André-Louis Cassé (m. 1763, d. 1781). Paris, 1763–4. *Mrs Harvey A. Firestone, Jr.* 105 Varicoloured gold. Unmarked. Paris, *c.* 1763. *California Palace of the Legion of Honor, San Francisco.* 106 Varicoloured gold. *Maker* Pierre-Nicolas Pleyard (m. 1759, w. 1793). Paris, 1762–3. *The Metropolitan Museum of Art.*

107 Gold-mounted tortoiseshell, set with miniatures. Marks indecipherable. Paris, *c.* 1760–5. *The Henry E. Huntington Library and Art Gallery, San Marino, California.* **108** Gold, set with enamel miniatures. On the cover, *Le Repos* after Greuze; on the bottom, a kitchen scene. *Maker Jean-Marie Tiron (m. 1748, w. 1775). Paris, 1763–4. Musée du Louvre, Paris.* **109** Varicoloured gold. Paris, 1764–5. *A La Vieille Russie, New York.* **110** Gold, diamond-studded and set with sepia enamel medallions, that on the cover signed *Mlle Duplessis.* Maker Jean George. Paris, 1759–62. *The Metropolitan Museum of Art.* **111** Gold and diamonds. On the cover, an enamelled allegorical scene of later date by Jean-François Tourcaty (b. 1763, w. 1784), signed *Tourcaty.* Maker Jean George. Paris, 1763–4. *Rijksmuseum, Amsterdam.* **112** Gold, enamelled; diamond thumbpiece. On the cover, inserted at a later date, portrait of Alexander I of Russia (1801–25). *Maker Jean George. Paris, 1763–4. The Metropolitan Museum of Art.* **113** Varicoloured gold. *Maker André-Louis Cassé. Paris, 1765–6.*

114 Gold. *Maker* Jean-Baptiste Bertin (m. 1740, d. 1771). Paris, 1764–5. *The Walters Art Gallery, Baltimore*. **115** Gold, enamelled. *Maker* Jean-Joseph Barrière. Paris, 1763–4. *Musée du Louvre, Paris*. **116** Gold, enamelled. Paris, 1762–3. **117** Gold, enamelled and set with enamel miniatures. The miniature on the cover is signed *Couniot*. Paris, 1765–6. *Musée du Louvre, Paris*. **118** Gold, with gouache miniatures. *Maker* Jean Ducrollay. Paris, 1760–1. *Musée du Louvre, Paris*. **119** Gold, set with Sèvres porcelain plaques. Paris, 1763–4. *Musée du Louvre, Paris*. Part of the body of the box is a replacement by P. F. Drais, 1774–5. Engraved on the rim *Madame du Barry au Bien-Aimé*. **120** Gold, enamelled. *Maker* Claude Perron (m. 1750, d. in or before 1777). Paris, 1763–4. *The Metropolitan Museum of Art*. **121** Gold, enamelled. *Maker* probably Julien Boulogne-Petit (m. 1765, living 1793). Inscribed on the rim *George à Paris*. Paris, 1764–5. *Musée Cognacq-Jay, Paris*.

122 Gold, enamelled. On the cover, portrait of Marie Antoinette by François Dumont (1751–1831). *Maker* Pierre-François-Mathis de Beaulieu (m. 1768, w. 1791). Paris, 1768–9. *The Cleveland Museum of Art.* **123** Gold. *Maker* Louis Philippe Demay (m. 1758, d. 1772). Paris, 1767–8. *The Walters Art Gallery, Baltimore.* **124** Varicoloured gold, enamelled. *Maker* Jean-Joseph Barrière. Paris, 1766–7. *Nationalmuseum, Stockholm.* Presented to Carl von Linné (1707–78) by Frederick Calvert, 7th Baron Baltimore. **125** Varicoloured gold, enamelled. *Maker* Jean-Joseph Barrière. Paris, 1765–6. *Musée du Louvre, Paris.* **126** Varicoloured gold, enamelled. *Maker* Philippe-Emmanuel Garbe (m. 1748, w. 1793). Paris, 1762–3. *The Metropolitan Museum of Art.* **127** Gold, enamelled. *Maker* Jean-Baptiste Carnay (m. 1764, living 1793). Paris, 1765–7. *The Metropolitan Museum of Art.* **128** Gold, enamelled. *Maker* Louis-Philippe Demay. Paris, 1766–7. *Musée du Louvre, Paris.* **129** Gold, enamelled; the enamel plaque is surrounded by diamonds. *Maker* Jean-Marie Tiron (m. 1748, w. 1781). Paris, 1767–8. *The Metropolitan Museum of Art.*

130 Gold, with gouache miniatures by Louis Nicolas van Blarenberghe (1716–94), signed and dated *van Blarenberghe* 1764. Paris, 1764–5 (the body of the box is a replacement, 1786–7). *Victoria and Albert Museum, London.* **131** Gold, with gouache miniatures of the royal chateaux. *Maker* Jean-Joseph Barrière. Paris, 1765–9. *Musée du Louvre, Paris.* On the cover, Versailles; on the front, Marly; on the end, Clagny; on the canted corner, the fountain of the Dômes, Versailles. On the remaining panels, Bellevue, Saint Hubert, Choisy and additional views of Versailles. **132** Gold, set with gouache miniatures. On the cover, an unidentified portrait. On the sides and bottom, grisaille river scenes by Louis Nicolas van Blarenberghe. The miniature on the bottom is signed and dated *van Blarenberghe* 1757. Paris, 1765–6. *Musée du Louvre, Paris.* **133** Gold, with gouache miniatures. *Maker* J. D. Paris, 1768–9. *The Metropolitan Museum of Art.* **134** Gold, with gouache miniatures. *Maker* Pierre-Nicolas Pleyard. Paris, 1765–6 and 1772–3. *The Metropolitan Museum of Art.* The box was altered or repaired in 1772–3 by a second goldsmith whose mark is indecipherable. **135** Gold, engine-turned and enamelled. *Maker* Jean-Joseph Barrière. Paris, 1765–6. *The Metropolitan Museum of Art.* **136** Gold. *Maker* Claude Héricourt (m. 1763, living 1785). Paris, 1768–9. *The Metropolitan Museum of Art.* **137** Gold, enamelled. Rim inscribed SAGERET A PARIS. Paris, 1766–7. *Musée du Louvre, Paris.* Charles Barnabé Sageret (m. 1752, living 1791) was one of the chief *fournisseurs* to Louis XV in the 1760s.

138 Gold, engine-turned and enamelled. On the cover, an unidentified portrait signed GS. Paris, 1768–74. *The Art Institute of Chicago.* 139 Lacquered tortoiseshell mounted in gold. Paris, 1765–6. Ex coll. René Fribourg. 140 Green lacquer and gold, set with a miniature. *Maker* possibly Henry Bodson (m. 1763, living 1789). Paris, 1766–7. *Musée Cognacq-Jay, Paris.* 141 Heliotrope mounted in gold. A portrait miniature on ivory is concealed beneath the hinged medallion on the cover. *Maker* Claude Héricourt. Paris, 1769–70. *The Metropolitan Museum of Art.* 142 Gold, enamelled. On the cover, a portrait of Maria Lescinska; inside, gold monogram ML. *Maker* Charles Le Bastier. Paris, 1768–9. *Antique Porcelain Company, New York.* 143 Gold, enamel and agate. Paris, 1767–8(?). *Musée Cognacq-Jay, Paris.* 144 Gold, enamelled. *Maker* Jean-Joseph Barrière. Paris, 1769–70. *The Metropolitan Museum of Art.*

145 Varicoloured gold, enamelled. On the cover, portrait of Catherine II of Russia. *Maker* Jean George. Paris, 1764–5. *The Metropolitan Museum of Art.* **146** Gold, set with enamel medallions. On the cover, Pierrot, Columbine and Harlequin. On the bottom, children blowing bubbles. *Maker* Jean-Joseph Barrière. Paris, 1765–6. *The Metropolitan Museum of Art.* **147** Gold, enamelled. Paris, 1769–70. *Musée Cognacq-Jay, Paris.* **148** Varicoloured gold. *Maker* Jean Formey. Paris, 1769–70. **149** Gold and red lacquer. On the cover, a miniature on ivory of Venus and Cupid. *Maker* Jean Formey. Paris, 1769–70. *California Palace of the Legion of Honor, San Francisco.* **150** Gold, with *piqué* lacquer panels. *Maker* Jean-Marie Tiron. Paris, 1761–3. *Musée du Louvre, Paris.* **151** Gold and lacquer. *Maker* Julien Rivard (m. 1720, d. before 1785). Paris, 1767–8. *The Wallace Collection, London.* **152** Gold, with *piqué* lacquer panels. *Maker* Louis Roucel (m. 1763, d. 1787). Paris, 1768. *Mr and Mrs Charles B. Wrightsman.* This is certainly the box described in the catalogue of the Gaignat sale in 1768 as '*presque quarrée, d'écaille coulée à charniere, le dessus représente un rhinoceros sur terrasse & arbres à côté*'. As was usual in the eighteenth century, the maker of the box was not mentioned.

153 Gold, with *piqué* lacquer panels. Paris, probably 1778. *Wartski, London.* **154** Gold, enamelled. *Maker* Jean-Joseph Barrière. Paris, 1768–9. *Rijksmuseum, Amsterdam.* **155** Gold, varicoloured and enamelled, set with plaques of agate. *Maker* Pierre-François Drais. Paris, 1770–1. *Musée du Louvre, Paris.* **156** Gold, enamelled and set with an enamel miniature. *Maker* Pierre-François Drais. Paris, 1769–71. *The Art Institute of Chicago.* **157** Gold, with miniatures in the style of Jacques Joseph DeGault (b. *c.* 1738, living 1812). *Maker* Pierre-François Drais. Paris, 1770–1. *A La Vieille Russie, New York.* **158** Gold, enamelled. Paris, 1768–75. *Henry E. Huntington Library and Art Gallery, San Marino, California.* A box of 1771–2 by P. F. M. de Beaulieu in the Louvre (Nocq and Dreyfus, *Catalogue . . .*, no. 92) is identical in design, but the two do not appear to be by the same maker. **159** Gold, enamelled. *Maker* Jean-Baptiste Beckers (m. 1753, w. 1793). Inscribed on the rim, *Beckers à Paris.* Paris, 1771–2. *The Metropolitan Museum of Art.* **160** Gold, enamelled in green and grey and set with an enamel portrait miniature. *Maker* Charles Le Bastier. Paris, 1771–2. *Mr and Mrs Charles B. Wrightsman.* An almost identical box, made by Le Bastier in the same year, is in the Louvre (Nocq and Dreyfus, *Catalogue . . .*, no. 65). It differs from this only in the miniature and in the substitution of rosettes for garlands on the cover and bottom. A third version is in a private collection; identical to the Louvre example, it is dated 1773–4. The miniatures on the two latter boxes are enamelled with classical subjects, suggesting that the miniature on this version is a replacement.

161 Varicoloured gold. *Maker* Pierre-François-Mathis de Beaulieu. Paris, 1770–1. *Wartski, London.* **162** Varicoloured gold. *Maker* Pierre Bidault (m. 1759, w. 1781). Paris, 1771–2. *The Metropolitan Museum of Art.* **163** Gold, the cover set with repoussé gold medallions of amorini. *Maker* probably Melchior-René Barré (m. 1751, w. 1791). Paris, 1771–2. *The Metropolitan Museum of Art.* **164** Composition, striped and mounted in gold and set with a cameo. *Maker* Pierre-Guillaume Sallot (m. 1750, w. 1793). Paris, 1770–1. *Antique Porcelain Company, New York.* **165** Gold, engine-turned and enamelled. Inscribed *Du Petit Dunkerque.* Paris, 1773–4. *Henry E. Huntington Library and Art Gallery, San Marino, California.* **166** Gold, with gouache miniatures. *Maker* Pierre-François-Mathis de Beaulieu. Paris, 1775–6. *Musée du Louvre, Paris.* **167** Gold, with gouache miniatures by Louis-Nicolas van Blarenberghe. Paris, *c.* 1770–5. *Henry E. Huntington Library and Art Gallery, San Marino, California.* **168** Gold, engine-turned and enamelled. On the cover, portrait of Lady Caroline Russell, Duchess of Marlborough, by Nicolas-André Courtois (*fl.* 1770–7), signed *Courtois. Maker* N.C.O. Paris, *c.* 1770–5. *The Art Institute of Chicago.*

169 Gold, enamelled. On the cover, an enamel miniature of a girl carrying a basket of flowers. *Maker* Jean-Louis Bouillerot (m. 1761, d. 1781). Paris, 1775–6. *Wartski, London.*   **170** Gold. *Maker* probably Louis Ray (m. 1772, w. 1786). Paris, 1775–6. *The Metropolitan Museum of Art.*   **171** Gold. *Maker* Paul-Nicolas Menière (m. 1775, d. 1826). Paris, 1775–6. *British Museum.* Horace Walpole was instrumental in procuring this box for Edward Gibbon shortly after the publication, in 1776, of the first volume of *The History of the Decline and Fall of the Roman Empire.*   **172** Gold, with Sèvres porcelain plaques painted with miniatures of the royal family. Inscribed on the rim, *Menierre Rue Mauconseille à Paris. Maker* Paul-Nicolas Menière. Paris, 1775–81. *Musée Cognacq-Jay, Paris.*   **173** Gold-mounted tortoiseshell. On the cover, a gouache miniature signed and dated *A(?)L.* 1776. Paris, 1778–9. *Musée Cognacq-Jay, Paris.*   **174** Mother-of-pearl and composition, mounted in gold and lined with tortoiseshell. On the cover, portrait of Madame Elisabeth, sister of Louis XVI. Paris, 1768–75. *The Metropolitan Museum of Art.*   **175** Tortoiseshell and varicoloured gold. Paris, 1775–6. *Musée du Louvre, Paris.*   **176** Textile Cone shell mounted in gold. *Maker* Pierre-François-Mathis de Beaulieu. Paris, 1768–75. *Antique Porcelain Company, New York.*

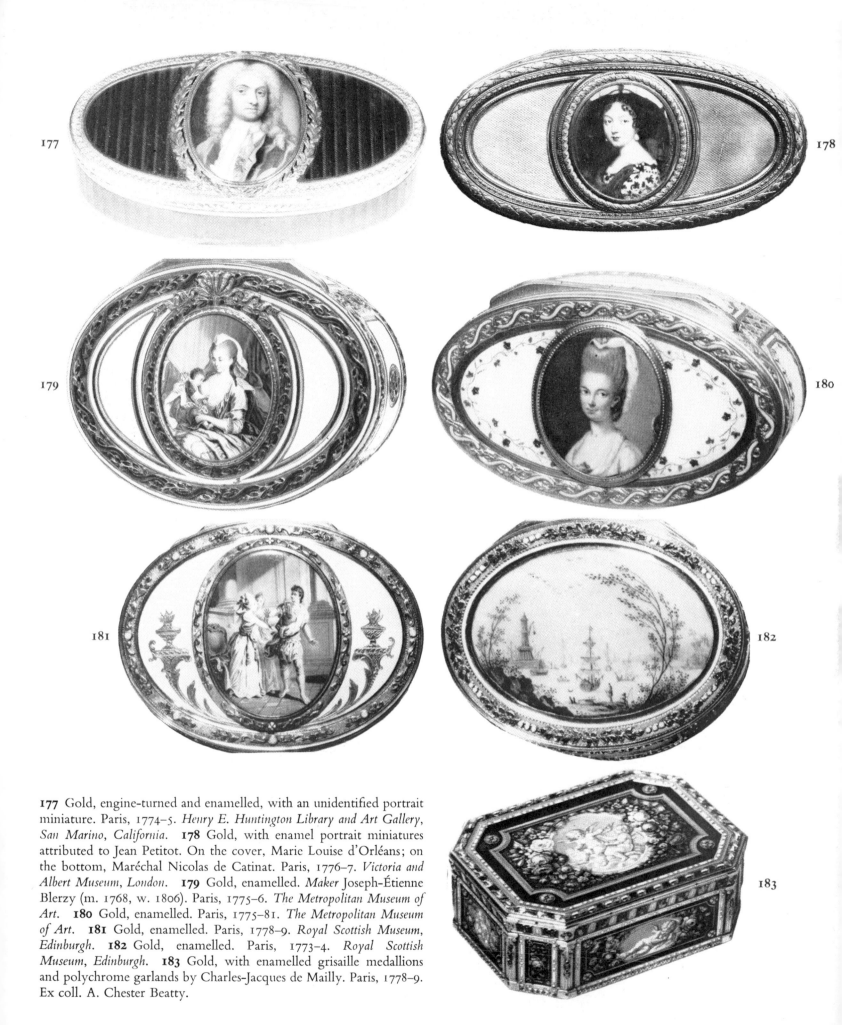

177 Gold, engine-turned and enamelled, with an unidentified portrait miniature. Paris, 1774–5. *Henry E. Huntington Library and Art Gallery, San Marino, California.* **178** Gold, with enamel portrait miniatures attributed to Jean Petitot. On the cover, Marie Louise d'Orléans; on the bottom, Maréchal Nicolas de Catinat. Paris, 1776–7. *Victoria and Albert Museum, London.* **179** Gold, enamelled. *Maker* Joseph-Étienne Blerzy (m. 1768, w. 1806). Paris, 1775–6. *The Metropolitan Museum of Art.* **180** Gold, enamelled. Paris, 1775–81. *The Metropolitan Museum of Art.* **181** Gold, enamelled. Paris, 1778–9. *Royal Scottish Museum, Edinburgh.* **182** Gold, enamelled. Paris, 1773–4. *Royal Scottish Museum, Edinburgh.* **183** Gold, with enamelled grisaille medallions and polychrome garlands by Charles-Jacques de Mailly. Paris, 1778–9. Ex coll. A. Chester Beatty.

184 Gold, enamelled. On the cover, a gouache miniature by Louis-Nicolas van Blarenberghe, signed *van Blarenberghe*. Unmarked. Paris, c. 1780. *Henry E. Huntington Library and Art Gallery, San Marino, California.* **185** Gold, with gouache miniatures (unsigned) by Louis-Nicolas van Blarenberghe. *Maker* Joseph-Étienne Blerzy. Paris, 1778–9. *The Metropolitan Museum of Art.* **186** Gold, enamelled and set with an enamel portrait of Marie Antoinette. *Maker* Joseph-Étienne Blerzy. Paris, 1776–7. *Musée Cognacq-Jay, Paris.* **187** Gold, enamelled and set with an enamel miniature. *Maker* probably Joseph-Étienne Blerzy. Paris, 1775–81. *Musée Cognacq-Jay, Paris.* **188** Gold, engine-turned and enamelled. On the cover, portrait of Louis XIV by Jean Petitot. *Maker* Charles Ouizille (m. 1771, w. 1806). Paris, 1778–9. Ex coll. George IV; Earl of Harrington; Demidoff; Pietri. *Musée du Louvre, Paris.* **189** Gold, with grisaille miniatures by Jacques-Joseph DeGault of the Triumphs of Alexander, after paintings by Charles Le Brun. On the cover, the entry of Alexander into Babylon. Inscribed *Le Brun* and signed *J J DeGault*. Paris, 1779–80(?). *The Cleveland Museum of Art.* The immediate source of DeGault's miniatures was undoubtedly a series of engravings by Sébastien Le Clerc (1637–1714) of Le Brun's paintings. They were reissued in Paris in 1784: it is thus possible that the miniatures on this box are later than the apparent date of the box itself. **190** Gold and red lacquer. On the cover, grisaille miniature in the style of Jacques-Joseph DeGault. Paris, 1781–2. *Wartski, London.* **191** Gold, the cover and bottom of opalescent glass painted in blue with chinoiserie landscapes. *Maker* Pierre-Claude Pottiers (m. 1778, living 1796). Paris, 1780–1. *Royal Scottish Museum, Edinburgh.* An identical box, made by Pottiers in the same year, is in a New York private collection.

192 Gold, engine-turned and enamelled and set with an enamel miniature. *Maker* probably Barthélemy Pillieux (m. 1774, w. 1790). Paris, 1781. *The Metropolitan Museum of Art.* **193** Gold, engine-turned and enamelled and set with an enamel miniature. *Maker* Charles Ouizille (m. 1771, w. 1809). Paris, 1780–1. *The Metropolitan Museum of Art.* **194** Gold, enamelled. On the cover, the cipher of Catherine II of Russia applied in diamonds on a glass plaque. *Maker* Jean-Joseph Barrière. Paris, 1782–3. *The Metropolitan Museum of Art.* **195** Gold, enamelled and set with diamonds. On the cover, portrait of Louis XVI by Louis-Marie Sicard (1746–1825), signed *Sicardy*. *Maker* Joseph-Étienne Blerzy. Paris, 1779–80. *The Metropolitan Museum of Art.* **196** Gold, enamelled. On the cover, portrait of Louis XVI by Pierre-Noël Violet (1749–1819), signed *Violet f.* *Maker* Paul-Nicolas Menière. Paris, 1779–80. *Musée du Louvre, Paris.* **197** Gold, enamelled. Paris, 1782–3. *Royal Scottish Museum, Edinburgh.* **198** Gold, the panels enamelled in light blue, yellow and white on a dark blue ground. *Maker* Pierre-Innocent Zurich (m. 1769, living 1793). Paris, 1782–3. *The Metropolitan Museum of Art.* **199** Gold, enamelled and studded with gold star-shaped *paillons*. *Maker* Jean-Marc-Antoine Écosse (m. 1755, w. 1791). Paris, 1775–81. *The Brooklyn Museum.*

200 Gold, with grisaille miniatures. *Maker* Paul-Nicolas Menière. Paris, 1781–2. *Musée du Louvre, Paris.* 201 Gold and lacquer. *Maker* Adrien-Jean-Maximilien Vachette (m. 1779, d. 1839). Paris, 1782–3. *Musée du Louvre, Paris.* 202 Gold, enamelled to simulate malachite. *Maker* Adrien-Jean-Maximilien Vachette. Paris, 1782–3. *The Metropolitan Museum of Art.* 203 Gold and agate. *Maker* Adrien-Jean-Maximilien Vachette. Paris, 1782–3. *Musée du Louvre, Paris.* 204 Gold, enamelled to simulate lapis lazuli. *Maker* Adrien-Jean-Maximilien Vachette. Paris, 1781–2. Ex coll. René Fribourg. *A La Vieille Russie, New York.* 205 Gold, enamelled and set with diamonds. *Maker* Joseph-Étienne Blerzy. Paris, 1785–6. Ex coll. René Fribourg. 206 Gold, enamelled. Paris, probably 1784–5. *Musée Cognacq-Jay, Paris.*

207 Gold and composition. On the cover, a *verre églomisé* medallion. *Maker* Charles Brisson (m. 1761, w. 1791). Paris, 1785–6. *The Metropolitan Museum of Art.* **208** Gold, set with portraits of the French royal family. *Maker* Adrien-Jean-Maximilien Vachette. Paris, 1784–5. *Musée du Louvre, Paris.* **209** Gold, with gouache miniatures. Paris, 1788–9. *Musée du Louvre, Paris.* **210** Tortoiseshell, gold-mounted and bordered with pearls. On the cover, gouache miniature by Gerard van Spaendonck (1746–1822), signed *Spaendonck. Maker* Adrien-Jean-Maximilien Vachette. Paris, 1784–5. *Musée du Louvre, Paris.* **211** Gold, with gouache miniatures of views of Lyon. Paris, 1788–9. Ex coll. René Fribourg. **212** Gold, enamelled. *Maker* possibly Pierre-Nicolas Marcault (m. 1733, d. 1789). *The Art Institute of Chicago.* **213** Gold, set with porcelain plaques painted in raised enamels. *Maker* Adrien-Jean-Maximilien Vachette. Paris, 1789–90. *The Metropolitan Museum of Art.* **214** Varicoloured gold, the cover set with a porcelain plaque painted on the outside with a flower still life, on the inside with children. The sides and base are enamelled pink on the outside, green inside. *Maker* Pierre-Denis Chaumont (m. 1777, w. 1793). Paris, 1789. *The Metropolitan Museum of Art.*

215 Gold, enamelled. Paris, 1797–8. Ex coll. Earl of Harewood. 216 Tortoise-shell, mounted in gold and set with a gouache miniature signed and dated *M De Suriny 1791*. French, end of the eighteenth century. *Musée Cognacq-Jay, Paris.* 217 Gold mounted tortoiseshell, the cover set with a gouache miniature by Jean-Baptiste-Jacques Augustin (1759–1832), signed and dated *augustin f. 1794(?).* Paris, 1775–81. *The Metropolitan Museum of Art.* 218 Gold, with gouache miniatures. Engraved on the rim, *Vachette et Ouizille Bijoutiers du Roi à Paris.* *Maker* Adrien-Jean-Maximilien Vachette. Paris, c. 1795. *A La Vieille Russie, New York.* Inscribed inside the cover and bottom, *Bhot et Baudoin Peint en 1770.* None of the miniatures appears to be signed or dated. Bhot is unrecorded; Baudoin is perhaps Pierre-Antoine Baudoin (1723–69), the engraved date being a faulty recollection. 219 Gold, enamelled and set with gouache miniatures. On the cover, the Crossing of the Rhine by Louis XIV in 1672, after a painting by van der Meulen, possibly by Henri-Joseph van Blarenberghe (1741–1826), signed BLARENBE. . . Engraved on the rim, *Vachette, Bijoutier, à Paris.* *Maker* Adrien-Jean-Maximilien Vachette. Paris, 1798–1809. *The Metropolitan Museum of Art.* 220 Gold, the exterior overlaid with tortoiseshell. A hinged medallion on the cover, inset with strands of hair, conceals a miniature of a woman's eye painted on ivory. *Maker* probably Joseph Lurat (recorded 1806). Paris, 1809–19. *The Metropolitan Museum of Art.* 221 Gold, inlaid with lapis, carnelian, turquoise, heliotrope and agate. *Maker* Étienne Alexandre Quinet (recorded 1806). Paris, 1809–19. *The Metropolitan Museum of Art.* 222 Gold, enamelled, the cover inset with a repoussé gold plaque. *Maker* Gabriel-Raoul Morel (w. 1798–c. 1827). Paris, c. 1810–20(?). *Musée du Louvre, Paris.* Although this box is struck with marks in use between 1791–8 its shape and style of decoration suggest a later date. It may have been worked from an older box, a not unusual practice.

223 Gold, with chased decoration emblematic of America. *Maker* Gabriel–Raoul Morel (w. 1798–c. 1827). Paris, 1809–19. *Musée du Louvre, Paris.* 224 Gold, enamelled. On the cover, an early nineteenth-century portrait of one of the natural children of Louis XIV. *Maker* Adrien-Jean-Maximilien Vachette. Inscribed on the rim, *Vachette et Ouizille Bijoutiers du Roi à Paris.* Paris, 1809–19. *Victoria and Albert Museum, London.* 225 Tortoiseshell and gold. On the cover, portrait on vellum reputedly of Madame de Maintenon, adapted from a portrait by Jean Petitot. *Maker* Pierre André Montauban (w. 1800–16). Paris, 1809–19. *Victoria and Albert Museum, London.* 226 Gold, the cover set with a portrait of Napoleon encircled with brilliants. Paris, c. 1815. *British Museum.* The box was presented by Napoleon to Mrs Anne Seymour Damer (1749–1828) on the occasion of his acceptance, 1 May 1815, of a bust of Charles James Fox by the sculptress. 227 Gold. On the cover is a hinged medallion inset with a miniature on ivory of the Empress Marie-Louise by Jean-Baptiste Isabey (1767–1855), signed and dated *Isabey 1812.* Concealed beneath the medallion are portraits of Napoleon, signed and dated *Isabey 1815,* and the King of Rome, signed and dated *M.1815. Maker* Gabriel–Raoul Morel. Paris, c. 1815. *The Metropolitan Museum of Art.* 228 Tortoiseshell and gold. *Maker* Adrien-Jean-Maximilien Vachette. Inscribed on the rim, *Vachette à Paris.* Paris, 1819–38. *Victoria and Albert Museum, London.* 229 Gold, the cover set with a portrait of Louis XIV attributed to Jean Petitot. *Maker* Augustin-André Héguin (m. 1785, recorded 1806). Paris, c. 1815(?). *Royal Scottish Museum, Edinburgh.* 230 Tortoiseshell, gold-mounted and set with a portrait on ivory of Louis XV by J. Parent after Hyacinthe Rigaud, signed and dated *I. Parent 1817.* Paris, c. 1817. *Victoria and Albert Museum, London.*

231 Gold. On the cover, a diamond-encircled topaz. *Maker* Adrien-Jean-Maximilien Vachette. Paris, *c.* 1825–30. *Musée du Louvre, Paris.* 232 Gold, enamelled. On the cover, diamond-set monogram of Charles X (1824–30). *Maker* Gabriel-Raoul Morel. Inscribed on the rim, *Petit-Jean & Ouizille Jou[aille]rs Bij[outier]rs de la Chambre du Roi.* Inscribed inside the cover, *Donnée par le Roi 1827.* Paris, *c.* 1827. Ex coll. René Fribourg. *A La Vieille Russie, New York.* 233 Gold, studded with brilliants. On the cover, portrait of Charles X by Daniel Saint (1778–1847), signed *Saint. Maker* Adrien-Jean-Maximilien Vachette. Paris, *c.* 1825. *Wartski, London.* 234 Gold, set with eighteenth-century gouache miniatures. *Maker* Alexandre Leferre (w. after 1838). Paris, *c.* 1840–50. *The Cleveland Museum of Art.* 235 Gold, enamelled by Philipp Ernst Schindler (1723–1810), the scene on the cover signed *Schindler.* In the large medallions, Flemish peasant scenes; between them, grisaille landscapes with figures. Austrian (Vienna), *c.* 1760. Formerly in the collections of the Maximilianmuseum, Augsburg. *A La Vieille Russie, New York.* 236 Gold, enamelled with Flemish peasant scenes by Philipp Ernst Schindler, signed *Schindler.* Austrian (Vienna), *c.* 1760–5. *Musée du Louvre, Paris.*

237 Gold, with enamel plaques by Philipp Ernst Schindler, signed *Schindler*. Austrian (Vienna), *c.* 1770. *The Metropolitan Museum of Art*. The box also bears a defaced maker's mark of three letters of which only the last, C, is legible. **238** Gold, enamelled and set on the cover with a white biscuit medallion bearing a portrait of Maria Anna of Austria (1738–89), daughter of the Empress Maria Theresa. Probably Austrian, *c.* 1770. *The Metropolitan Museum of Art*. **239** Gold, enamelled. Probably Austrian, *c.* 1780. Ex coll. Empress Maria Theresa (1717–80). *Musée du Louvre, Paris*. **240** Gold, enamelled. On the cover, an enamel medallion depicting a Sacrifice to Venus. *Maker* I.W.S. Austrian (Vienna), *c.* 1785–90. *The Art Institute of Chicago*. **241** Gold, with a portrait of Alexander I of Russia (1801–25), signed *PR*. Austrian (Vienna), 1816. *The Art Institute of Chicago*. **242** Varicoloured gold, enamelled and studded with rhinestones. *Maker* A.M. Austrian (Vienna), 1832. *The Metropolitan Museum of Art*.

243, 244 Gold and tortoiseshell. German, *c.* 1720–30. *Private collection.* **245** Gold, the cover set with an agate. Probably German, *c.* 1730. *The Metropolitan Museum of Art.* **246** Double box, gold and mother-of-pearl. German, *c.* 1740–50. *Wartski, London.* **247** Gold, overlaid with plaques of mother-of-pearl, carved and engraved and decorated with gold appliqués. German, *c.* 1745–50. *The Metropolitan Museum of Art.* **248** Gold, studded with diamonds and set on the cover with an enamel portrait of Frederick II of Prussia, after a painting by Antoine von Pesne (1683–1757). German (Berlin), 1746. *Verwaltung der Staatlichen Schlösser und Gärten, Berlin.* Furnished on 25 February 1746 by Johann Ernst Gotzkowsky, the king's commissioner, the box was presented by Frederick to Prince Leopold of Anhalt-Dessau. **249** Gold, set with plaques of agate over pink foil appliquéd in varicoloured mother-of-pearl and ivory; diamond thumbpiece. *Maker* D.B. German (Stettin), *c.* 1755–60. *The Metropolitan Museum of Art.*

250 Gold, inlaid with varicoloured mother-of-pearl and ivory. *Maker* P.C. (or G.). Probably German, *c.* 1755–60. *The Metropolitan Museum of Art.* The scene on the cover is of the Place Maubert, after a painting by Étienne Jeaurat (1699–1789) exhibited in the Salon of 1753. 251 Gold, enamelled. German (Berlin), *c.* 1760. Ex coll. Queen Charlotte (1744–1818). *British Museum.* 252 Gold, enamelled, with diamond thumbpiece. Engraved *Baudeson* on the rim. *Maker* Daniel Baudesson (*fl. c.* 1730–80). German (Berlin), *c.* 1760. *The Metropolitan Museum of Art.* 253 Gold, enamelled, with diamond thumbpiece. Unmarked. *Maker* possibly Daniel Baudesson. German (Berlin), *c.* 1760. *Mr and Mrs Charles B. Wrightsman.* 254 Gold, enamelled with scenes from the story of Diana by Daniel Chodowiecki (1726–1801), signed on the cover *D. Chodowiecki. Maker* possibly Daniel Baudesson. German (Berlin), *c.* 1760–5. *Musée du Louvre, Paris.* 255 Gold, decorated in flat translucent and raised opaque enamels. Unmarked. German, *c.* 1750–60. *The Metropolitan Museum of Art.* 256 Gold, enamelled, with diamond thumbpiece. German, *c.* 1760–5. *The Wallace Collection, London.* 257 Onyx mounted in gold. Unmarked. German, *c.* 1750–60. *The Metropolitan Museum of Art.*

258 Gold, enamelled, with diamond thumbpiece. German, *c.* 1755–60. *Victoria and Albert Museum, London.* 259 Gold, the cover with a scene of Venus and Mercury instructing Cupid executed in layers of mother-of-pearl and gold. German, *c.* 1760. *A La Vieille Russie, New York.* 260 Gold, with enamel miniatures. Probably German, *c.* 1765–70. *The Metropolitan Museum of Art.* 261 Gold. On the cover, portrait of a woman by an unknown, probably French, miniaturist. German, *c.* 1760. *Rijksmuseum, Amsterdam.* 262 Gold, with enamel plaques attributed to Gottfried Chodowiecki, signed *Chodowiecki.* German, *c.* 1760. *Rijksmuseum, Amsterdam.* The plaques appear to be about ten years later in date than the goldwork. 263 Gold, enamelled. *Maker* I. R. German, *c.* 1775–80. *The Metropolitan Museum of Art.* 264 Gold, with enamel placques. German, *c.* 1765–70. *Musée du Louvre, Paris.*

265 Gold. *Maker* Louis Mestejer (w. 1730–50). Dutch (Amsterdam),
1747. *Wartski, London.* 266 Gold. *Maker* N.Z. Dutch (Amsterdam),
1752. Ex coll. A. Chester Beatty. 267 Gold. Dutch, *c.* 1755–60.
Rijksmuseum, Amsterdam. 268 Gold. *Maker* Barend Enzering (recorded 1807–16). Dutch (Amsterdam), 1825. *Rijksmuseum, Amsterdam.*
269 Gold, engraved with the cypher AS. *Maker* G.A. English, *c.* 1710.
Antique Porcelain Company, New York. The maker's mark appears to
be the same as that, recorded by Jackson, on a tobacco box of 1709–10;
an earlier variant of the mark occurs in 1702–3. 270 Gold, engraved
with the arms of Lockwood. English, *c.* 1720. 271 Gold. On the
cover, a portrait of Mary Queen of Scots, perhaps one of several copies
made by Bernard Lens (1682–1740) of a painting then owned by the
Duke of Hamilton. Engraved on the bottom are the arms of Cotton
with Craggs in pretence. English, *c.* 1720. *Victoria and Albert Museum,
London.*

272 Gold. English, *c.* 1720–30. Ex coll. A. Chester Beatty.   273, 274 Gold. The cover is signed along the front edge BVREL FECIT. English, *c.* 1730. *Private collection.*   275 Gold. English, *c.* 1720–30. Ex coll. René Fribourg.   276 Gold. *English, c.* 1735–40. *Antique Porcelain Company, New York.*   277 Gold. *Maker P.P., English, c.* 1750. *Museum of Fine Arts, Boston.* 278, 279 Gold. English, *c.* 1740–50. *Private collection.*

280 Gold. English, *c.* 1740–50. **281, 282** Gold. *Maker* F.H. English (London), 1751–6. *Private collection.* **283** Gold. English, *c.* 1745–50. *A La Vieille Russie, New York.* **284** Gold. English, *c.* 1750. *Wartski, London.* **285** Gold. English, *c.* 1750–60. *A La Vieille Russie, New York.* **286** Gold-mounted agate, studded with diamonds. English, *c.* 1750–60. *A La Vieille Russie, New York.* **287** Gold and dendritic agate. An unsigned watch is set on the front; the back panel is hinged and conceals a painted moving landscape. English, *c.* 1765. *A La Vieille Russie, New York.*

288 Horn, lined and mounted with gold. On the cover, portrait miniature on ivory of Anne, first Marchioness of Donegal (*c.* 1739–80) by Richard Cosway (1742–1821). English, *c.* 1765–70. *The Metropolitan Museum of Art.* 289 Gold. Inside the lid, an unidentified portrait. English, *c.* 1775. *A La Vieille Russie, New York.* 290 Gold. On the cover, an enamel portrait of a lady. Inside, the monogram L. English, *c.* 1780. *Charles Angell, Bath.* Said to have been presented to Elizabeth Stewart (1769–1851) by her grandmother, Elizabeth Viscountess Langford. 291 Tortoiseshell, gold-mounted. On the cover, an enamel portrait miniature signed and dated *S* 177. . . . English, 1771–9. *The Cooper Union Museum, New York.* 292 Gold, enamelled. *Maker* James Morriset (w. 1773–8). English (London), *c.* 1775. *Wartski, London.* 293 Double box, gold and enamel. *Maker* John Innocent (w. 1773–92). English (London), 1778–9. *The Walters Art Gallery, Baltimore.*

294 Tortoiseshell, mounted in gold and set on the cover with a Wedgwood jasper plaque of The Muses Watering Pegasus in Helicon designed by John Flaxman (1755–1826). English, *c.* 1780–90. *The Metropolitan Museum of Art.* **295** Gold and agate. On the cover, a Wedgwood blue and white jasper portrait medallion of Catherine II of Russia. Probably English, *c.* 1780. *The Trustees of the Lady Lever Art Gallery, Port Sunlight.* This box may perhaps be an example of the work of the Birmingham firm of Boulton and Fothergill. Boulton is known to have set Wedgwood's cameos in faceted steel jewellery, and it is not unlikely that he would have produced snuff boxes commemorative of so illustrious an occasion as the visit of Catherine the Great to the Soho factory in 1776. It may also be noted that commercial relations among the three were close: Boulton and Fothergill engaged an agent who represented them, and also Wedgwood, at the Russian court. **296** Gold, enamelled. English (London), 1801–2. **297** Gold, enamelled and set with an unidentified portrait. English (London), 1808–9. *Royal Scottish Museum, Edinburgh.* **298** Gold. *Maker* William Eley (w. 1795–1808/9). English (London), 1806–7. *Queen's College, Oxford.* **299** Gold. English (London), 1815–16. *Antique Porcelain Company, New York.* **300** Gold, the cover set with an Italian mosaic landscape. English (London), 1818–19.

301 Gold. On the cover, a portrait of an unidentified man by James Scouler (1740?–1812), signed and dated *Scouler 1777*. *Maker* A. J. Strachan. English (London), 1818–19. *The Art Institute of Chicago*. **302** Gold. English (London), 1822–3. *Wartski, London*. **303** Gold, decorated with emblems of the United Kingdom. English (London), 1824–5. *The Walters Art Gallery, Baltimore*. **304** Varicoloured gold and diamonds. On the cover, the monogram of William IV (1830–37). English, *c*. 1830. *The Metropolitan Museum of Art*. **305** Gold. Inscribed: The Inhabitants of Kilkenny Unanimous in their Gratitude present this Box to JAMES WEMYS ESQ^r Mayor 1795. *Maker* James Keating (w. 1792–1811). Irish (Dublin), 1795. *The Metropolitan Museum of Art*. **306** Gold, chased and enamelled with the arms of Scholey. *Maker* I.E. Irish (Dublin), 1813–14. According to an engraved inscription on the bottom, this box was presented to George Scholey, Lord Mayor of London, in 1813.

307 Gold. *Maker* Frantz Bergs (w. 1725–77). Swedish (Stockholm), c. 1745. **308** Gold. *Maker* Catherine Kedjeström (w. 1762, d. 1773). Swedish (Stockholm), c. 1770. *The Metropolitan Museum of Art*. The maker's mark on the box is that of Catherine's husband, Anders (w. 1735, d. 1762). After his death his wife continued to use his mark. **309** Gold, enamelled. *Maker* Peter Johan Ljungstedt (w. 1778–1804). Swedish (Stockholm), c. 1780. **310, 311** Gold and dendritic agate. Inside the lid, portrait of Prince Ferdinand, Duke of Brunswick-Luneburg (1721–92) by an unknown miniaturist. *Maker* Frederik II Fabritius (1740–89). Danish (Copenhagen), probably 1767–8. *Museum of Decorative Art, Copenhagen*. **312** Gold, enamelled. *Maker* C.H. Possibly Danish, c. 1780. *The Metropolitan Museum of Art*. **313** Gold, enamelled. Possibly Scandinavian, c. 1780–90. *Antique Porcelain Company, New York*.

314 Varicoloured gold. *Maker* D.M.C. Swiss, 1765–70. *The Metropolitan Museum of Art.* 315 Varicoloured gold. The enamel plaque on the cover is hinged and encloses a watch. A music mechanism is set in the bottom. *Maker* D.M.C. Swiss, *c.* 1770. *Victoria and Albert Museum, London.* 316 Varicoloured gold, the cover set with a hinged medallion concealing a watch. *Maker* possibly D.M.C. Swiss, *c.* 1770. *Rijksmuseum, Amsterdam.* 317 Varicoloured gold. *Maker* D.M.C. Swiss, 1765–70. Ex coll. René Fribourg. 318 Gold, enamelled. *Maker* possibly D.M.C. Swiss, 1765–70. *Musée du Louvre, Paris.* 319 Gold, enamelled. *Maker* D.M.C. Swiss, 1770–5. *The Metropolitan Museum of Art.* 320 Gold, enamelled. *Maker* R. R. Swiss, 1775–80. Ex coll. Earl of Harewood.

321 Gold, enamelled. *Maker P.G. Swiss, c.* 1785. **322** Gold and enamelled singing-bird box. The mechanism is inscribed *Jacob Frisard. Maker G.R.G.* (or C?) for Jacob Frisard (1753–1812). Swiss (Geneva), *c.* 1806. *The Art Institute of Chicago.* In addition to the maker's mark, the box also bears the Vienna mark for gold, 1806–7. **323, 324, 325** Gold and enamelled singing-bird box. Engraved inside the outer cover, *Jaquet Droz & Leschot London N 29. Maker G.R.C.* for the firm of Jaquet Droz and Leschot. Swiss (Geneva), *c.* 1810. *A La Vieille Russie, New York.* The firm, which had a branch in London, often inscribed its boxes as having been made in that city (see p. 42). **326** Gold, enamelled. *Maker F.J. Swiss,* 1810–20. *The Art Institute of Chicago.* **327** Gold, enamelled. *Maker F.J. Swiss,* 1810–20. *Henry E. Huntington Library and Art Gallery, San Marino, California.*

328 Gold, enamelled, set with pearls and an enamel miniature. *Maker R.L. & C. Swiss, c. 1810–20. Wartski, London.*
329 Gold, enamelled. Swiss, *c. 1810–20. Mr. E. Marcus.* **330** Gold, enamelled. *Maker G.W. Swiss, c. 1810–20. Antique Porcelain Company, New York.* **331** Gold and enamelled singing-bird box with music mechanism. Swiss (Geneva), *c. 1820. A La Vieille Russie, New York.* **332** Gold and enamelled musical automaton box. *Maker G.G.R. Swiss (Geneva), c. 1820. A La Vieille Russie, New York.* While the music plays, the two gardeners in the foreground clip the trees; another gardener moves across the background with a full wheelbarrow, disappears behind the pavilion (which encloses a waterfall) and emerges with the wheelbarrow empty. **333** Gold and enamelled automaton box set with a watch. Swiss (Geneva), *c. 1820. Ex coll A. Chester Beatty.*

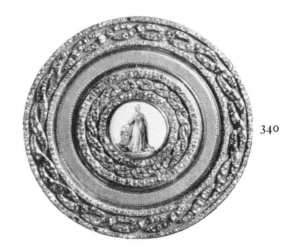

334 Gold and diamonds, with the monogram of the Empress Elizabeth. *Maker* Jérémie Pauzié (w. 1740–64). Russian (St Petersburg), *c.* 1745–50. *State Hermitage Museum, Leningrad.* **335** Gold and diamonds. *Maker* Johann Balthasar Gass (w. 1760–93). Russian (St Petersburg), *c.* 1770–5. *State Hermitage Museum, Leningrad.* **336, 337** Varicoloured gold. On the cover, a medallic portrait of Catherine II signed WÆCHTER; on the base, a medal commemorating the accession of the Empress in 1762. *Maker* Jean-Pierre Ador (w. 1770–85). Russian (St Petersburg), 1774. *Wartski, London.* There were two medallists named Waechter active in St Petersburg during Catherine's reign, Georg Christian (1729–89) and his brother, Johann Georg (1724–97). While both executed medals in honour of Catherine's accession in 1762, the medals on this box are probably by Georg Christian who is recorded as having executed several other medals commemorative of the Empress's reign. **338** Gold, set with precious stones and an enamel miniature. *Maker* Alexander Lang (w. 1773–7). Russian (St Petersburg), *c.* 1775. *State Hermitage Museum, Leningrad.* **339** Gold and diamonds, set with the monogram of Catherine II. *Maker* Jean-Jacques Duc (w. 1770–85). Russian (St Petersburg), *c.* 1775. *State Hermitage Museum, Leningrad.* **340** Gold and diamonds, with an enamel miniature set in the cover. *Maker* Johann Gottlieb Scharff (w. 1772–1808). Russian (St Petersburg), *c.* 1780. *State Hermitage Museum, Leningrad.*

341 Gold, engine-turned and enamelled, and studded with diamonds. On the cover, enamel miniature of *Le Ramoneur* after Jean-Baptiste Greuze (1725–1805). Russian (St Petersburg), 1781. *Musée du Louvre, Paris.* **342** Gold, engine-turned and enamelled. On the cover, enamel portrait of Louis XVI by Louis-Marie Sicard, signed and dated *Sicardy 1790. Maker* P.M.C. Russian (Moscow), *c.* 1790. *The Metropolitan Museum of Art.* **343** Gold, enamelled. On the cover, a scene of a royal musical party. Inscribed on the front rim, *Bouddé Saint-Petersburg. Maker* Jean-François Xavier Bouddé (w. 1769–after 1789). Russian (St Petersburg), *c.* 1790. *Musée du Louvre, Paris.* **344** Gold, enamelled. Russian (St Petersburg), 1800. **345, 346** Varicoloured gold. Inscribed *Kolb a St Petersburg. Maker* Johann Friedrich Kolb (w. 1806–24). Russian (St Petersburg), first quarter nineteenth century. *The Walters Art Gallery, Baltimore.* **347** Gold, set on the cover with a diamond-framed portrait of a man, signed B. Russian, *c.* 1830. *The Cleveland Museum of Art.*

348 Tortoiseshell, piqué and mounted in gold. On the cover, miniature of Charles III of Spain (1759–88) after the portrait of 1786 by Goya. The dog's collar is inscribed *Reyn Sc.* Probably Spanish, *c.* 1786. *Royal Scottish Museum, Edinburgh.* **349** Vari-coloured gold inset with enamel plaques. *Maker* A.P. Italian, *c.* 1770–5. *Victoria and Albert Museum, London.* **350** Gold, silver and agate. Italian(?), *c.* 1775. *Musée du Louvre, Paris.* **351** Tortoiseshell mounted in gold and set with an unidentified miniature. Probably Italian, beginning of the nineteenth century. *Museo Stibbert, Florence.* **352** Gold double box with thumbpiece. Possibly Czechoslovakian (Kaschau), 1800. *Private collection.* **353, 354** Gold. *Maker* Jacob Hurd (1702–58). American (Boston), *c.* 1725. *Museum of Fine Arts, Boston.* Engraved with the arms of William Dummer, Lt.-Governor of Massachusetts 1716–30, who bequeathed it to his nephew, William Powell, in 1756. Dummer was the son of the silver-smith Jeremiah Dummer and nephew of John Coney. **355** Gold. *Maker* Peckham & Grinell (w. 1839). American (New York), *c.* 1835. *Philip Hammerslough.*

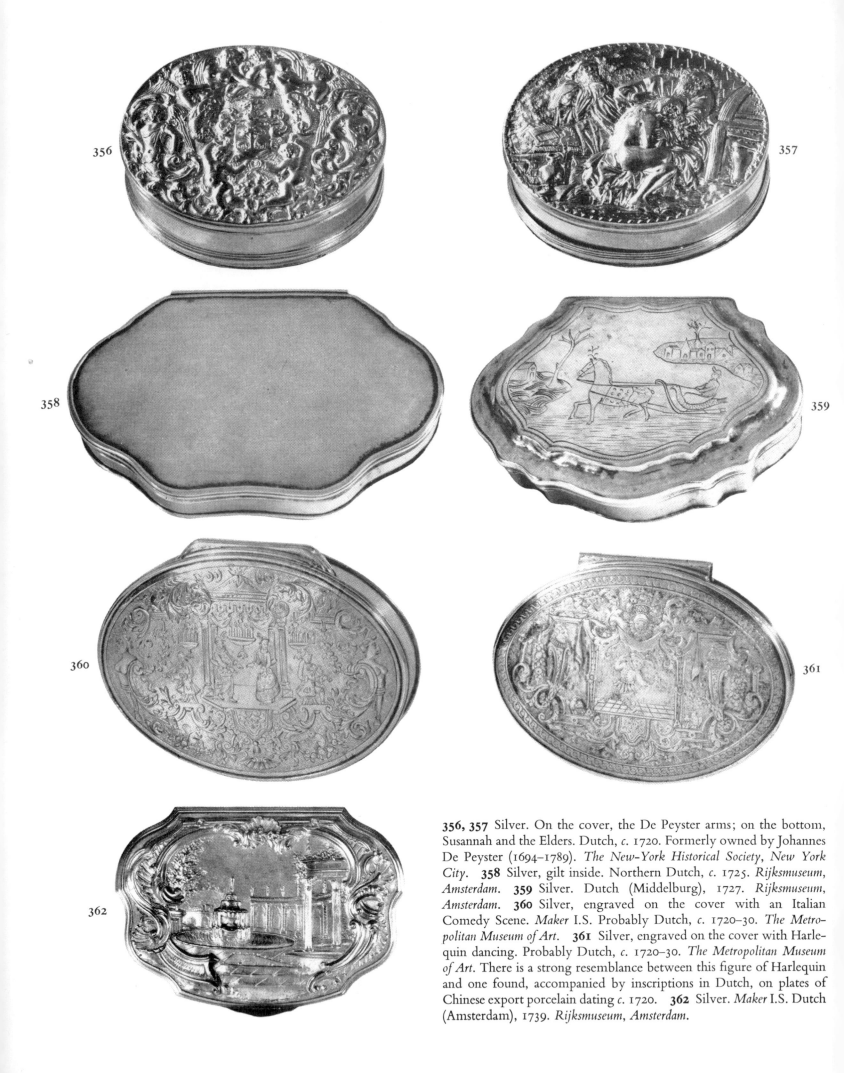

356, 357 Silver. On the cover, the De Peyster arms; on the bottom, Susannah and the Elders. Dutch, *c.* 1720. Formerly owned by Johannes De Peyster (1694–1789). *The New-York Historical Society, New York City.* **358** Silver, gilt inside. Northern Dutch, *c.* 1725. *Rijksmuseum, Amsterdam.* **359** Silver. Dutch (Middelburg), 1727. *Rijksmuseum, Amsterdam.* **360** Silver, engraved on the cover with an Italian Comedy Scene. *Maker* I.S. Probably Dutch, *c.* 1720–30. *The Metropolitan Museum of Art.* **361** Silver, engraved on the cover with Harlequin dancing. Probably Dutch, *c.* 1720–30. *The Metropolitan Museum of Art.* There is a strong resemblance between this figure of Harlequin and one found, accompanied by inscriptions in Dutch, on plates of Chinese export porcelain dating *c.* 1720. **362** Silver. *Maker* I.S. Dutch (Amsterdam), 1739. *Rijksmuseum, Amsterdam.*

363

363 Silver tobacco box engraved with the arms of Christopher Blakiston. *Maker* Soane or Soame. English (London), 1699–1700. *Master and Fellows of St John's College, Cambridge*. There was, at this early date, little distinction between snuff and tobacco boxes. In the absence of the former, this piece is included as stylistically representative of both types of box. **364** Silver. *Maker* David Willaume (w. 1710–31). English (London), 1709–10. *The Brooklyn Museum*. Engraved at a later date with the Royal arms as used from 1801 to 1816, and the inscription *To H.R.H. the Duke of Sussex*. Although unusually large (diam. 3¾ in.), especially for this early date, this may have been a table snuff box. **365** Silver-gilt double-lidded box. Engraved on the outer cover with the story of the Good Samaritan. On the inner cover, the arms of the Goldsmiths' Company. Inscribed *Jno. Derussat London, Fecit. 1756, and bequeathed it to the Worshipful Company of Goldsmiths*, 1807. *Maker* John Derussat (unrecorded). English (London), 1756. *The Worshipful Company of Goldsmiths, London*. **366** Silver, the lid set with mother-of-pearl. English, *c*. 1760. *The Metropolitan Museum of Art*. **367** Silver, the lid set with Egyptian jasper. English, *c*. 1760. *Castle Museum, Norwich*. This box and the preceding one are certainly of the same, probably provincial, provenance. **368** Silver, with shell lid. Inscribed on the base *Jeremiah Goold 1785*. English, *c*. 1785. *Castle Museum, Norwich*. **369** Silver-mounted Cypraea shell, the lid engraved with the monogram SH, and the inscription *Step^n Horst Hull*. English (probably Hull), *c*. 1790. *Castle Museum, Norwich*.

364

365

366

367

368

369

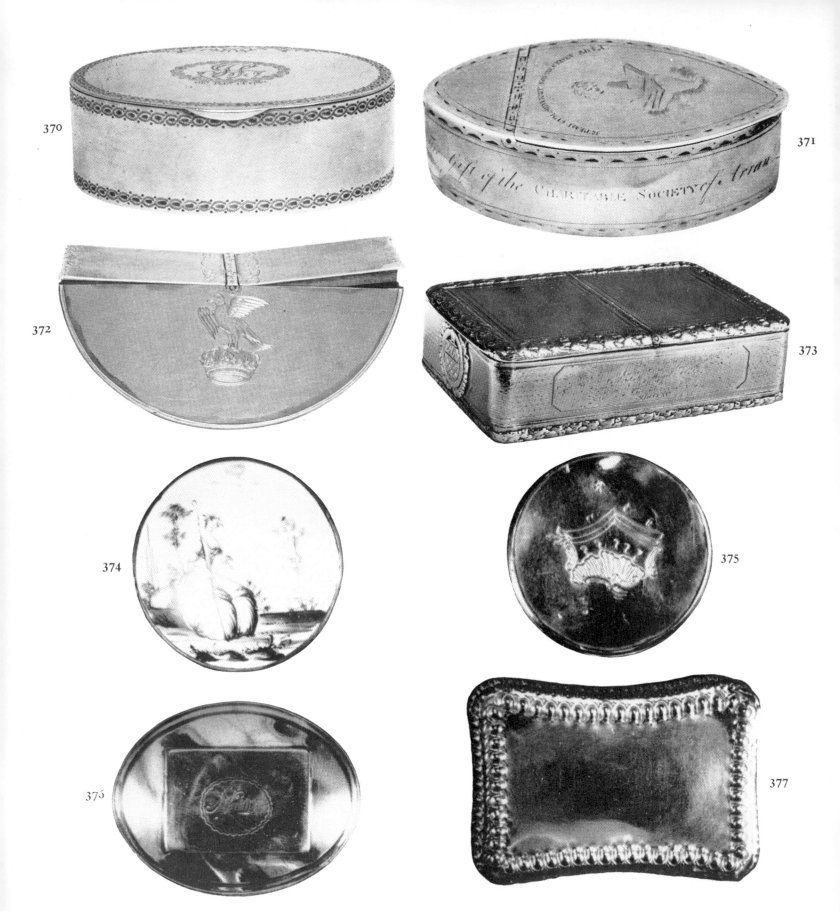

370 Silver, the cover engraved with the monogram IS and the inscription *Ob^t Feby 14. 1780. Maker* A.L. English(?), *c. 1780. The Metropolitan Museum of Art.* **371** Silver. Irish (Dublin), *c. 1794. Maker* James Keating. *The Metropolitan Museum of Art.* Inscribed *The Gift of the Charitable Society of Arran Quay Chapel to the Rev. Josh Charles Finn. A.D. 1794.* **372** Silver, gilt inside. English, 1790–1800. *The Metropolitan Museum of Art.* Engraved with an unidentified ducal crest. **373** Silver-gilt double box chased with the Waynflete arms and engraved with those of Berners. *Maker* A. J. Strachan. English (London), 1814–15. *Magdalen College, Oxford.* **374, 375** Silver plate, the cover set with an enamel plaque. English (Sheffield), *c. 1760. Sheffield City Museum.* **376** Silver plate, the inside tinned. English (Sheffield), *c. 1770. Sheffield City Museum.* **377** Silver plate. English (Sheffield), *c. 1785. Sheffield City Museum.* Owned, and probably made, by Joseph Wilson (1723–96), plater and snuff manufacturer. An associate of Thomas Boulsover, Wilson was also founder of Wilson's Snuff Mills, Sharrow, Sheffield; the 'No. 1' engraved on the cover of the box probably refers to a grade of snuff.

378, 379 Silver, the cover gilded on both sides. Unmarked. American (probably New York State), c. 1720. *The Henry Ford Museum, Dearborn, Michigan.* The body of the box is probably a replacement. The inscribed name is of Catherina De Peyster who married her kinsman, Abraham De Peyster, in 1684. **380, 381** Silver. *Maker S.R. Inscribed Ann: Parcivell: Her Box.* *1729.* American, c. 1729. *The Henry Ford Museum, Dearborn, Michigan.* **382** Silver. Unmarked. American, c. 1730. *The Brooklyn Museum.* **383** Silver, engraved with the Wentworth arms. *Maker* John Coney (1655–1722). American (Boston), c. 1720. *Yale University Art Gallery.* The arms are probably those of John Wentworth (1671–1730), Lieutenant-Governor, and later Acting Governor, of New Hampshire. **384** Silver. *Maker* Benjamin Brenton (1695–1749). American (Newport, R.I.), c. 1725. *Henry Francis du Pont Winterthur Museum.* **385** Silver. *Maker* Samuel Vernon (1685–1737). American (Newport, R.I.), c. 1725. *Philip Hammerslough.*

386 Silver. *Maker* A.C. American (Albany, N.Y.), c. 1735. *John Devereux Kernan*. The initials are said to be those of Catharyna Cuyler who married the silversmith Jacob Ten Eyck in 1736. **387** Silver. *Maker* William Huertin, Jr. (1703–71). American (probably New York City), c. 1740. *Philip Hammerslough*. Huertin, whose name has also been spelled Heurtin, became a freeman in New York in 1731 and later worked in Newark, N.J. **388** Silver. *Maker* Jacob Gerritse Lansing (1736–1803). American (Albany, N.Y.), c. 1760. *John Devereux Kernan*. **389** Silver. Unmarked. American (probably New England), c. 1750. *John Devereux Kernan*. **390** Silver. *Maker* William Whittemore (1710–70). American (Portsmouth, N.H.), c. 1740. *Henry Francis du Pont Winterthur Museum*. **391** Silver. *Maker* Barent Ten Eyck (1714–95). American (Albany, N.Y.), c. 1740. *Henry Francis du Pont Winterthur Museum*. **392** Silver. Unmarked. American, c. 1740. *Henry Francis du Pont Winterthur Museum*. **393** Silver. Unmarked. American (probably New England), c. 1770. *John Devereux Kernan*.

394, 395 Silver. Engraved on the bottom with the cipher MC, and inscribed inside the cover, *Gov! Dinwiddle to Mary Coates jun! 1757. Maker Joseph Richardson (1711–84). American (Philadelphia), 1757. Philadelphia Museum of Art.* Robert Dinwiddie (*c.* 1690–1770), was Colonial Governor of Virginia 1752–8. **396** Silver-mounted shell. *Maker Joseph Richardson.* American (Philadelphia), *c.* 1760. *Elliott Richardson, Jr.* **397** Silver-mounted cowrie shell. *Maker John Leacock (recorded 1748–59). American (Philadelphia), c. 1759. Philip Hammerslough.* **398** Silver. *Maker Daniel Dupuy (1719–1807). American (Philadelphia), c. 1770. Philip Hammerslough.* **399** Silver. *Maker William Whetcroft (1735–99). American (Annapolis, Md.), c. 1765. Philip Hammerslough.* **400** Silver, with agate base; gilt inside. Unmarked. American(?), *c.* 1765. *The Henry Ford Museum, Dearborn, Michigan.*

401 Silver, the cover and base of tortoiseshell. *Maker* Samuel Parmelee (1737–1807). American (Guilford, Conn.), 1775–1800.
Philip Hammerslough.   402 Silver mounted cowrie shell. *Maker* Paul Revere (1735–1818). American (Boston), *c.* 1780.
Philip Hammerslough.   403, 404 Silver-mounted cowrie shell. Unmarked. American (attributed to Norfolk, Va.), *c.* 1800.
Norfolk Museum.   405 Silver, inscribed with the name of Abraham Van Nest (1777–1864). Unmarked. American, early
nineteenth century. *The New-York Historical Society, New York City.*   406 Silver-mounted horn. Inscribed *The owners of
the Hero Grateful present this to Cap! Wm Cuthbert 1802. Maker* Jacob Jennings (1739–1817). American (Norwalk, Conn.),
1802. *Philip Hammerslough.*   407 Silver. Unmarked. American(?), *c.* 1800. *The Henry Ford Museum, Dearborn, Michigan.*
408 Silver. Inscribed with the name of Dr Joseph White (1763–1832), a President of the New York State Medical Society.
Maker Shepherd and Boyd (w. 1806–1829/30). American (Albany, N.Y.), *c.* 1810. *Philip Hammerslough.*

409 Silver gilt. *Maker* Laurent Amiot (1764–1839). Canadian (Quebec), *c.* 1790. *Paul Gouin.* **410** Silver. *Maker* James Godfrey Hanna (1780–1851). Canadian (Quebec), *c.* 1810. *Musée de la Province, Quebec.* **411** Silver. *Maker* François Sasseville (1797–1864). Canadian (Quebec), *c.* 1825. *Musée de la Province, Quebec.* **412, 413** Silver, gilt inside. French (Lille), probably 1730. *The Henry Ford Museum, Dearborn, Michigan.* Formerly owned by Francis Lewis (1713–1802), a signer of the Declaration of Independence. The box is struck with a defaced maker's mark of which the letters are possibly PI (or J) F. **414** Silver. French (Paris), 1727–32. *Musée du Louvre, Paris.* **415** Silver gilt. French (Paris), 1737–8. *A La Vieille Russie, New York.*

416 Silver. *Maker* Antoine Daroux (m. 1735, d. 1789). French (Paris), 1745–6. *The Metropolitan Museum of Art.* 417 Silver gilt. *Maker* Antoine Daroux. French (Paris), 1755–6. *The Metropolitan Museum of Art.* 418 Silver, set with plaques of black lacquer inlaid with tinted mother-of-pearl. *Maker* Antoine Daroux. French (Paris), 1743–4. *A La Vieille Russie, New York.* 419 Silver, set with plaques of inlaid mother-of-pearl. *Maker* C(?).I(or T). French (Paris), 1768–75. *The Brooklyn Museum.* The mounts bear a date later than the style of the box would suggest and are perhaps a replacement. 420 Silver, partly gilt. *Maker* Gabriel Vougny (m. 1719, d. 1752). French (Paris), 1748–9. *Private collection.* The battle scenes are perhaps allusive to the War of Austrian Succession (1740–8). 421 Silver, the trophies of varicoloured gold. *Maker* Louis Charonnat (m. 1748, retired 1780). French (Paris), 1760–1. *A La Vieille Russie, New York.* 422 Silver, the reserved scenes of varicoloured gold. *Maker* Charles Le Bastier. French (Paris), 1760–1. *The Metropolitan Museum of Art.*

423 Silver. Continental, c. 1725. *Museo Nazionale, Naples.*
424 Silver, Probably Swedish, c. 1735. *Röhsska Konstslöjdmuseet, Göteborg.* 425 Silver. Probably Swedish, dated 1766. *Röhsska Konstslöjdmuseet, Göteborg.* 426 Silver. *Maker* F(?).P. Italian (probably Padua), c. 1750. *The Metropolitan Museum of Art.* 427 Silver, enamelled and set with plaques of moss agate. The interior is gilded. German(?), c. 1770. *The Metropolitan Museum of Art.* 428, 429, 430 Silver, with decoration in niello. *Maker* A. S. Popoff (unrecorded). Russian, dated 1769. *The Walters Art Gallery, Baltimore.*

431 Silver, with niello maps of northern Siberia on the cover and base. On the cover, the western half; the island at the upper left is Novaya Zemlya. Russian (Moscow), *c.* 1780. *The Metropolitan Museum of Art.* **432** Silver, with niello decoration. Russian (Moscow), 1784. *The Metropolitan Museum of Art.* **433** Silver, gilt inside. Swiss (Zürich), *c.* 1820. *Schweizersches Landesmuseum, Zürich.* **434** Brass. Dutch, 1700–25. *Museo del Palazzo di Venezia, Rome.* **435** Steel. English, dated 1735. *Museum of the City of New York.* **436** Brass. English, 1725–50. *Colonial Williamsburg, Virginia.*

437 Steel. German, c. 1750. *Musée Le Secq des Tournelles, Rouen.* **438** Steel. German, c. 1755. *Musée Le Secq des Tournelles, Rouen.* **439** Brass. English (probably Birmingham), c. 1775. *The Metropolitan Museum of Art.* **440** Pewter. English, c. 1750(?). *Colonial Williamsburg, Virginia.* **441** Pewter. English or Continental, c. 1800. *Colonial Williamsburg, Virginia.* **442** Pewter. Probably Continental, c. 1800. *Colonial Williamsburg, Virginia.* **443** Pewter. English, early nineteenth century. *Colonial Williamsburg, Virginia.* **444** Pewter. English, c. 1815. *Colonial Williamsburg, Virginia.*

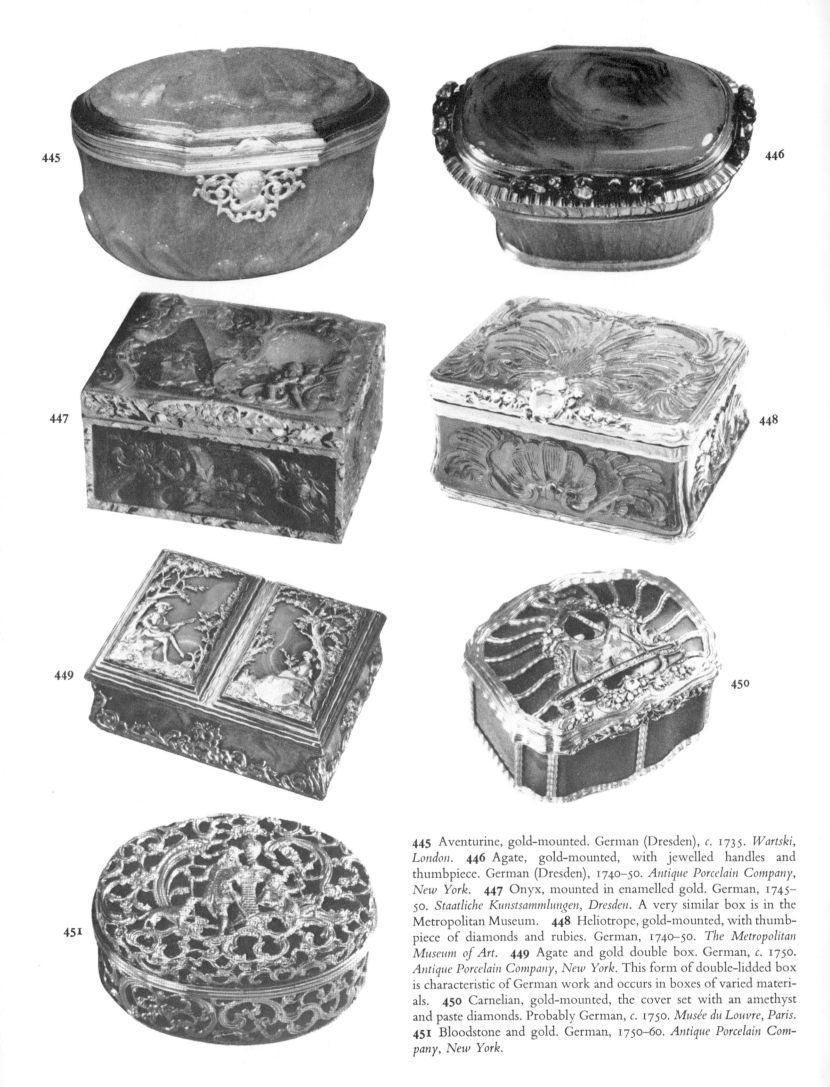

445 Aventurine, gold-mounted. German (Dresden), *c.* 1735. *Wartski, London.* 446 Agate, gold-mounted, with jewelled handles and thumbpiece. German (Dresden), 1740–50. *Antique Porcelain Company, New York.* 447 Onyx, mounted in enamelled gold. German, 1745–50. *Staatliche Kunstsammlungen, Dresden.* A very similar box is in the Metropolitan Museum. 448 Heliotrope, gold-mounted, with thumbpiece of diamonds and rubies. German, 1740–50. *The Metropolitan Museum of Art.* 449 Agate and gold double box. German, *c.* 1750. *Antique Porcelain Company, New York.* This form of double-lidded box is characteristic of German work and occurs in boxes of varied materials. 450 Carnelian, gold-mounted, the cover set with an amethyst and paste diamonds. Probably German, *c.* 1750. *Musée du Louvre, Paris.* 451 Bloodstone and gold. German, 1750–60. *Antique Porcelain Company, New York.*

452 Amethyst quartz and gold. English, 1750–60. Ex coll. René Fribourg. **453** Puddingstone and gold. German, 1750–60. **454** Striated agate mounted in gold. English, c. 1765. *Wartski, London.* **455** Bloodstone, mounted in enamelled gold. German, c. 1755. *The Metropolitan Museum of Art.* **456** Agate, mounted in enamelled gold. On the cover, portrait of Henriette Duchesse d'Orléans, after Jean Petitot. Probably German, c. 1750. *The Art Institute of Chicago.* **457** Rock crystal mounted in gold with thumbpiece of paste diamonds. Probably German, c. 1750. *Wallace Collection, London.* **458** Jasper, with applied gold decoration, gold rims and thumbpiece of paste jewels. *Maker* I.W.S. Austrian (Vienna), 1774. *Antique Porcelain Company, New York.*

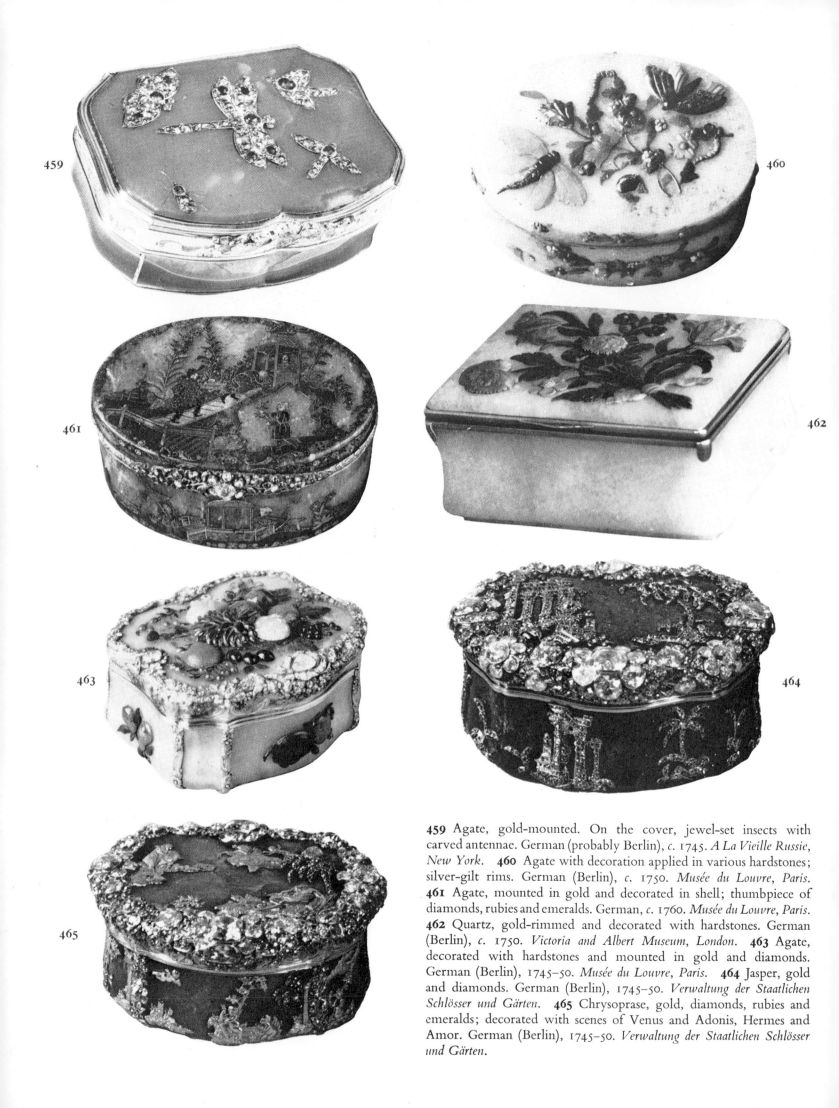

459 Agate, gold-mounted. On the cover, jewel-set insects with carved antennae. German (probably Berlin), c. 1745. *A La Vieille Russie, New York.* **460** Agate with decoration applied in various hardstones; silver-gilt rims. German (Berlin), c. 1750. *Musée du Louvre, Paris.* **461** Agate, mounted in gold and decorated in shell; thumbpiece of diamonds, rubies and emeralds. German, c. 1760. *Musée du Louvre, Paris.* **462** Quartz, gold-rimmed and decorated with hardstones. German (Berlin), c. 1750. *Victoria and Albert Museum, London.* **463** Agate, decorated with hardstones and mounted in gold and diamonds. German (Berlin), 1745–50. *Musée du Louvre, Paris.* **464** Jasper, gold and diamonds. German (Berlin), 1745–50. *Verwaltung der Staatlichen Schlösser und Gärten.* **465** Chrysoprase, gold, diamonds, rubies and emeralds; decorated with scenes of Venus and Adonis, Hermes and Amor. German (Berlin), 1745–50. *Verwaltung der Staatlichen Schlösser und Gärten.*

466–470 Chrysoprase, varicoloured gold and diamonds. German (Berlin), c. 1745. *A La Vieille Russie, New York.*
471 Chrysoprase, gold and diamonds. Designed by John William George Kruger (b. 1728) for Frederick II of Prussia. German (Berlin), c. 1750. *Verwaltung der Staatlichen Schlösser und Gärten.*

472

473

474

475

476

477

478

479

472 Hardstone, mounted in gold. On the cover, an enamelled pearl-bordered bouquet. *Maker* Johann Christian Neuber (m. 1762, d. 1808). German (Dresden), *c.* 1775. *Royal Scottish Museum, Edinburgh.* Accompanying the box is a small book entitled *Spécification d'une Tabattière composé d'un Cabinet des Pierres dans la quelle on trouve LXXVIII pièces des pierres précieuses qui se trouve dans l'Electorat de Saxe. Faite par Jean Chretien Neuber.* **473** Hardstone, gold and enamel with pearl-bordered rosette on the cover. *Maker* probably Johann Christian Neuber. German (Dresden), *c.* 1775. *Musée Cognacq-Jay, Paris.* **474** Hardstone, mounted in gold. *Maker* Christian Gottlieb Stiehl (*c.* 1708–92). German (Dresden), 1775. *Musée du Louvre, Paris.* **475** Hardstone and simulated pearls. On the cover, miniature on ivory of Marie Antoinette. German (Dresden), *c.* 1780. *Victoria and Albert Museum, London.* **476** Agate, gold-mounted and inset with an enamel portrait miniature framed in diamonds. *Maker* probably Johann Christian Neuber. German (Dresden), *c.* 1775. *Wartski, London.* **477** Hardstone and gold. On the cover, a Meissen porcelain plaque. *Maker* Johann Christian Neuber. German (Dresden), *c.* 1785. *Wartski, London.* The trellis pattern is inlaid directly into the quartzite body of the box. **478** Hardstone, gold-mounted. German (Dresden), 1780–90. *Antique Porcelain Company, New York.* Around the bottom rim are engraved numbers from 1 to 16 suggesting that the mounts were originally intended for a box with a radiating pattern of hardstones. **479** Jasper, gold-mounted. German, 1780–90. *Musée Nissim de Camondo, Paris.*

480 Moss agate double box with gold mounts. *Maker* Noël Hardivilliers. French (Paris), 1737–8. *The Walters Art Gallery, Baltimore.*
481 Bloodstone, gold-mounted. French (Paris), 1738–44. *Victoria and Albert Museum, London.* **482** Sardonyx, mounted in chased and enamelled gold. French (Paris), 1743–4. *Musée du Louvre, Paris.*
483 Carnelian, with enamelled gold mounts. French (Paris), 1753–4. *Musée du Louvre, Paris.* **484** Rock crystal, mounted in enamelled gold. French (Paris), *c.* 1780. *Wartski, London.* **485** Malachite, gold-mounted. On the cover, a plaque of petrified wood decorated with varied hardstones. *Maker* Adrien-Jean-Maximilien Vachette. French (Paris), 1789. *Musée du Louvre, Paris.* **486** Gold, with mosaic hardstone panels. Italian, first half nineteenth century. *Royal Scottish Museum, Edinburgh.*

480

481

482

483

484

485

486

487 Porcelain, gold-mounted. Painted by Christian Friedrich Herold (1700–79). German (Meissen), *c.* 1735. *Victoria and Albert Museum, London.* **488** Porcelain, gold-mounted. German (Meissen), *c.* 1735. *State Hermitage Museum, Leningrad.* **489** Porcelain, gold-mounted. German (Meissen), *c.* 1735. *State Hermitage Museum, Leningrad.* **490** Porcelain, gold-mounted. Painted by Christian Friedrich Herold. German (Meissen), 1735–40. *Victoria and Albert Museum, London.* **491** Porcelain, gold-mounted. German (Meissen), 1735–40. *Antique Porcelain Company, New York.* **492** Porcelain, gold-mounted. German (Meissen), *c.* 1740. *Antique Porcelain Company, New York.*

493, 494 Porcelain, gold-mounted. On the cover is a view of Meissen showing the Albrechtsburg fortress in which the porcelain factory was established. German (Meissen), 1735–40. *Victoria and Albert Museum, London.* 495, 496 Porcelain, gold-mounted. German (Meissen), *c.* 1750. 497 Porcelain, silver-mounted. Painted by Christian Friedrich Herold. German (Meissen), 1745–50. *Cecil Higgins Art Gallery, Bedford.* 498 Porcelain, gold-mounted. Decorated by Johann Martin Heinrici (1711–86). German (Meissen), 1745–50. *The Metropolitan Museum of Art.*

499 Porcelain, with gilt-metal mounts. German (Meissen), c. 1750. **500** Porcelain, gold-mounted. German (Meissen), c. 1750. *Museo Nazionale, Naples.* The subject of the painting inside the cover may have been the source of similar compositions by Robert Hancock in England. **501** Porcelain, gold-mounted; painted with views of Dresden. German (Meissen), c. 1750. Ex coll. A. Chester Beatty. **502** Porcelain, with silver-gilt mounts. Painted with scenes of Saxon miners attributed to Bonaventura Gottlieb Häuer (1710–82). German (Meissen), c. 1760. **503** Porcelain, gold-mounted and painted with Italian Comedy figures. German (Meissen), c. 1760. Ex coll. René Fribourg.

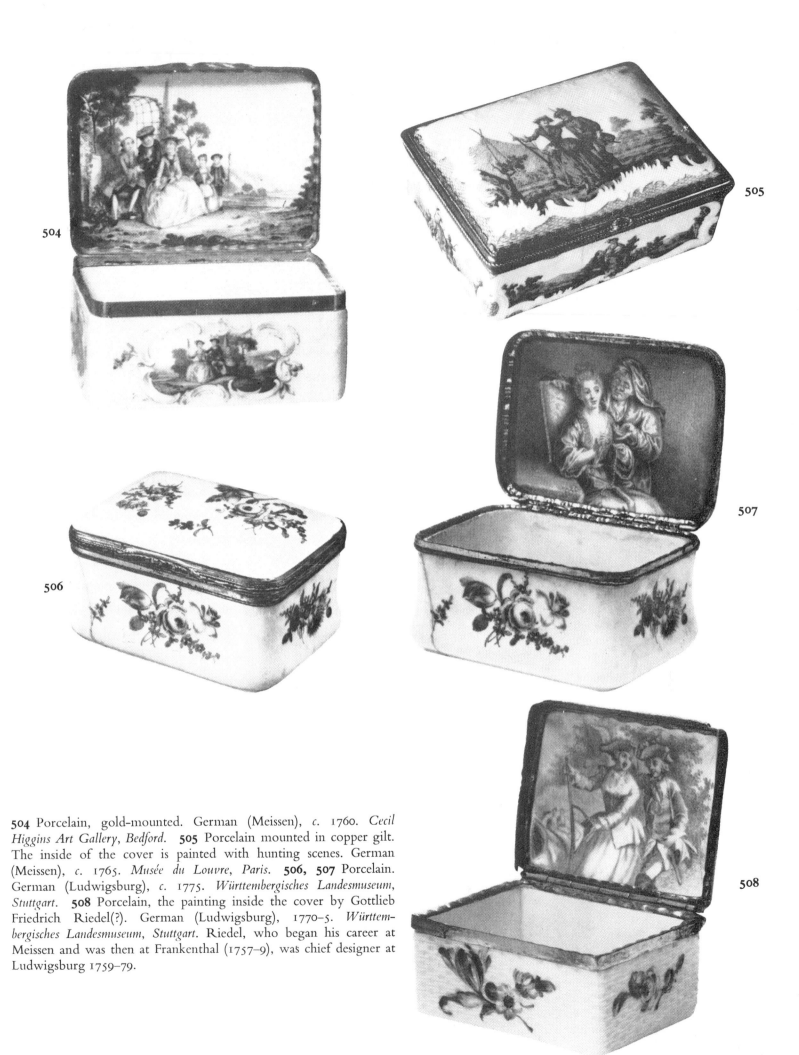

504 Porcelain, gold-mounted. German (Meissen), c. 1760. *Cecil Higgins Art Gallery, Bedford.* 505 Porcelain mounted in copper gilt. The inside of the cover is painted with hunting scenes. German (Meissen), c. 1765. *Musée du Louvre, Paris.* 506, 507 Porcelain. German (Ludwigsburg), c. 1775. *Württembergisches Landesmuseum, Stuttgart.* 508 Porcelain, the painting inside the cover by Gottlieb Friedrich Riedel(?). German (Ludwigsburg), 1770–5. *Württembergisches Landesmuseum, Stuttgart.* Riedel, who began his career at Meissen and was then at Frankenthal (1757–9), was chief designer at Ludwigsburg 1759–79.

509 Porcelain double box lacking its mounts and covers. German (Berlin?), *c.* 1750. *Cecil Higgins Art Gallery, Bedford.* The figure was possibly inspired by Watteau's *Italian Entertainment*, acquired by Frederick II in 1750, in which it appears reversed, with variations in the details of the costume and instrument. **510** Porcelain. German (Frankenthal), *c.* 1750. *Museo Nazionale, Naples.* **511** Porcelain. On the cover, a raised portrait bust of Charles I, Duke of Brunswick; inside, a variety of symbols including a coffeepot, cup and saucer, artists' and gardening tools and a figure of Time. German (Furstenberg), 1750–60. *The Metropolitan Museum of Art.* **512** Porcelain. German (Nymphenburg), *c.* 1760. *Museo Nazionale, Naples.* **513, 514** Two porcelain boxes with relief portraits of Maximilian III of Bavaria. German (Nymphenburg), 1765–70. *Antique Porcelain Company, New York* (**513**).

515 Porcelain, silver-mounted. German, *c.* 1730. *Landesgewerbeamt Baden-Württemberg, Stuttgart.* 516 Porcelain box lid. On the exterior, a harbour scene in the style of C. F. Herold; inside, an unidentified portrait. German (Kelsterbach), *c.* 1765. *Grossherzogliche Privatsammlung, Darmstadt.* 517 Porcelain. German (Kelsterbach), *c.* 1766. *Grossherzogliche Privatsammlung, Darmstadt.* 518 Porcelain. German (Kelsterbach), *c.* 1766. *Grossherzogliche Privatsammlung, Darmstadt.* 519 Porcelain. German (Kelsterbach), *c.* 1766. *Grossherzogliche Privatsammlung, Darmstadt.* 520 Porcelain. German (Kelsterbach), *c.* 1767. *Grossherzogliche Privatsammlung, Darmstadt.*

521 Porcelain, with raised gilded and painted decoration. French (Saint-Cloud), c. 1730. *Musée des Arts Décoratifs, Paris.*
522 Porcelain, the chinoiseries painted on a yellow ground. French (Saint-Cloud), c. 1730. *Musée des Arts Décoratifs, Paris.*
523 Porcelain. French (Saint-Cloud), 1730–40. *Musée des Arts Décoratifs, Paris.* 524 Porcelain. French (Chantilly), 1730–40. *Antique Porcelain Company, New York.* 525 Porcelain. French (Chantilly), 1730–40. *Antique Porcelain Company, New York.*
526 Porcelain, with Paris silver mounts of 1738–9. French (Chantilly), c. 1738. *Victoria and Albert Museum, London.* Figural boxes of this type were probably used more for sweetmeats than for snuff (see p. 10). This figure is known in several versions, each slightly different in details of position and colouring.

527 Porcelain, mounted in silver (originally gilt). French (Chantilly), c. 1745. *The Metropolitan Museum of Art.* 528 Porcelain, mounted in silver gilt. French (Mennecy), 1740–5. *The Metropolitan Museum of Art.* 529 Porcelain double box with Paris silver mounts dated 1750–6. French (Mennecy), c. 1750. *The Metropolitan Museum of Art.* 530 Porcelain, with Paris silver mounts dated 1750–6. French (Mennecy), c. 1755. *The Metropolitan Museum of Art.* 531 Porcelain. French (Mennecy), c. 1750. *Mrs Harvey A. Firestone, Jr.* 532 Porcelain. French (Mennecy), c. 1760. *Mrs Harvey A. Firestone, Jr.*

533

533 Porcelain, with carved rock crystal cover. French (Mennecy), 1760–5. Ex coll. Mrs Henry Walters. *The Metropolitan Museum of Art.* 534, 535 Porcelain, with Paris gold mounts dated 1750–1. French (Vincennes), 1750–1. *Mrs Harvey A. Firestone, Jr.* 536 Porcelain. French (Vincennes), c. 1750. *Cahiers de la Céramique du Verre et des Arts du Feu, Sèvres.* 537 Porcelain, with Paris gold mounts dated 1784–5. French (Sèvres), c. 1784. Ex coll. René Fribourg. 538 Porcelain. French (Sèvres), c. 1780. *Museo Nazionale, Naples.* 539 Porcelain. French (Sèvres), early nineteenth century. *Museo Nazionale, Naples.*

540, 541 Porcelain. Italian, *c.* 1740. **542** Porcelain. Italian (Doccia), 1740–60. *State Hermitage Museum, Leningrad.* **543** Porcelain. Italian (Capodimonte), *c.* 1745–50. *Museo Nazionale, Naples.* **544** Porcelain, gold-mounted. Italian (Capodimonte), 1750–5. *The Metropolitan Museum of Art.* **545** Porcelain. Italian (Venice), *c.* 1760. *Museo Nazionale, Naples.* **546** Porcelain. Italian (Venice), late eighteenth century. *Museo Nazionale, Naples.*

547 Porcelain. Italian (Naples), late eighteenth century. *Museo Nazionale, Naples.* 548 Porcelain. Italian (Naples), early nineteenth century. *Museo Nazionale, Naples.* 549 Porcelain. On the cover, a portrait of Ferdinand IV of Naples (1751–1825), who reigned (with the title of Ferdinand I) as King of the Two Sicilies from 1816. Italian (Naples), *c.* 1816. *Museo Nazionale, Naples.* 550, 551 Porcelain, Spanish (Buen Retiro), *c.* 1760–70. *Museo Arqueológico Nacional, Madrid.* 552, 553 Porcelain. Spanish (Buen Retiro), *c.* 1760–70. *Museo Arqueológico Nacional, Madrid.*

554 Porcelain. Russian (St Petersburg), 1752. *State Hermitage Museum, Leningrad.* 555 Porcelain, gold-mounted. Russian (St Petersburg), *c.* 1755. *State Hermitage Museum, Leningrad.* 556 Porcelain, gold-mounted. Russian (St Petersburg), *c.* 1760. *State Hermitage Museum, Leningrad.* 557 Porcelain. Russian (St Petersburg), *c.* 1760. *State Hermitage Museum, Leningrad.* The shape is undoubtedly copied from Mennecy porcelain; it is also known in English enamel. 558 Porcelain. Russian (St Petersburg), 1760–5. *State Hermitage Museum, Leningrad.* 559 Porcelain, gold-mounted. Russian (St Petersburg), *c.* 1760. *State Hermitage Museum, Leningrad.*

560 Porcelain 'envelope' box. Inscribed on the cover, A MADAME, MADAME DE N . . . A SON LOGIS. Russian (St Petersburg), *c.* 1760. Ex coll. Blohm. **561** Porcelain 'envelope' box. Inscribed on the cover, A SON EXCELLENCE MADAME LA COMTESSE DE FIEVERS NEE DE KROUS: A BELL ACOMPAGNA. Russian (St Petersburg), *c.* 1760. Ex coll. Blohm. **562** Porcelain. Swiss (Zürich), *c.* 1770–80. *Schweizerisches Landesmuseum, Zürich.* **563** Porcelain. Swiss (Zürich), *c.* 1770–80. *Schweizerisches Landesmuseum, Zürich.* **564** Porcelain. Swiss (Zürich), *c.* 1785. *Schweizerisches Landesmuseum, Zürich.* **565** Enamelled earthenware. English (Bristol), 1763. *Glaisher Bequest, The Fitzwilliam Museum, Cambridge.* **566** Lead-glazed earthenware, with screw lid. On the cover, a portrait of John Wilkes (1727–97). Incised inside the cover, *Samuel Bawl, 1769.* English (Leeds), 1768–9. *Glaisher Bequest, The Fitzwilliam Museum, Cambridge.* The box was probably a souvenir of the Middlesex elections of 1768 in which Wilkes—the exiled politician and founder of the newspaper *The North Briton*—was thrice victor over his opposition and thrice denied his seat by the House of Commons.

567 Enamel. German, *c.* 1725–30. *Museo Nazionale, Naples.* **568** Enamel. German (Berlin), *c.* 1730. Ex coll. Blohm. **569** Enamel. German (Berlin), *c.* 1735. Ex coll. René Fribourg. *A La Vieille Russie, New York.* **570** Silver, the cover of enamelled copper. Decorated by Christian Friedrich Herold, signed *Herold fecit*. German, *c.* 1730–5. *British Museum.* In a discussion of Herold's career as a *Hausmaler* whilst at the Meissen factory, Hugh Tait (*British Museum Quarterly*, XXV, 1962) offers this piece as an example of his outside work executed shortly after his establishment at Dresden in 1726. **571** Silver, the cover of enamelled copper. Decoration attributed to Christian Friedrich Herold. German, *c.* 1740. *The Cooper Union Museum, New York.* **572** Enamel. Decorated in the style of Christian Friedrich Herold. German, *c.* 1740. **573** Enamel cane handle with a hinged snuff compartment. On the cover, a harbour scene in the style of Christian Friedrich Herold. German, *c.* 1740–5. Ex coll. Blohm.

574 Enamel double box. German(?), mounted in Paris silver rims dated 1744–50. *The Brooklyn Museum, New York.* **575** Enamel. Continental, *c.* 1745. *Museo Nazionale, Naples.* **576** Enamel. On the cover, Tobias and the Angel. German, *c.* 1740–5. *Victoria and Albert Museum, London.* **577** Enamel, painted with a battle plan of the Potsdam region. The map is drawn with north at the front of the box. German, *c.* 1760. *Antique Porcelain Company, New York.* **578** Enamel. Decorated with a portrait of Frederick the Great surrounded by the names of his victorious battles in the first two Silesian and Seven Years Wars. The latest date is that of the battle of Zorndorf (25 August 1758). German, *c.* 1758. *Antique Porcelain Company, New York.* **579, 580** Enamel, with Paris silver-gilt mounts dated 1748–9. *The Cleveland Museum of Art.* Of French enamel boxes little is known. It is likely that the enamel bodies of most boxes with Parisian mounts were German, made for the French market, e.g., **574** which combines a Parisian motif (*cf.* **15**) with the characteristically German form of double lid. The oddly graceful decoration of this box, however, seems more akin to French work.

581, 582 Gold-mounted enamel 'envelope' box with a portrait inside the lid of Crown Prince Christian (later Christian VII) by Josias Brecheisen (w. 1757–63). Danish (Copenhagen), *c.* 1760. *Rosenborg Castle, Copenhagen.* **583, 584** Gold-mounted enamel 'envelope' box with a portrait inside the lid of Prince Frederick, brother of Christian VII, by Josias Brecheisen. Danish (Copenhagen), *c.* 1760. *Rosenborg Castle, Copenhagen.* This box and the preceding one were made as a pair for the father of the brothers, Frederick V. **585, 586** Enamel, mounted in silver. Inside the cover, a portrait of Frederick II of Prussia. Decorated by Josias Brecheisen, signed and dated (on the tablet on the front of the box) *Brecheisen a Kopenhage 1757.* Danish (Copenhagen), 1757. *Rosenborg Castle, Copenhagen.*

587, 588 Enamel, with monochrome transfer-printed decoration. On the cover, *Paris Awarding the Apple to Hibernia*, engraved by Simon-François Ravenet (1706–74) after James Gwim. Inside the cover, a portrait of Maria Gunning, Countess of Coventry, attributed to John Brooks after a painting (1751) by Francis Cotes. English (Battersea), 1753–6. *Raby Bequest, Manchester City Art Gallery*. 589, 590 Enamel, with painted decoration. On the cover, a battle scene; inside, a portrait of the Empress Elizabeth of Russia. English, c. 1760. *Raby Bequest, Manchester City Art Gallery*. The battle scene appears to represent a victory of the English over Russia during the Seven Years War (the inscription is unintelligible). 591 Enamel, transfer-printed and over-painted. On the cover, an adaptation by Robert Hancock (1730–1817) of Boucher's *Pensent-ils au raisin* painted (and also engraved by J. P. LeBas) in 1747. English (Battersea), 1753–6. *Victoria and Albert Museum, London*. 592 Enamel, with painted decoration. English (Battersea), 1753–6. *Victoria and Albert Museum, London*. 593 Carved mother-of-pearl, the enamel lid with painted decoration. English, the lid Battersea, 1753–6. *Cecil Higgins Art Gallery, Bedford*.

594 Enamel, printed in black, with an almanac for 1759. Inscribed, *Made by Anth. Tregent in Denmark Street*. English (London), 1759. *Victoria and Albert Museum, London*. 595 Enamel, printed in black with songs and musical instruments. English (probably London), *c.* 1760. *The Metropolitan Museum of Art*. Variants of this box, in the Schreiber and Ionides collections, also bear a portrait of Mrs Brooks, wife of John Brooks the engraver at Battersea. 596 Enamel, printed in black. On the cover, an adaptation of an engraving by P. Aveline of Boucher's *La Bonne Aventure*; on the front, an allegory of Britannia. English (probably London), *c.* 1761. *Victoria and Albert Museum, London*. The dating is suggested by the fact that the same allegorical vignette occurs on a box commemorating the marriage of George III and Queen Charlotte. 597 Enamel, printed in purple. On the cover, an adaptation of *Les Amours Pastorales*, engraved by Claude Duflos after Boucher. On the sides, pastoral scenes; on the bottom, a girl blowing bubbles. English (South Staffordshire), *c.* 1760. *Victoria and Albert Museum, London*. 598 Enamel, with painted decoration. On the cover, an Italian Comedy Scene. English, *c.* 1755–60. *Cecil Higgins Art Gallery, Bedford*. 599 Enamel, with painted decoration. English (South Staffordshire), *c.* 1760. *Victoria and Albert Museum, London*. 600 Enamel, with painted decoration. English (South Staffordshire), *c.* 1765. *Victoria and Albert Museum, London*.

601 Enamel double box, with painted decoration. Inside each lid, a scene of amorous pug dogs. English, *c.* 1760. *The Cooper Union Museum, New York*. Both the shape of the box and its decoration are imitative of German examples dating *c.* 1750–5. Curiously, pug dogs—which were in fashion in England from 1688 when they were introduced by William III—do not appear on English porcelain and enamel as they do in Germany where they became the vogue *c.* 1750. The scenes on this box thus represent an amusing 'borrowing' of a native taste. **602** Enamel, with painted decoration. English (South Staffordshire), *c.* 1760–70. *The Metropolitan Museum of Art*. The scenes of water birds are in the style of, and possibly copied after, Charles Fenn. Two volumes of his designs have not been traced; some were published by Robert Sayer in 1757 and 1760 (*The Ladies Amusement*). **603** Enamel, with painted decoration. On the cover, a portrait of John Wilkes after an engraving (1754) by James Watson of a painting by Robert Edge Pine. On the sides, landscape reserves. English (South Staffordshire), *c.* 1763. *Victoria and Albert Museum, London*. **604** Enamel, printed and painted. On the cover, a scene adapted from the title vignette to the song 'My Grandmother's Cot', published in *Clio and Euterpe* (1758). English (South Staffordshire), *c.* 1760–70. *The Metropolitan Museum of Art*. **605** Enamel, printed and painted. On the cover, *Le Matin*, after a painting by Nicolas Lancret (1690–1743) engraved by Nicolas de Larmessin. The sides and bottom are painted with vignettes from *The Ladies Amusement* and with a variation of Boucher's *Pensent-ils au raisin*. English (South Staffordshire), *c.* 1765–75. *Victoria and Albert Museum, London*.

606 Enamel, printed and painted. On the cover, *Les Amants*, from an engraving (1751) of a painting by Jean-Marc Nattier (1685–1766). On the sides, vignettes from *The Ladies Amusement* (1760). English (South Staffordshire), *c.* 1765–75. *Raby Bequest, Manchester City Art Gallery.* **607** Enamel, with painted decoration. On the cover, a fortune-telling scene; on the sides, landscapes. English (South Staffordshire), *c.* 1765–75. *Beauchamp Galleries, London.* **608** Enamel, printed and painted. On the front is a view of the Thames near Twickenham; the domed building is the Orleans House Octagon built by James Gibbs in 1730. English (South Staffordshire), *c.* 1770–5. *Victoria and Albert Museum, London.* **609** Enamel, printed and painted. On the cover, *L'Après Dîner*, after Nicolas de Larmessin's engraving of a painting by Lancret. English (South Staffordshire), *c.* 1770–80. *The Metropolitan Museum of Art.* **610** Enamel, printed and painted. English (South Staffordshire), *c.* 1765–75. *The Metropolitan Museum of Art.* **611** Enamel, printed and painted. English (South Staffordshire), *c.* 1765–75. *The Metropolitan Museum of Art.*

612 Enamel, with painted decoration. English (South Staffordshire), *c.* 1770–80. *The Metropolitan Museum of Art.* A luminous blue-grey background and unusually subtle technique characterise these still lifes which occur, with variations, on several boxes. **613** Enamel, printed and painted. English (South Staffordshire), *c.* 1770–80. *The Metropolitan Museum of Art.* **614** Enamel, with painted decoration. English (Bilston), *c.* 1770. *Castle Museum, Norwich.* **615** Enamel, with painted decoration. English (Bilston), *c.* 1780. *Cecil Higgins Museum, Bedford.* **616** Enamel, with painted decoration. English (South Staffordshire), *c.* 1775–85. *The Metropolitan Museum of Art.* **617** Enamel, English, made for the American market, *c.* 1765. *Museum of the City of New York.* Evert Bancker (1721–1803) was a New York merchant who, from 1769 to the Revolution, was a major supplier for English troops and also barrackmaster for New York City.

618 Tortoiseshell, mounted and *piqué* in silver. Probably Continental, early eighteenth century. *The Metropolitan Museum of Art.* **619, 620, 621** Tortoiseshell box with double lid, mounted and *piqué* in gold. On the bottom, the arms of Affleck executed in *piqué point*. Inside, a miniature portrait of a woman by Lawrence Crosse (*c.* 1654–1724), signed with the monogram LC. English, *c.* 1720. *A La Vieille Russie, New York.* **622** Tortoiseshell, mounted and *piqué* in silver. German or Dutch, *c.* 1720–30. *The Metropolitan Museum of Art.* **623** Tortoiseshell, mounted and *piqué* in silver. Continental or English, 1725–50. *The Metropolitan Museum of Art.* **624** Tortoiseshell, engraved and mounted in silver. On the cover, Adam and Eve; on the bottom, a couple dressed in costumes of the early eighteenth century. *Maker Peter Van Dyck (1684–1750). American (New York City), c.* 1730. *The Mabel Brady Garvan Collection, Yale University Art Gallery.* **625** Tortoiseshell, mounted in silver and *piqué* in silver and mother-of-pearl. Probably German, *c.* 1730–40. *The Metropolitan Museum of Art.*

626

627

629

631

626 Tortoiseshell, mounted and *piqué* on silver. On the cover, a medal, probably by John Croker, commemorating the Treaty of Utrecht in 1713; on the bottom, the royal monogram. Said to have been given by Queen Anne to Admiral Bodham. English, *c*. 1713. *Castle Museum, Norwich.* **627** Tortoiseshell and gold. Signed, *Gouers a Paris.* Maker Daniel Govaers. French (Paris), 1725–6. *Wartski, London.* **628** Tortoiseshell, mounted in silver and *piqué* in silver and mother-of-pearl. French, *c*. 1730–40. *Castle Museum, Norwich.* **629** Tortoiseshell, silver and silver gilt. Inside the cover, an enamel miniature of a man. French, *c*. 1765. *Antique Porcelain Company, New York.* **630** Tortoiseshell, mounted and *piqué* in silver. Continental, mid-eighteenth century. *Museo Nazionale, Naples.* **631** Tortoiseshell, mounted in silver and *piqué* in silver and mother-of-pearl. English or Continental, mid-eighteenth century. *Castle Museum, Norwich.* **632** Tortoiseshell, mounted and *piqué* in silver. On the cover, a free adaptation of *La Terre* (generally known as *The Cherry Pickers*) by Nicolas Lancret. Continental, 1750–75. *Museo Nazionale, Naples.*

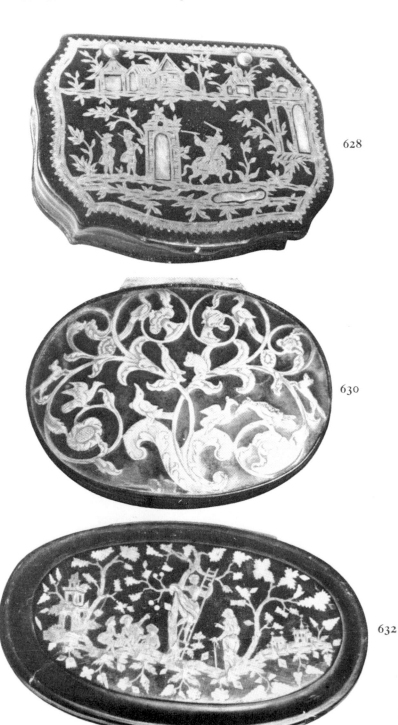

628

630

632

633 Tortoiseshell, mounted and *piqué* in gold. French, *c.* 1750. Ex coll. A. Chester Beatty. **634** Tortoiseshell, with *piqué* decoration in gold. Italian (Naples), *c.* 1750. Ex coll. A. Chester Beatty. **635** Tortoiseshell, with *piqué* decoration in gold. Italian (Naples), *c.* 1750. *Mrs Harvey A. Firestone, Jr.* **636** Tortoiseshell, mounted and *piqué* in silver and varicoloured gold. French (Paris), 1762–3. Ex coll. René Fribourg. **637** Tortoiseshell, mounted and *piqué* in silver. Continental, mid-eighteenth century. *Staatliche Kunstsammlungen, Dresden.* **638** Black composition, mounted and *piqué* in gold. *Maker* Pierre-François Drais. French (Paris), 1767–8. Ex coll. René Fribourg. **639** Tortoiseshell, mounted and *piqué* in gold and set on the cover with a repoussé gold plaque. Marks illegible. Inscribed on the rim, *Vachette à Paris. Maker* Adrien-Jean-Maximilien Vachette. French (Paris), early nineteenth century(?). *The Worshipful Company of Goldsmiths, London.*

633

634

635

636

637

638

639

640 Tortoiseshell, mounted and *piqué* in gold. *Maker* Adrien-Jean-Maximilien Vachette. French (Paris), early nineteenth century.
641 Yellow horn, *piqué* in gold. French, *c.* 1790. *The Brooklyn Museum.*
642 Horn. On the cover, pressed portraits of William and Mary. Unsigned. *Maker* John Obrisset (w. 1705–28). English (London), early eighteenth century. *British Museum.*

643, 644 Tortoiseshell, mounted in silver, with cast and chased portraits of William and Mary. Unsigned. *Maker* John Obrisset. English (London), early eighteenth century. *British Museum.* **645** Tortoiseshell, silver-mounted. On the cover, cast and chased portrait of Queen Anne signed and dated *OB 1705*. *Maker* John Obrisset. English (London), 1705. *The Metropolitan Museum of Art.* **646** Tortoiseshell plaques, mounted in a silver frame to form a snuff box. On the cover and bottom, pressed portraits of Prince George of Denmark and Queen Anne. Unsigned. *Maker* John Obrisset. English (London), early eighteenth century. *British Museum.*

647 Horn, with pressed decoration of the arms and name of Sir Francis Drake and the ships of his voyage. Signed and dated JOHN·OBRISSET· FECIT· 1712. *Maker* John Obrisset. English (London), 1712. Ex coll. P. A. S. Phillips. *The London Museum.* The *raison d'être* of the box is undetermined, but is presumably connected with either the successful political campaign of Francis Henry Drake (later 5th Bart.) in 1713, or his coming of age the following year. **648** Horn, with pressed equestrian portrait of George II, signed and dated *OBri/set Londini Fecit 1727*. *Maker* John Obrisset. English (London), 1727. Ex coll. P. A. S. Phillips. *The London Museum.*

647   648

649

649 Ivory, lined with tortoiseshell. Continental, first half eighteenth century. *Schweizerisches Landesmuseum, Zürich.* **650** Ivory, with silver hinge. The cover is set with a silver plaque engraved JONᴺ DALE and (apparently at a different time) 1738. Scottish, *c.* 1738. *Mrs H. B. Findlay.* **651** Ivory and ebony, silver-mounted and engraved on the cover *Thoˢ Carruthers PERSHORE.* Scottish, *c.* 1740–50. *Mrs H. B. Findlay.* **652** Ivory and ebony, silver-mounted. Scottish, *c.* 1740–50. *Mrs H. B. Findlay.* **653** Ivory, carved, lined with tortoiseshell, and mounted in gold. French (Paris), 1768–9. **654** Ivory, carved and mounted in gold. German, *c.* 1765–75. *A La Vieille Russie, New York.*

650

651

652

653

654

655 Ivory, gold-mounted, the cover with an allegorical figure after Martin de Vos (1538–1603). *Maker* possibly C. Coppin (w. 1798–?). French (possibly Marseilles). Ex coll. James Hazen Hyde. *The Cooper Union Museum, New York.*
656 Tortoiseshell, gold-mounted, the cover appliquéd in hardstones. German (Berlin), *c.* 1750–60. *Victoria and Albert Museum, London.* **657** Tortoiseshell, inlaid in mother-of-pearl. Continental, 1750–1800. *Museo Nazionale, Naples.*
658 Tortoiseshell. Continental, *c.* 1810–20. *Österreichische Tabakregie, Vienna.* **659** Silver-mounted box of striated agate with horn cover. Engraved on the shield is the monogram of Hester C. Bussing who was married in 1794. American, *c.* 1794. *Museum of the City of New York.* **660** Horn, with cast and engine-turned decoration. On the cover, the monogram of Louis XVIII and the inscription *Boite Royale de France Année 1825.* French, 1825. *The Cooper Union Museum, New York.*
661 Ivory. On the cover, portrait of Frederick II of Prussia. Probably German, *c.* 1760–70. *Österreichische Tabakregie, Vienna.*
662 Ivory, mounted in gold and set with an unidentified portrait miniature. French (Paris), 1775–81. *The Brooklyn Museum.*

663 Tortoiseshell, gold-mounted. On the cover, a miniature by Louis-Marie Sicard, signed *Sicardi*. French, *c.* 1790. *Musée du Louvre, Paris.* **664** Ivory, gold-mounted. On the cover and bottom, portraits called those of the Jousserand children. French, *c.* 1790. *Musée du Louvre, Paris.* **665** Tortoiseshell. On the cover, a miniature portrait by François Dumont, signed and dated *Dumont a Rome 1786*. French, *c.* 1786. *Musée du Louvre, Paris.* **666** Tortoiseshell. On the cover a portrait of a man signed *Dufour*. English(?), *c.* 1790. *The Brooklyn Museum.* The miniaturist has been tentatively identified as William Dufour, who exhibited in London in 1765. **667** Tortoiseshell. On the cover, a portrait of a man signed and dated *Villers-f. 1791*. French, 1791. *The Cooper Union Museum, New York.* **668** Tortoiseshell, gold-mounted. On the cover, a miniature signed and dated *H.V. 1811*. French, 1811. *Musée du Louvre, Paris.* **669** Tortoiseshell, gold-mounted. On the cover, a portrait miniature called that of the Maréchale Bessières and the duc d'Istrie Delaplace. *Maker* Pierre-André Montauban. French (Paris), *c.* 1805. *Musée du Louvre, Paris.* **670** Ivory. On the cover, a portrait of a member of the Bleeker family. The miniature American, the box probably English, *c.* 1800. *Museum of the City of New York.*

671 *Vernis Martin*, with silver-gilt rims and tortoiseshell lining. On the cover, the Rape of Europa. French, *c.* 1760–70. *Musée du Louvre, Paris.* 672 *Vernis Martin* with gold rims. French, *c.* 1765. *Antique Porcelain Company, New York.* 673 *Vernis Martin*, lined with tortoiseshell and mounted in silver gilt. On the cover, a scene of men playing bowls. French, *c.* 1765–70. *The Metropolitan Museum of Art.* 674 *Vernis Martin*, lined with tortoiseshell and mounted in silver gilt. French, *c.* 1770. *The Metropolitan Museum of Art.* 675 *Vernis Martin*, lined with tortoiseshell and mounted in gold. On the cover, an unidentified portrait miniature. French (Paris), 1771–2. *Musée du Louvre, Paris.* 676 Lacquered wood. Italian (Venice), *c.* 1750–75. *The Walters Art Gallery, Baltimore.*

677, 678, 679 Lacquered wood, decorated in gold and mother-of-pearl. German, *c.* 1770. *Landesgewerbeamt Baden-Württemberg, Stuttgart.* The decoration appears to refer to an ecclesiastical elector of Swabia. **680** Tin, lacquered in imitation of tortoiseshell. Welsh (Pontypool), dated 1749. *The National Museum of Wales, Cardiff.* **681, 682** Plated tin, lacquered and gilt-painted. Inscribed inside with the initials of the owner and, in Welsh, the unidentified 'Stone Cottage'. Welsh (Pontypool), 1772. *The National Museum of Wales, Cardiff.*

683 Papier-mâché, with gilt decoration on imitation tortoiseshell ground. *Maker* Jean Guérin (d. 1797). German (Brunswick, Stobwasser factory), 1763–72. *State Museum, Brunswick.* A native of Clermont, Guérin settled in Brunswick in 1763 and married a sister of J. H. Stobwasser four years later. This box must have been made before 1772 when Guérin established a branch of the factory in Berlin. Like the majority of papier-mâché snuff boxes its shallowness is compensated for by greater length (5¾ in.). **684** Papier-mâché. On the cover, a portrait of Friedrich Christian Ludwig Henneberg (b. 1748), after a painting executed between 1810 and 1815 by Johann Helarius Krevel (1776–1846). Signed in red inside, *303 Stobwassers Fabrik*. German (Brunswick, Stobwasser factory), *c.* 1815. *State Museum, Brunswick.* **685** Papier-mâché painted with a view of the Brockenhaus after an anonymous engraving (*c.* 1810). Signed in red: *16168 Stobwassers Fabrik*. German (Brunswick, Stobwasser factory), *c.* 1810. *State Museum, Brunswick.* The Brocken is one of the peaks of the Harz Mountains; the building was evidently a focal point for excursionists. **686** Papier-mâché. Continental (Italian?), *c.* 1800. *Museo Nazionale, Naples.* **687** Papier-mâché, painted by Samuel Raven (1775–1847) with the arms of the Plane Makers Society. English (Birmingham), *c.* 1820. *City Museum and Art Gallery, Birmingham.* The Plane Makers Society does not appear to be recorded and was presumably a mutual benefit society rather than a formal trade union. **688** Papier-mâché, with a painting by Samuel Raven of George IV after Lawrence. Inscribed inside the lid, *J. Machin. Union Commercial Room. S. Raven Pinxt.* English (Birmingham), probably 1825. *Victoria and Albert Museum, London.* John Machin (*fl.* 1825–58) became landlord of the inn called the Union Commercial Room in 1825; he is thought to have commissioned this box on that occasion.

689 Burr maple with silver hinge. French, *c.* 1745. *Pinto Collection of Wooden Bygones.* **690** Wood, with pressed portraits of Voltaire and Rousseau. French, probably 1778. *British Museum.* Undoubtedly made to commemorate the death of the two philosophers in the same year. **691** Wood, the cover pressed with a scene entitled *Henri IV chez Michau.* French, early nineteenth century. *British Museum.* **692** Wood, the cover pressed with an allegorical scene of the battle of Austerlitz (the battle of the three emperors). French, 1805. *British Museum.* **693** Wood, lined with tortoiseshell, in the shape of Napoleon's tricorne. French, early nineteenth century. *Pinto Collection of Wooden Bygones.* **694** Wood, with pressed decoration. French, *c.* 1815. *British Museum.* Franz Joseph Gall (1758–1828) was the founder of phrenology. **695** Wood, pressed with a portrait of Louis XVIII (1814–24). French, *c.* 1814. *British Museum.*

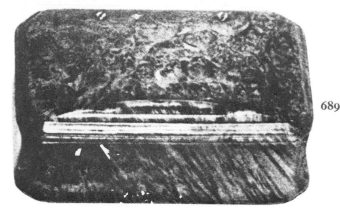

689

690

691

692

693

694

695

696 Cedar, horn-rimmed and inlaid in bone. English, dated 1706. *Pinto Collection of Wooden Bygones.* 697 Wood, veneered in mahogany, satinwood, boxwood and ebony. English, *c.* 1775. *Pinto Collection of Wooden Bygones.* 698 Birch. Scandinavian(?), *c.* 1800. *Pinto Collection of Wooden Bygones.* 699 Birch. Probably Scottish, *c.* 1800–10. *Pinto Collection of Wooden Bygones.* 700 Birch. Scandinavian or Scottish, *c.* 1800–10. *Pinto Collection of Wooden Bygones.* 701 Wood, painted in black. On the cover, a scene representing Burns's poem *Cotter's Saturday Night* (1785). Scottish (Mauchline), early nineteenth century. *Mrs H. B. Findlay.* Allusions to Burns's work on this and other Mauchline boxes are particularly appropriate: he was himself the son of a cotter; and for three years (1788–91), while he was living near Dumfries, his wife lived in Mauchline. 702 Ischia lava, the cover set with a mosaic view of Tivoli. Presented to Sir Thomas Lawrence during his visit to Rome in 1819. Italian, *c.* 1819. *Victoria and Albert Museum, London.* 703 Verre églomisé, silver-mounted. On the cover, a skating scene signed *zeuner inv.* Dutch (Amsterdam), probably 1803. *Victoria and Albert Museum, London.*

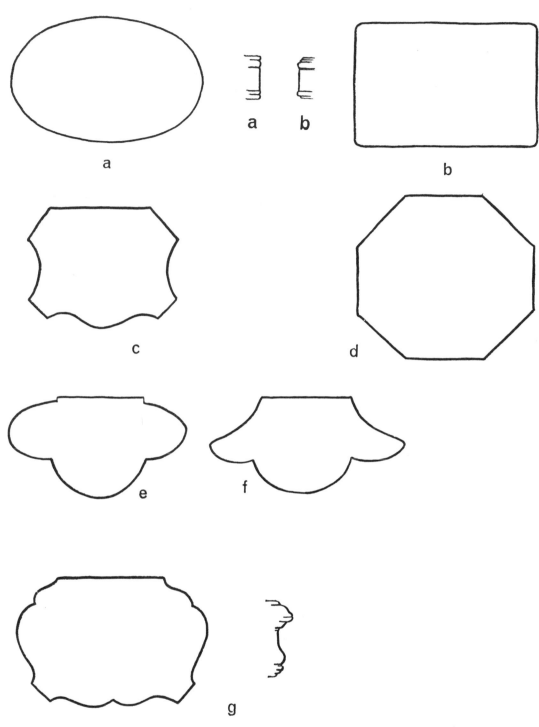

In this and the following three plates a survey indicating the major changes in the shapes of snuff boxes is offered. Except where noted, the examples are composite, and may be considered representative of boxes of any material at a given date.

a) English and Continental, *c.* 1720–30. Oval boxes of the late seventeenth century were probably similar in proportion, although smaller in overall size.
b) English and Continental, *c.* 1720–30.
c) Continental, *c.* 1730.
d) English and Continental, *c.* 1735.
e) A box of this shape is illustrated in the 1733 trade card of the Parisian goldsmith Jean de Haynault (Nocq, *Le Poinçon de Paris*, II, pp. 27–8); it is presumably illustra-

tive of the box 'en trefle' in the collection of the duchesse d'Orléans (see p. 9).
f) Clearly a variation of the preceding, this form appears in the trade card, *c.* 1740(?), of the London goldsmith Thomas Clark. A somewhat similar shape occurs in Meissen porcelain about this time.
g) Continental, *c.* 1735; and English, *c.* 1735–40. The cartouche shape retained its popularity in provincial centres until *c.* 1775.

II

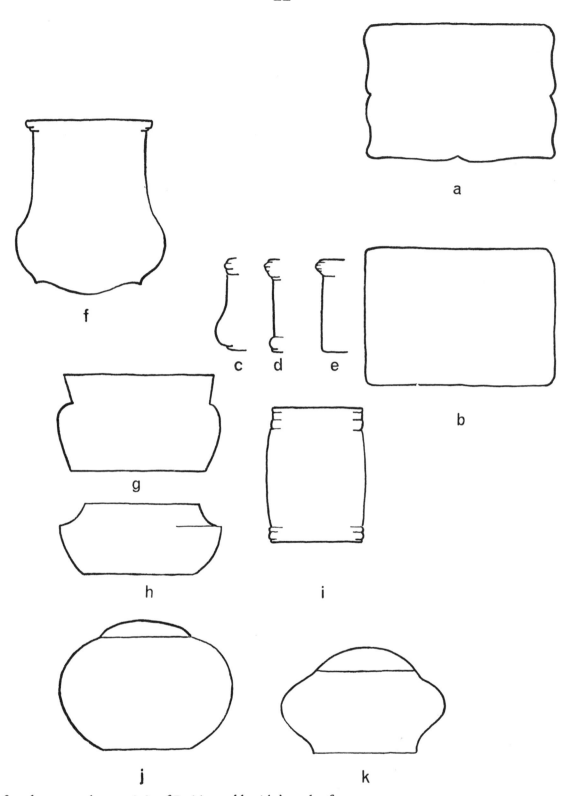

The first five shapes are characteristic of Parisian goldsmiths' work of 1740–50.

a) *c.* 1745.
b) 1740–50.
c) *c.* 1740–5.
d) *c.* 1745.
e) *c.* 1745–50.
f) English, *c.* 1750. An agate box of similar shape is in Amalienborg Castle; it is probably a Danish adaptation of the English form.

g) Continental, *c.* 1735–40.
h) Continental, *c.* 1740–50. The shape occurs most often in Meissen porcelain.
i) Continental and English, *c.* 1745–60.
j) French, *c.* 1750. More apple-shaped variants of the *boîte à ballon* occur *c.* 1760–5 in Continental porcelain and English enamel.
k) Continental, *c.* 1765. A ceramic form.

III

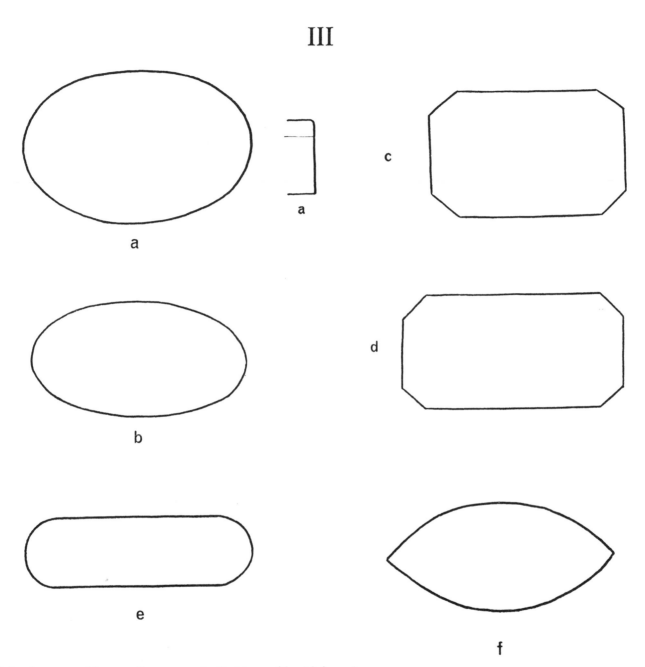

All the shapes on this page first appear in Parisian goldsmiths' work.

a) *c.* 1750–70.
b) *c.* 1770–85.
c) *c.* 1765–80.

d) *c.* 1780–1800. The shape was adopted by Swiss gold-smiths *c.* 1810.
e) *c.* 1785. A broader variant appears in England *c.* 1790.
f) Continental, *c.* 1785–90.

IV

a

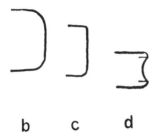

b   c   d

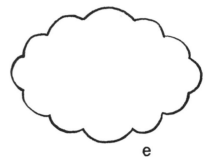

e

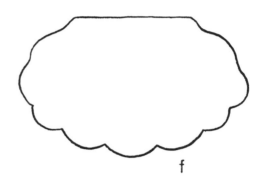

f

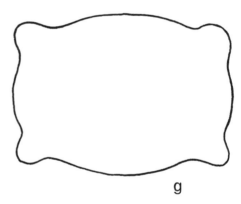

g

a) Continental and English, *c.* 1800–30.
b) English, *c.* 1800–15.
c) Continental, *c.* 1810–30.
d) English, *c.* 1820.

e) Continental and English, *c.* 1825–30. The form appears
    to have originated in Switzerland in watches made for
    the Turkish market.
f) Continental, *c.* 1830.
g) Continental (chiefly Austrian), *c.* 1830–40.

V

MARKS

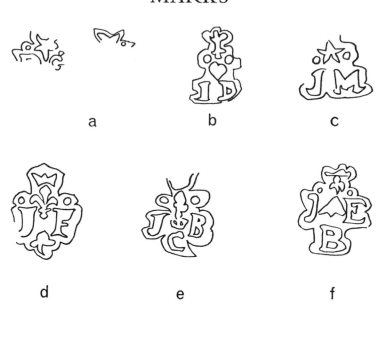

Included on this page are the marks of some of the most active Parisian goldsmiths, as well as several guild and tax marks which are to be expected on a Parisian box. The somewhat random choice of examples has been dictated by the availability of clear strikes.

a) Daniel Govaers. A complete strike of the mark is unusual. Unlike most of his colleagues Govaers did not include the traditional crowned fleur-de-lis (symbolising Paris) in his mark.

b) Jean Ducrollay. The identification of a goldsmith's punch often depends on distinct peculiarities of the shape of its reserve. Ducrollay's mark is characterised by the upward slope of the D and its outline.

c) Jean Moynat.

d) Jean Formey.

e) Jean-Baptiste Carnay.

f) Jean-Etienne Blerzy.

g) Adrien-Jean-Maximilien Vachette (mark after the Revolution).

h) Gabriel-Raoul Morel.

i) Warden's letter for 1757–8.

j) Charge mark for gold and small silver work, 1762–8: crossed laurel branches.

k) Discharge mark for gold and small silver work, 1750–6: a hen's head.

l) Discharge mark for work intended for export, 1733(?)–75: a cow.

m) Tax mark for 20-carat gold, Vienna, 1806–7. This is included here as it is one of the most recurrent nineteenth-century marks.

VI

INSCRIPTIONS AND SIGNATURES

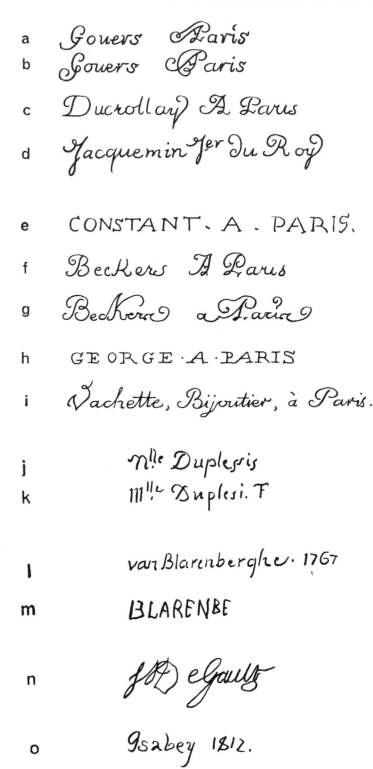

a   *Gouers Paris*

b   *Gouers Paris*

c   *Ducrollay A Paris*

d   *Jacquemin Jer Du Roy*

e   CONSTANT . A . PARIS.

f   *Beckers A Paris*

g   *Beckers a Paris*

h   GEORGE · A · PARIS

i   *Vachette, Bijoutier, à Paris.*

j   *Mlle Duplessis*

k   *Mlle Duplesi. F*

l   *van Blarenberghe . 1767*

m   BLARENBE

n   *DeGault*

o   *Isabey 1812.*

Unless otherwise noted, all appear on boxes in the Metropolitan Museum.

a,b) Daniel Govaers. The first inscription is engraved on a box in the Metropolitan Museum, the second on one in the Wrightsman collection.

c) Jean Ducrollay.

d) Pierre-André Jacquemin (see p. 58). Engraved on a box by Ducrollay (*38*).

e) Constant, presumably a *marchand mercier*, is unidentified; his name is engraved on a box by Ducrollay (*80*).

f,g) Jean-Baptiste Beckers.

h) Jean George.

i) Adrien-Jean-Maximilien Vachette.

j,k) Mlle Duplessis (see p. 28). The first signature occurs on a miniature painted in the grisaille manner traditionally associated with this artist. The second, which appears to be that of the same painter, occurs on an atypical polychrome genre scene, on a box in the Wrightsman collection.

l) Louis-Nicolas van Blarenberghe. The signature appears on a box, in the Wrightsman collection, painted with views of the Chateau de Chanteloup. Despite the absence of initials, the signature is that of Louis-Nicolas, who had been appointed *Peintre de Batailles au Departement de la Guerre* by his patron the duc de Choiseul, owner of the chateau.

m) Probably Henri-Joseph van Blarenberghe.

n) Jacques-Joseph DeGault.

o) Jean-Baptiste Isabey.

Bibliography

Introduction: Primary Sources

A General Description of All Trades, London, 1747.

Arbuckle, James, *Snuff, A Poem*, Edinburgh, 1719.

Aumont, Louis Marie Augustin, duc d', Collection, *Sale Catalogue*, Paris, 1782.

Baillard, Edme, *Discours du tabac*, Paris, 1668.

Baretti, Joseph, *An Account of the Manners and Customs of Italy*, 2 vols., London, 1768.

Baruffaldi, Girolamo, *La Tabaccheide*, Ferrara, 1714.

Burrish, Onslow, *Batavia Illustrata*, 2 vols., London, 1728. Provides a record of the Dutch role in the tobacco trade, as well as of the materials imported by the East India Company for use in the manufacture of boxes.

Conti, Prince de, *Catalogue d'une riche collection*, Paris, 1777.

Foreman, Charles, *A Letter to the Right Honourable Sir Robert Walpole*, London, 1732.

Gibson, John, *The History of Glasgow*, Glasgow, 1777.

Goldsmith, Oliver, *The Life of Richard Nash, of Bath, Esq.*, London, 1762.

Howell, James, *Epistolae Ho-Elianae*, London, 1650.

Mander, Karel van, *Lauwercrants voor alle Lieffhebbers des Loffwaerden Snuyfftoebacks*, 1665.

Mercure de France, 1672–1832.

Moore, Dr John, *A View of Society and Manners in France, Switzerland and Germany*, 2 vols., Paris, 1803 (the first edition appeared in 1779). *A view of Society and Manners in Italy*, 2 vols., London, 1790.

Pandora's Box: a Satyr against Snuff, London, 1718.

[Perrault, Charles], *Les Souhaits ridicules. Avec l'exercice de la Tabatière*, Guibray, n.d. [c. 1750]. Although published together, only the *Souhaits* is by Perrault; the satire on the use of the snuff box is anonymous.

Riesbeck, Baron Caspar, *Travels through Germany*, 2 vols., Dublin, 1787.

Spectator, London, 1711–14.

Tatler, London, 1709–11.

Thiebault, Dieudonné, *Original Anecdotes of Frederick the Second King of Prussia*, 2 vols., London, 1805.

Walpole, Horace, *Correspondence*, ed. W. S. Lewis, New Haven, 1937–to date.

[Walpole, Horace], *Catalogue of the Classic Contents of Strawberry Hill*, London, 1842.

Whipping-Tom: or, a Rod for a Proud Lady, 6th edn., London, 1722. (Discourse I. The Foppish Mode of taking Snuff.)

Zucchi, Francesco, *La Tabaccheide*, Ascoli, 1636.

Introduction: Secondary Sources

Allemagne, Henri René d', *Les Accessoires du costume et du mobilier*, 3 vols., Paris, 1928.

Bellaigue, Geoffrey de, 'Engravings and the French Eighteenth-century Marqueteur—I', *Burlington Magazine*, Vol. CVII (1965), pp. 240–50.

Boehn, Max von, *Modes and Manners: Ornaments*, London, 1929.

Cordey, Jean, ed., *Inventaire des biens de Madame de Pompadour*, Paris, 1939.

Dickson, Sarah Augusta, *Panacea or Precious Bane. Tobacco in Sixteenth Century Literature*, New York, 1954.

Bibliography

Evans, George, *The Old Snuff House of Fribourg & Treyer 1720–1920*, London, 1921.
Guilmard, D., *Les maîtres ornemantistes*, 2 vols., Paris, 1880–1.
[Hill, Benson Earle], Dean Snift, of Brazen-nose, *A Pinch—of Snuff*, London, 1840.
Mackenzie, Compton, *Sublime Tobacco*, New York, 1958.
MacLysaght, Edward, *Irish Life in the Seventeenth Century*, Cork, 1950.
Maze-Sencier, Alphonse, *Le livre des collectionneurs*, Paris, 1885. *Les fournisseurs de Napoléon Ier*, Paris, 1893.
Robert, Joseph C., *The Story of Tobacco in America*, New York, 1949.
Weiss, Harry B. and Grace M., *The Early Snuff Mills of New Jersey*, Trenton, 1962.

French Gold Boxes

Azur, J. A., *Almanach des fabricans*, Paris, 1810.
Berry-Hill, Henry and Sidney, *Antique Gold Boxes*, London, New York, Toronto, 1960.
Bara, Aline, 'Petits objets précieux du legs H. Verhaege de Naeyer', *Bulletin des Musées royaux d'art et d'histoire*, 4th series, Vol. XIX (1947), pp. 50–61.
Darmon, J.-E., *Dictionnaire des peintres miniaturistes sur vélin, parchemin, ivoire et écaille*, Paris, n.d. [*c.* 1930].
Demoriane, Hélène, 'Les tabatières Louis XV vues sous toutes leurs faces', *Connaissance des Arts*, 1962, pp. 112–23.
Duvaux, Lazare, *Livre-journal*, 2 vols., Paris, 1873. Introduction by Louis Courajod.
Finlay, Ian, 'Some Silver and Gold Work Recently Acquired by the Royal Scottish Museum. Part II', *Apollo*, Vol. LIII (1951), pp. 69–72.
Franklin, Alfred, *Dictionnaire historique des arts, métiers et professions exercés dans Paris depuis le treizième siècle*, Paris and Leipzig, 1906.
Fribourg, René, collection, *Sale Catalogue*, London, Sotheby & Co., 14 October 1963.
Furetière, Antoine, *Dictionnaire universel*, 2 vols., La Haye and Rotterdam, 1694.
Hulot, M., père, *L'Art du tourneur mécanicien*, Paris, 1775.
Jeannerat, Carlo, 'DeGault et Gault de Saint-Germain', *Bulletin de la Société de l'histoire de l'art français*, 1935, pp. 221–35.
Julia de Fontenelle, *Manuel complet du bijoutier, du joaillier, de l'orfèvre*, 2 vols., Paris, 1832.
Handbook of the Art Collections, Henry E. Huntington Library and Art Gallery, San Marino, 1953. Does not provide specific attributions.
LeRoy, Pierre, *Statuts et privilèges du corps des marchands orfèvres-joyailliers*, Paris, 1759.
Manuel du tourneur, 2 vols., Paris, 1792 and 1796.
Marquet de Vasselot, J. J., *Bibliographie de l'orfèvrerie*, Paris, 1925.
Maze-Sencier, Alphonse, *Le livre des collectionneurs*, Paris, 1885. *Les fournisseurs de Napoléon Ier*, Paris, 1893.
Musée Cognacq-Jay, *Catalogue*, Paris, 1930. No illustrations; many attributions open to question.
Nocq, Henry and Dreyfus, Carle, *Tabatières, boîtes et étuis . . . des collections du Musée du Louvre*, Paris, 1930.
Norton, Martin. 'Gold Snuff boxes of the XVIIIth Century', *Apollo*, Vol. XXXV (1942).
Norton, Richard and Martin, *A History of Gold Snuff Boxes*, London, 1938.
Secrets concernant les arts et métiers, 4 vols., Paris, 1790. Methods of working and tinting gold are given in Vol. I.
Tait, Hugh, 'Eighteenth-century Gold Boxes', *Connoisseur*, Vol. CLIV (1963), pp. 216–25.
Verlet, Pierre, *Le commerce des objets d'art et les marchands merciers à Paris au XVIIIe siècle*, Paris, 1958.
Vidal, Pierre, and Duru, Léon, *Histoire de la corporation des marchands merciers, grossiers, jouailliers*, Paris, 1913.
Watson, F. J. B., *The Choiseul Box*, London, 1963.

Other Continental, English and American Gold Boxes

Bäcksbacka, L., *St. Petersburgs juvelerare, guld- och Silversmeder 1714–1870*, Helsingfors, 1951. Incorporates, and adds to, information first published by Foelkersam.

Berry-Hill, Henry and Sidney, *Antique Gold Boxes*, London, New York, Toronto, 1960.

Chapuis, Alfred, *Histoire de la boîte à musique*, Lausanne, 1955.

Chapuis, Alfred, and Gélis, Edouard, *Le monde des automates*, 2 vols., Paris, 1928.

Das Grune Gewölbe zu Dresden, Dresden, 1937. An unillustrated guide.

Foelkersam, Baron A. de, 'L'Orfèvrerie à Saint-Pétersbourg de 1714 à 1814', *Starye Gody*, Vol. I (1907), supplement at the end of each monthly issue. Especially valuable for photographs of boxes not generally accessible.

Foskett, Daphne, *British Portrait Miniatures*, London, 1963.

Foster, J. J., *A Dictionary of Painters of Miniatures 1525–1850*, London, 1926.

Heal, Ambrose, *The London Goldsmiths*, Cambridge, 1935.

Klar, Martin, 'Berliner Golddosen aus Friderizianischer Zeit', *Pantheon*, Vol. IX (1932), pp. 60–2. With English summary.

Munthe, Gustaf, *Falk Simons silversamling*, Stockholm, 1938.

Prideaux, Sir Walter Sherburne, *Memorials of the Goldsmiths' Company*, 2 vols., London, n.d. [c. 1896].

Prachoff, Adrien, *Album de l'exposition retrospective d'objets d'art, de 1904, à St. Pétersbourg*, St Petersburg, 1907.

Schneeberger, Pierre-F., *Les peintres sur émail genevois au XVIIᵉ et au XVIIIᵉ siècle*, Geneva, 1958.

Scott, H. A. (comp.), *Extracts from Notices which Appeared in London Newspapers Referring to Objects of Fine and Decorative Arts 17th and 18th Centuries, Made . . . from the Burney Collection of Papers in the British Museum*, 11 vols., London, 1937. Typewritten; a bound copy is in the Metropolitan Museum. Vols. V, VI, VIII, IX and XI include references to snuff boxes.

Tait, Hugh, 'Eighteenth-century Gold Boxes', *Connoisseur*, Vol. CLIV (1963), pp. 216–25.

Wenham, Edward, 'Snuff-Boxes by English Goldsmiths', *Connoisseur*, Vol. XCVII (1936), pp. 72–5.

Silver Boxes

Bradbury, Frederick, *History of Old Sheffield Plate*, London, 1912.

Buhler, Kathryn C., *American Silver*, Cleveland and New York, 1950.

Catalogus van het Goud- en Zilverwerk, Amsterdam (Rijksmuseum), 1952. No illustrations.

Clarke, Hermann Frederick, *John Coney, Silversmith 1655–1722*, Boston and New York, 1932.

Descamps, Jean, *Histoire de la Corporation des Orfèvres de Lille*, Lille, 1926.

Dow, George Francis, *The Arts & Crafts in New England*, Toppsfield (Mass.), 1927.

Exhibition of Russian Art, London, 1935. No illustrations.

Fales, Martha Gandy, *American Silver in the Henry Francis Du Pont Winterthur Museum*, Winterthur, 1958.

Frederiks, J. W., *Dutch Silver*, Vols. II and III, The Hague, 1958 and 1960.

French, Hollis, *Jacob Hurd and his Sons Nathaniel and Benjamin, Silversmiths 1702–1781*, Cambridge (Mass.), 1939.

Gans, M. H., and Duyvené de Wit-Klinkhamer, Th.M., *Dutch Silver*, London, 1961. A useful general account; there are no illustrations of snuff boxes.

Gottesman, Rita Susswein, *The Arts and Crafts in New York 1726–1776*, New York, 1938.

Hammerslough, Philip H., *American Silver*, 2 vols., Hartford, 1958 and 1960.

Hughes, G. Bernard, *Small Antique Silverware*, London, 1957.

Langdon, John Emerson, *Canadian Silversmiths and their Marks 1667–1867*, Lunenberg (Vt.), 1960.

Phillips, John Marshall, *American Silver*, New York, 1949.

Prime, Alfred Coxe, *The Arts & Crafts in Philadelphia, Maryland and South Carolina 1721–1785*, London, 1929.
Rice, Norman S., *Albany Silver 1652–1825*, Albany Institute of History and Art, 1964. Indispensable.
Scott, H. A. (comp.), *Extracts from Notices which Appeared in London Newspapers Referring to Objects of Fine and Decorative Arts 17th and 18th Centuries, Made . . . from the Burney Collection of Papers in the British Museum*, 11 vols., London, 1937. Typewritten; one bound set is in the Metropolitan Museum. Vols. V, VI, VIII, IX and XI include references to snuff boxes.
Traquair, Ramsay, *The Old Silver of Quebec*, Toronto, 1940.

Marking Gold and Silver Boxes

Andrén, Erik, Hellner, Brynolf, Hernmarck, Carl, and Holmquist, Kersti, *Svenskt Silversmide 1520–1850*, Stockholm, 1963.
Bäcksbacka, L., *St. Petersburgs Juvelerare, Guld- och Silversmeder 1714–1870*, Helsingfors, 1951.
Beuque, Emile, *Dictionnaire des poinçons officiels français et étrangers*, 2 vols., Paris, 1925–8.
Beuque, Emile, and Frapsauce, M., *Dictionnaire des poinçons de maîtres-orfèvres français*, Paris, 1929.
Bøje, Chr. A., *Danske Guld og Solv Smedemaerker*, Kjøbenhavn, 1946.
Bulgari, Costantino G., *Argentieri Gemmari e Orafi d'Italia*, 2 vols., Rome, 1949.
Currier, Ernest M., *Marks of Early American Silversmiths*, Portland, Maine and London, 1938.
Darling Foundation of New York State Early American Silversmiths and Silver, *New York State Silversmiths*, Eggerstville, 1964. Illustrated by photographs.
Dennis, Faith, *Three Centuries of French Domestic Silver*, 2 vols., The Metropolitan Museum of Art, New York, 1960. The second volume is devoted to Parisian and provincial marks illustrated by photographs.
Douet, S. P., *Tableau des symboles de l'orfèvrerie de Paris*, Paris, 1806 and 1809.
Hipkiss, Edwin J., *The Philip Leffingwell Spalding Collection of Early American Silver*, Museum of Fine Arts, Boston, 1943. Illustrated by photographs.
Jackson, Sir Charles James, *English Goldsmiths and their Marks*, 2nd edn., London, 1921.
Munthe, Gustaf, *Falk Simons Silversamling*, Stockholm, 1938.
Nocq, Henry, *Le poinçon de Paris*, 5 vols., Paris, 1926–31.
Nocq, Henry, et Dreyfus, Carle, *Tabatières, boîtes et étuis . . . des collections du Musée du Louvre*, Paris, 1930.
Rice, Norman S., *Albany Silver 1652–1825*, Albany Institute of History and Art, 1964. Illustrated by photographs.
Rosenberg, Marc, *Der Goldschmiede Merkzeichen*, 4 vols., Frankfurt am Main, 1922–8.
Traquair, Ramsay, *The Old Silver of Quebec*, Toronto, 1940.
Voet, Elias Jr., *Merken van Friesche Goud- en Zilversmeden*, The Hague, 1932. *Merken van Haagsche Goud- en Zilversmeden*, The Hague, 1941. *Nederlandse Goud- en Zilvermerken, 1445–1951*, The Hague, 1951.

Base-Metal Boxes

Allemagne, H. R. d', *Rouen, Musée Le Secq des Tournelles. Ferronnerie ancienne*, 2ᵐᵉ partie, Paris, 1924.
Beard, Charles R., 'Lancashire Snuff and Tobacco Boxes', *Apollo*, Vol. XVII (1933), pp. 261–4.
Leader, Robert Eadon, *History of the Company of Cutlers in Hallamshire*, 2 vols., Sheffield, 1905.
Linden, Julien van der, 'Les boîtes en cuivre dites tabatières hollandaises', *Annales de la Société d'Archéologie de Bruxelles*, Vol. XV (1901), pp. 199–229. In an otherwise precise discussion, 'tabatière' is applied indiscriminately to snuff and tobacco boxes.
Massé, H. J. L. J., *Chats on Old Pewter*, New York, n.d. [*c.* 1910].
Michaelis, Ronald F., 'Collecting Old Pewter Snuffboxes', *Apollo*, Vol. XLV (1947), pp. 23–4.

Hardstone Boxes

Caire-Morand, A., *La science des pierres précieuses*, 2nd edn., Paris, 1833.

Holzhausen, Walter, 'Johann Christian Neuber', *Apollo*, Vol. LII (1950), pp. 104–6.

Klar, Martin, 'Die Tabatieren Friedrichs des Grossen', *Der Cicerone*, Vol. XXI, Pt. I (1929), pp. 7–18. 'Berliner Galanteriewaren aus Friderizianischer Zeit', *Pantheon*, Vol. V (1930), pp. 69–72. (With English summary.)

Weinstein, Michael, *Precious and Semi-Precious Stones*, 4th edn., New York and Chicago, 1946.

Porcelain Boxes

Alfassa, Paul, and Guérin, Jacques, *Porcelaine française du XVIIe au milieu du XIXe siècle*, Paris, n.d. [*c.* 1932].

Blohm, Otto and Magdalena, *Collection, Sale Catalogue*, Pts. II and III, Sotheby & Co., London, 24–5 April 1961, 9–10 October 1961.

Chavagnac, Comte X. de, et Grollier, Marquis de, *Histoire des manufactures françaises de porcelaine*, Paris, 1906.

Daydi, M. Olivar, *La Porcelana en Europa*, 2 vols., Barcelona, 1953.

Fourest, Henry-Pierre, 'Les boîtes en porcelaine tendre au Musée Adrien-Dubouché', *Cahiers de la Céramique*, Vol. IV (1961), pp. 44–51.

Frothingham, Alice Wilson, *Capodimonte and Buen Retiro Porcelains*, New York, 1955.

Hackenbroch, Yvonne, *Meissen and Other Continental Porcelain, Faience and Enamel in the Irwin Untermyer Collection*, New York, 1956.

Heine, Axel, *Porcelaens-tabatièren i det 18. Aarhundrede*, Copenhagen, 1937.

Honey, W. B., *European Ceramic Art*, 2 vols., London, 1949. *French Porcelain of the Eighteenth Century*, London, 1950. *Dresden China*, new edn., London, 1954. *German Porcelain*, 3rd printing, London, 1954.

Kaznakov, S. N., *Paketovyya tabakerki Imperatorskago farforovago zavoda* [*Snuff boxes from the Imperial Porcelain Factory*], St Petersburg, 1913. (Text in Russian only.)

Lane, Arthur, *Italian Porcelain*, London, 1954.

Lechevallier-Chevignard, Georges, *La manufacture de porcelaine de Sèvres*, Paris, 1908.

Loukomski, Georges, 'Russian Porcelain', *Apollo*, Vol. XLV (1947), pp. 8–13.

Menzhausen-Handt, Ingelore, 'Christian Friedrich Herold', *Keramik-freunde der Schweiz*, No. 50 (1960), pp. 35–8.

Pazaurek, Gustav E., *Deutsche Fayence- und Porcellan-Hausmaler*, 2 vols., Leipzig, 1925.

Röder, Kurt, *Das Kelsterbacher Porzellan*, Darmstadt, 1931.

Schmidt, Robert, *Porcelain as an Art and a Mirror of Fashion*, Trans. and ed. by W. A. Thorpe, London, 1932.

Troïnitsky, S., *Tabatières en porcelaine à l'Ermitage Impérial*, Leningrad, 1915.

Enamel Boxes

Cook, Cyril, 'James Gwin and his Designs on Battersea Enamels', *Apollo*, Vol. LV (1952), pp. 66–9. 'John Brooks and his Engravings on Battersea Enamels', *ibid.*, pp. 147–9, 153.

Hayward, J. F., 'A Berlin Enamel Box Commemorating the Battle of Leuthen', *Apollo*, Vol. XLI (1945), pp. 118–19, 121. 'German Commemorative Enamel Boxes', *Apollo*, Vol. XLIII (1946), pp. 113–14, 121. 'Signed Enamels by C. A. von Zirnfeld', *Freunde der Schweizer Keramik*, No. 17 (1950), pp. 11–12.

Honey, W. B., 'New Light on Battersea Enamels. I, II', *Connoisseur*, Vol. LXXXIX (1932), pp. 82–9, 164–70.

Hughes, Therle and Bernard, *English Painted Enamels*, London and New York, 1951.

Hughes, W. W., 'Authorship of Some Designs on Porcelain and Enamel and Robert Hancock's Connection with Battersea and Bow', *Transactions of the English Ceramic Circle*, No. III (1935), pp. 85–96.

Mew, Egan, *Battersea Enamels*, London and Boston, 1926.

Rackham, Bernard, *Catalogue of the Schreiber Collection. Vol. III. Enamels and Glass.* London (Victoria and Albert Museum), 1924. 'Porcelain as a Sidelight on Battersea Enamels', *Transactions of The English Ceramic Circle*, No. IV (1932), pp. 45–58.

Tait, Hugh, 'Herold and Hunger', *British Museum Quarterly*, Vol. XXV (1962), pp. 39–41.

The Ladies Amusement; or, Whole Art of Japanning Made Easy, 2nd edn., London, 1762. Facsimile edn., London, 1959. The first edition was evidently published late in 1759 or in January 1760, as it was first advertised, in the *Gentleman's Magazine*, in February 1760.

Toppin, Aubrey J., 'Battersea: Ceramic and Kindred Associations', *Transactions of The English Ceramic Circle*, No. IX (1946), pp. 165–78. 'Notes on Janssen, and the Artists at the Battersea Factory', *ibid.*, No. IV (1932), pp. 58–68.

Lacquered and Varnished Boxes

Boyer, Martha, *Japanese Export Lacquers from the Seventeenth Century in the National Museum of Denmark*, Copenhagen, 1959.

Dickinson, George, *English Papier-Mâché*, London, 1925.

Fuhse, F., *Vom Braunschweiger Tischlerhandwerk. Stobwasserarbeiten. Werkstude aus Museum, Archiv und Bibliotek der Stadt Braunschweig*, Vol. I), Braunschweig, 1925. (Detailed account of Stobwasser and his predecessors.)

Gibbs, F. W., 'Historical Survey of the Japanning Trade', *Annals of Science*, Vol. VII (1951), pp. 401–16, Vol. IX (1953), pp. 88–95, 197–213, 214–32.

Holzhausen, Walter, *Lackkunst in Europa*, Braunschweig, 1959.

Hughes, G. B., 'Domestic Metalwork', *Connoisseur Period Guides: The Early Georgian Period 1714–1760*, London, 1957, pp. 104–8. (Brief account of Baskerville.)

Hutton, William, *The History of Birmingham*, 4th edn., London, 1819. (Originally published 1782, contains valuable, though short, accounts of Taylor and Baskerville.)

John, W. D., *Pontypool and Usk Japanned Wares*, Newport, Monmouthshire, 1953. (Essential to any discussion of lacquer in Great Britain.)

Jullian, Philippe, 'Comment identifier le vernis Martin', *Connaissance des Arts*, No. 119 (1962), pp. 43–9.

Manifesto Camerale, Turin, 1763. (Arents Coll., N.Y. Public Library.)

McClinton, Katharine, 'American Engravings on Papier-Mâché Snuffboxes', *Antiques*, Vol. XLVIII (1945), pp. 284–5.

Phillips, Philip A. S., 'Samuel Raven', *Connoisseur*, Vol. LXXXIII (1929), pp. 29–39. 'Stobwasser Ware', *ibid.*, Vol. LXXXV (1930), pp. 166–73 (adapted from Fuhse). 'Stobwasser and Stockmann', *ibid.*, Vol. LXXXV (1930), pp. 232–40. *Collection, Sale Catalogue*, Sotheby & Co., London, 4 July 1934.

Secrets concernant les arts et métiers, Vol. II, Paris, 1790.

Stalker, John, and Parker, George, *A Treatise of Japanning and Varnishing*, Oxford, 1688. (Facsimile edn., Chicago, Ill., 1960).

Toller, Jane, *Papier-Mâché in Great Britain and America*, Newton, Mass., 1962. (Chiefly concerns mid-nineteenth-century work.)
Venice, Ca' Rezzonico, *Mostra Temporanea Lacche Veneziane del Settecento*, Venice, 1938 (text by Giulio Lorenzetti).
Volker, T., 'Japanese Export Lacquer', *Oriental Art*, N.S. Vol. III (1957), pp. 60–4.

Tortoiseshell, Ivory and Horn Boxes

Dent, Herbert C., *Piqué: A Beautiful Minor Art*, London, 1923.
Finlay, Ian, 'Scottish Snuffboxes—A Link with America', *Antiques*, Vol. LXV (1954), pp. 394–6.
Fisher, F. J., *Short History of the Worshipful Company of Horners*, London, n.d. (c. 1936).
Kunz, George Frederick, *Ivory and the Elephant*, New York, 1916.
Phillips, P. A. S., *John Obrisset*, London, 1931.
Read, C. H., 'English Work in Impressed Horn', *Some Minor Arts as Practised in England*, New York, 1894, pp. 1–7.

Wood Boxes

Finlay, Ian, 'Scottish Snuffboxes—a Link with America', *Antiques*, Vol. LXV (1954), pp. 394–6. (Mauchline boxes.)
Hughes, Therle, 'Tunbridge Ware', *The Concise Encyclopedia of Antiques*, Vol. IV, New York, 1955, pp. 78–84.
Maze-Sencier, Alphonse, *Le livre des collectionneurs*, Paris, 1885. (Pressed wood boxes.)
Pinto, Edward H., *Wooden Bygones of Smoking and Snuff Taking*, London, 1961.
Symonds, R. W., 'Tunbridge Ware', *Connoisseur*, Vol. LXXIX (1927), pp. 23–9.

The Elusive and the Rare

Copper-Royer, Jacqueline, *La marqueterie de paille*, Paris, 1954.
Notes and Queries, Series VII, Vol. 8 (1889); Series X, Vol. 5 (1907); Series XII, Vol. 12 (1923). For leather boxes.

Appendix I

Index of the Makers of Gold and Silver Boxes

		Fig. no.
FB	Frantz Bergs	307
Two sizes of this mark are recorded. Bergs also used a third mark, BERGS		
FF	Frederik II Fabritius	310–11
FH	unidentified English maker	281–2
FJ three fleurs-de-lis	unidentified Swiss maker	326, 327
F(?)P	unidentified Italian maker	426
FS	François Sasseville	411
FSC (or G)	unidentified	39–40
FTG fleece	François-Thomas Germain	71–3
GA	unidentified English maker	269
GG laurel leaf	Gabriel Gallois	11
GL crescent	Guillaume Loir	44
GRC incuse	unidentified Swiss maker	323–5
GRG (or C?)	unidentified Swiss maker	322
GRM ear, in a lozenge	Gabriel-Raoul Morel	222, 223, 227, 232
GV crowned heart	Gabriel Vougny	420
GW	unidentified Swiss maker	330
HB device not known	possibly Henry Bodson	140
the device in Bodson's mark was a chevalier's cross		
Hurd in oval	Jacob Hurd	353–4
This is the third of six marks used by Hurd. The others are: Jacob/Hurd; I HURD; HURD (2 sizes); Hurd in cartouche		
IA crown	Jean-Pierre Ador	336–7
Two versions of the mark are recorded: IA within a crown; and IA, a crown above		
IC	John Coney	383
IG sun	Jean Gaillard	25

		Fig. no.
IGH	James Godfrey Hanna	410
IGS pellets between	Johann Gottlieb Scharff	340
II star between	John Innocent	293
the mark is recorded by Jackson as being probably Innocent's		
IK pellet between	James Keating	305, 371
IL pellet between	Jacob Gerritse Lansing	388
For a discussion and illustration of the several punches used by the two Lansings of this name, see Norman S. Rice, *Albany Silver*, 1964, p. 23		
IL pellet between	John Leacock	397
IR	unidentified German maker	263
IS swan	unidentified Dutch maker	360
IWS	unidentified Viennese maker	240, 458
JB bird(?)	probably Jacques Brillant or Briant	13
JBB device indecipherable	unidentified	82
JBB star	Jean-Baptiste Bertin	114
JBB sun	Jean-Baptiste Beckers	159
JBC crown	Jean-Baptiste Carnay	127
JBP	Julien Boulogne-Petit	121
JCD heart	Jean-Charles Simphorien Dubos	94
JD device indecipherable	unidentified	133
JD heart	Jean Ducrollay	9, 15, 35, 38, 43, 59, 60, 80, 84, 93, 118
JE star	Jean-Marc-Antoine Écosse	199

			Fig. no.				*Fig. no.*
JEB	level	Joseph-Etienne Blerzy	179, 185, 186, 187, 195, 205	LC	ear of wheat	Louis Charonnat	421
				LM		Louis Mestejer	265
	Blerzy's mark after the Revolution was JEB, a pansy, in a lozenge			LM	hammer	Louis Mailly	2–3
				LM	star	Louis Michelin	58
JF	eagle's head	Jean Frémin	41, 95	LP(?)		unidentified French maker	27
JF	trefoil	Jean Formey	64, 65, 83, 90, 97, 148, 149	LPD	tree	Louis-Philippe Demay	123, 128
JFB	star	Jean-François Breton	17, 18, 42	LR	crown	Louis Roucel	152
				LR	ray	Louis Ray	170
JFG	star	Jean-François Garand	49	MC	quince	Mathieu Coiny	88
				MDL	flame	Michel de Lassus	23, 29
JG	star	Jean George	57, 68, 76–8, 79, 91, 92, 110, 111, 112, 145	MRB	greyhound	Melchior-René Barré	163
				MRH	sun	Michel-Robert Hallé or Hallet	32
JJB	no device	Jean-Joseph Barrière	108, 115, 124, 125, 131, 135, 144, 146, 154, 194	NCO	device unknown	unidentified French maker	168
				NH	cock	Noel Hardi-villiers	62, 63, 480
JL	a half oak leaf and the point of a spear, in a lozenge	Joseph Lurat	220	NZ		unidentified Amsterdam maker	266
				PAM	palm tree, in a lozenge	Pierre-André Montauban	225, 669
JLB	crown	Jean-Louis Bouillerot	169	PB	tiara	Pierre Bidault	162
JM	star	Jean Moynat	33, 34, 53, 61, 66, 69, 85	PC (or G)	crown above	unidentified German maker	250
				PCP	cross	Pierre-Claude Pottiers	191
JML	shell	Jacques-Michel Lemaire	1, 101		After the Revolution the device in Pottier's mark was altered to 3 stars in a triangle		
JMQ	shell	Jacques-Malquis Le Quin	36	PD	helmet	Pierre-François Delafons	30
JMT	spirit level	Jean-Marie Tiron	129, 150	PDC	heart	Pierre-Denis Chaumont	214
JR	lamp	Julien Rivard	151	PEG	cock	Philippe-Emmanuel Garbe	126
JR	pellet between	Joseph Richard-son	394–5, 396	PFD	heart	Pierre-François Drais	119, 155, 156, 157
JTL	branch of mire	Jacques-Toussaint Lemire	15	PG		unidentified Swiss maker	321
JV	lance	Joseph Vallayer	48	P & G	incuse, an eagle in an octagon above	Peckham & Grinnell	355
LA		Laurent Amiot	409				

Appendix I

		Fig. no.
PG crown above (or C)	unidentified German maker	250
PGS crown	Pierre-Guillaume Sallot	164
PIL pellets between, in rectangle	Peter Johan Ljungstedt	309
Two variants of this mark are recorded. Ljungstedt also used the mark LIUNGSTEDT		
PIZ grenade	Pierre-Innocent Zurich	198
PMB star	Pierre-François-Mathis de Beaulieu	122, 161, 166, 176
PMC	unidentified Russian maker	342
PNM bird(?)	possibly Pierre-Nicolas Marcault	212
PNM pine cone	Paul-Nicolas Menière	171, 172, 196, 200
PNP sheaf of wheat	Pierre-Nicolas Pleyard	106, 134
PP incuse	unidentified English maker	277
PR rose	Paul Robert	87, 98
PVD pellet, in trefoil	Peter Van Dyck	624

		Fig. no.
REVERE	Paul Revere	402
RL in rectangle & C	unidentified Swiss maker	328
RR	unidentified Swiss maker	320
SHEPHERD & BOYD	Robert Shepherd & William Boyd	408
SO in an oval	Soane or Soame	363
SP in shaped cartouche	Samuel Parmelee	401
SR	unidentified American maker	380–1
SV a pellet, in heart-shaped frame	Samuel Vernon	385
TLL mitre	Thomas-Louis Levesque	20
WE in serrated rectangle	William Eley	298
WH in oval	William Huertin, Jr.	387
Whittemore	William Whittemore	390
WI 2 stars above, fleur-de-lis below	David Willaume	364
WW conjoined	William Whetcroft	399

Appendix II

Cycles of Date Letters in Paris, London and Birmingham

As only the year of its registration is given, it should be remembered that each letter straddled two years, usually being put into service in mid-year.

PARIS

A	1718	1741	1764	Q	1733	1756	1779
B	1719	1742	1765	R	1734	1757	1780
C	1720	1743	1766	S	1735	1758	1781
D	1721	1744	1767	T	1736	1759	1782
E	1722	1745	1768	V	1737	1760	
F	1723	1746	1769	X	1738	1761	
G	1724	1747	1770	Y	1739	1762	
H	1725	1748	1771	Z	1740	1763	
I	1726	1749	1772				
K	1727	1750	1773	U			1783
L	1728	1751	1774	P_{84}			1784
M	1729	1752	1775	P_{85}			1785
N	1730	1753	1776	P_{86}			1786
O	1731	1754	1777	P_{87}			1787
P	1732	1755	1778	P_{88}			1788
				P_{89}			1789

LONDON

	Roman capitals	lower case	Gothic	lower case	Roman capitals	lower case
A	1716	1736	1756	1776	1796	1816
B	1717	1737	1757	1777	1797	1817
C	1718	1738	1758	1778	1798	1818
D	1719	1739	1759	1779	1799	1819
E	1720	1740	1760	1780	1800	1820
F	1721	1741	1761	1781	1801	1821
G	1722	1742	1762	1782	1802	1822
H	1723	1743	1763	1783	1803	1823
I	1724	1744	1764	1784	1804	1824
K	1725	1745	1765	1785	1805	1825
L	1726	1746	1766	1786	1806	1826
M	1727	1747	1767	1787	1807	1827
N	1728	1748	1768	1788	1808	1828
O	1729	1749	1769	1789	1809	1829
P	1730	1750	1770	1790	1810	1830
Q	1731	1751	1771	1791	1811	1831
R	1732	1752	1772	1792	1812	1832
S	1733	1753	1773	1793	1813	1833
T	1734	1754	1774	1794	1814	1834
U	1735	1755	1775	1795	1815	1835

BIRMINGHAM

	Roman capitals	Roman lower case	Gothic		Roman capitals	Roman lower case	Gothic
A	1773	1798	1824	N	1785	1811	1836
B	1774	1799	1825	O	1786	1812	1837
C	1775	1800	1826	P	1787	1813	1838
D	1776	1801	1827	Q	1788	1814	1839
E	1777	1802	1828	R	1789	1815	1840
F	1778	1803	1829	S	1790	1816	1841
G	1779	1804	1830	T	1791	1817	1842
H	1780	1805	1831	U	1792	1818	1843
I	1781	1806	1832	V	1793	1819	1844
J		1807		W	1794	1820	1845
K	1782	1808	1833	X	1795	1821	1846
L	1783	1809	1834	Y	1796	1822	1847
M	1784	1810	1835	Z	1797	1823	1848

Glossary of Recurrent Terms

The following list is meant to include the terms most often met with in a general discussion of snuff boxes. Terms of more restricted occurrence are defined in the body of the text, to which the reader is referred in the index.

Agate, dendritic. Varieties of agate—e.g., moss agate, mocha stone—having inclusions of iron or manganese oxide resembling trees (Greek, *dendra*) or moss.

Basse taille. Literally, 'shallow carving', an enamelling technique in which translucent enamels are fired on a carved surface. The term began to give way—at least in sculpture—to *bas relief* in the late seventeenth century. A survival or revival extends its usage in enamelling.

Boîte à portrait. A diamond-studded gold box set on or inside the cover with a royal portrait.

Camaïeu, en. A term in use by the middle of the eighteenth century to describe monochrome painting in any colour in imitation of cameos.

Chasing. The technique of working a metal surface from the top or outside with small hammers (*ciselets*) to produce raised decoration. *Ciselure*, chiselling and tooling are equivalent terms. The English verb *chase* apparently derives from the French *enchâsser*, the medieval *châsse*—a reliquary box—having set the precedent for this technique.

Cuvette, en. 'Basin-shaped'; a term commonly used in the eighteenth century to describe boxes made of porcelain or formed of a hollowed-out piece of hardstone.

Embossing. Ornamenting with a boss or protuberance—a term loosely used to designate any raised decoration.

Fantasy boxes. Snuff boxes in unusual shapes, as human or animal figures, sedan chairs, etc.

Freedom boxes. Boxes of the dimensions of snuff boxes made to enclose a scroll presenting the Freedom of a city. Common in Great Britain and America.

Guilloché. Engine-turned; apparently entirely unrelated to *guilloche* (used at least from the late seventeenth century to describe a continuous border of intertwined ribbons).

Grisaille. Monochrome painting in pastel shades of grey.

Incuse. Said of a mark on metal of which the letters, instead of appearing raised in a sunken reserve, are incised or stamped into the surface (from the Latin *incūs*, 'anvil'). Marks of this type are common in central Europe, occur sporadically in England and America, and never in France.

Integral hinge. A hinge constructed of small metal cylinders soldered alternately along the edge of a box and its cover and held in place by a metal pin. Admiration of the precision with which these hinges were made in Paris occupies almost the whole of Diderot's essay on the *tabatière* in the *Encyclopédie*.

Matte. French, 'dull'. A lustreless granulated finish obtained by hammering a metal surface with a small chiselling hammer (*matoir*) that has a pattern of grains on the striking end. Also known as *sablé* ('sanded').

Moss agate. See **Agate, dendritic.**

Paillons. (From the French *paille*, 'straw'.) Shaped pieces of very thin beaten gold placed between layers of translucent enamel (*199*). Introduced on gold boxes in Paris *c.* 1780.

Paste. Imitation precious or semi-precious stones usually made of glass, often backed or fused with coloured or metal foils. Their manufacture (by *voirriers*) in Paris is documented from 1292; the English word does not make its appearance until 1662. Paste diamonds were later known as strass (after George-Frédéric Strass, 1700–73, who began marketing his imitations in Paris in 1766) or as rhinestones; they are common on nineteenth-century gold boxes.

Pinchbeck. An alloy of three parts zinc to four of copper which, on account of its soft gold colour, was often used for the mounts of enamel snuff boxes. Named after its English inventor, Christopher Pinchbeck (1670–1732).

Piqué. (French—'pricked'.) Decoration in strips (*piqué posé*) or pinpoints (*piqué point*) of gold or silver embedded in a soft material such as tortoiseshell, horn, ivory, or leather.

Plein, en. Decoration in opaque enamel colours painted on the surface of a gold box. In this technique the enamel does not fill in prepared recesses but floats, as it were, on the surface of the gold, defining a layer of its own.

Porcelain, hard-paste. A ceramic material composed of a non-fusible clay (kaolin) and a calcareous flux (petuntse) fired at a temperature high enough to produce vitrification. Most German porcelain snuff boxes are hard paste, as are those of Sèvres.

Porcelain, soft-paste. A ceramic material composed of a white clay (e.g., soapstone) and a frit (e.g., ground glass), fired at a low temperature.

Quatrecouleur. (Traditionally spelt without a final *s*.) Varicoloured gold; although literally 'four-colour' it is generally used to designate any number of tints of gold.

Repoussé. ('Pushed back'.) Raised decoration achieved by hammering from within. Repoussé gold plaques occur on Continental and English boxes after *c.* 1775.

Reserve. In porcelain, an area left in the white amidst coloured decoration; by extension, any plain area set off from a 'worked' surface.

Sablé. See **Matte.**

Semi-precious. A modern term of convenience designating any jewel stone except the diamond, ruby, emerald, and sapphire.

Tabatière à cage. A snuff box whose sides are plaques of any material, set in a metal (usually gold) frame.

Zellenmosaik. *Cloisonné* hardstone decoration in which the stones are fixed in gold cells (*Zellen*). A technique characteristic of boxes made in Dresden from *c.* 1760.

Index

Index

Treatise of Japanning, A, 78
Treaty of Paris, 52
Tregent, Anthony, 74, 75; **594**
Tunbridge Wells, wood boxes, 89–90
Turin, lacquer boxes, 82
Turkey, porcelain trade, 67

United Kingdom, emblems of, **303**
United States, see America
Untermyer, Irwin, 69
Urban VII, 4
Usefulness of Experimental Philosophy, 78
Usk, lacquer boxes, 79

V., H., **668**
Vachette, Adrien-Jean-Maximilien, 27, 30, 31, 58, 64, 85; **201–4, 208, 210, 213, 218, 224, 228, 231, 233, 485, 639, 640**
  Mark, **Vg**
  Signature, **VI i**
Vairlet, Jean-Etienne, 53
Vallayer, Joseph, 58; **28, 48**
Van Dyck, Peter, 51, 87; **624**
Van Loo, Carle, 76
Varnish, composition of, 78, 79, 81
Varnished boxes
  Continental, **686**
  English, 79–80; **687, 688**
  French, 81–2; **671–5**
  German, 81; **677, 683–5**
  Italian, 82; **676**
  Welsh, 78–9; **680–2**

Venice
  Lacquered boxes, 82; **676**
  Porcelain boxes, 70; **545, 546**
Vernet, Joseph, 80
Vernis Martin, 21, 81–2
Vernon, Samuel, **385**
Verre églomisé, 91; **703**
Victoria, Queen of England, 17
Vienna
  Gold boxes, 32; **235–7, 240–2**
  Hardstone box, **458**
  Tax Mark, **Vm**
Villegagnon, Nicolas Durand de, 1
Villers, **667**
Villers, Claude de, **28**
Vincennes, porcelain boxes, 69–70; **534–6**
Violet, Pierre-Noël, 30; **196**
Vologda, maps of, 55
Voltaire (François-Marie Arouet), portrait of, 88; **690**
Vos, Martin de, **655**
Vougny, Gabriel, **420**

W., G., **330**
Waddesdon Manor, 11
Waechter, Georg Christian, **336**
Waechter, Johann Georg, **336**
Waghorne, John, 80
Wakelin, Edward, 37
Waldseemüller, Martin, 1
Wales, see Pontypool
Wales, Frederick, Prince of, 17

Walpole, Horace, 7, 10, 11, 13, 29, 36, 37, 42, 61, 91; **171**
  Portrait, 75
Walpole, Sir Robert
  Letter to . . ., A, 12
  Portrait of, 75
Walpole, Thomas, 13
Washington, George, 39, 80
Watches, set in boxes, **287, 316**
Watson, F. J. B., 27
Watson, James, **603**
Watt, James, 61, 86
Watteau, Jean-Antoine, miniatures after, 76; **2, 509**
Waynflete, arms of, **373**
Wedgwood, Josiah, 16, 38, 71, 86
Wedgwood plaques, set in boxes, **294, 295**
Weigel, Jean-Christophe, 11
Weinziener, J. E. A., 81
Wemys, James, **305**
Wenman, John, 92
Wentworth, John, arms of, **383**
Whetcroft, William, **399**
Whieldon, Thomas, 71
Whipping Tom, 9, 13, 88
White, Dr Joseph, **408**
Whittemore, William, 51; **390**
Wilkes, John, **566**
  Portrait, 76; **603**
Wilkie, Sir David, 80, 81
Willaume, David, **364**
William III and Mary of England, portraits of, **642, 643**

William IV of England, monogram, **304**
Williams, Robert, 48
Wilson, Joseph, **376**
Wilson, R. Thornton, 69
Wilson, T. B., 17
Wirgman, Peter, 38
Wobbe, Willem, 46
Wolfsburg, Carl Ferdinand von, 73
Wood, petrified, 63
Wood boxes
  Continental, **700**
  English, **696–8**
  French, **689–95**
  Scottish, **699, 701**
Woollett, William, 76
Wright, Joseph, 51
Wuest, Jean Leonhard, 11

York House, Battersea, 73–5
Ystad, silver box, 54

Z., N., **266**
Zellenmosaik, 65, 66, 114
Zenger, John Peter, 39
Zeuner, **703**
Zirnfeld, Anton von, 73
Zucchi, Francesco, 8, 45, 63, 83
Zürich
  Porcelain boxes, **562–4**
  Silver box, **433**
Zurich, Pierre-Innocent, **198**